The Looking Glass Brother

The Looking Glass Brother

Peter von Ziegesar

ST. MARTIN'S PRESS • NEW YORK

Author's Note: This is a true story, though in a few cases names and details have been changed.

THE LOOKING GLASS BROTHER. Copyright © 2013 by Peter von Ziegesar. All rights reserved. Printed in the United States of America. For information, address St. Martin's Press, 175 Fifth Avenue, New York, N.Y. 10010.

www.stmartins.com

ISBN 978-0-312-59298-1 (hardcover)
ISBN 978-1-4299-8990-9 (e-book)

St. Martin's Press books may be purchased for educational, business, or promotional use. For information on bulk purchases, please contact Macmillan Corporate and Premium Sales Department at 1-800-221-7945 extension 5442 or write specialmarkets@macmillan.com.

First Edition: June 2013

10 9 8 7 6 5 4 3 2 1

To my father, whose advice I took:
I never went to Wall Street.

The Looking Glass Brother

Part One

Sins cannot be undone, only forgiven.

—Igor Stravinsky

Chapter One

March 12, 1995
New York City

The phone at my desk rang and a crusty, vaguely familiar, tobacco-hoarse voice crackled in my ear.

"Peter, it's Peter. Your stepbrother," said the voice. "Your stepbrother, Peter, who you haven't seen in many years. Little Peter, meet Big Peter. Isn't that funny? Anyway, it's me."

I looked out my window. It was a gray winter's afternoon in Greenwich Village. I felt like I was listening to a lost recording of the Beat poets.

"Peter?" I said, helplessly. "Peter?" If this really was my stepbrother, it was the first time I'd heard his voice since the early eighties. Obviously terrible things had happened to him in the meantime. Things that had turned him from the alert, blue-eyed violin prodigy, the apple of his mother's eye, who attended one elite school after another—Dalton; Saint Ann's, in New York City; and then my father's alma mater, the Choate school, in Wallingford, Connecticut—into a drooling specimen of New York City's homeless. Something out of Bob Dylan: "Bent out of shape from society's pliers . . ."

There was nothing on the line now but the distant honking of cars.

And then the crackly voice started again. "My mother gave me your number, because she said you were a good person. How my mother would know anything about that I don't understand. She never liked you and always said you were spoiled rotten and no damn good, especially when you had long hair. But she's changed her tune now, if you want to see me, and I hope you do. If you care about me at all."

"Peter, where are you?" I asked, fearing the line would cut off.

"It doesn't matter where I am," he said. "And it's probably better if you don't know."

"Can you get to the corner of Eighth Avenue and Fourteenth Street in half an hour?"

"Sure."

"Do you have a watch?" I asked.

"I don't need a watch. Give me forty-five minutes. I'll see you there."

"Who was that?" asked Hali, coming into my office, drying her hair in a towel.

"That was Peter."

"Your *stepbrother* Peter?" she asked, with disbelief.

"I'm going out to meet him right now."

"Oh. Be careful," she said, placing a pair of black cat's-eye glasses embedded with tiny diamonds on her nose. The glasses made her look like the excuses secretary at a suburban high school. She wore flowered long johns and a loose, ripped Princeton T-shirt. "Be sure to call me if it gets too late."

It was almost dark by the time I reached Fourteenth Street, and the broad strip of cheap clothing outlets and check-cashing stores looked grim and windswept. Still, I wasn't far from my apartment. If Peter clubbed me over the head unexpectedly with a piece of scrap wood, I could probably make my way back by crawling.

Various rumors had come to me over the years of Little Peter's fantastical exploits—we called him "Little" Peter, since I was "Big" Peter—how he'd run screaming down East Ninety-sixth Street in a bathrobe after escaping from the Mount Sinai Hospital psychiatric ward, only to be knocked down by a careening taxi and dragged back to the hospital by two cops. How he'd spent six months in a lockup in Blaine County, Idaho, after trying to break open his mother's head with a piece of firewood. How one night in Indianapolis he was clocked in a new car going 110 miles an hour past the governor's mansion. Convinced that pursuing cops were in league with a ring of automobile thieves, he crashed into a massive police roadblock at the town center, totaling his car—but walking away unharmed. How he'd fallen asleep drunk one afternoon in a Montana wheat field, and had woken to the gentle, but mysterious, susurration of the blades of a harvest combine, which a moment later came thundering down over his head. How he'd lifted his hands instinctively to protect himself, only to see them severed at the wrists. How he'd scrambled to a lake by the field and lain down in ice-cold water, seeking only peace and death, while his hands flapped back and forth on bits of skin from their bloody stumps. How a helicopter had flown him to Salt Lake City, where a team of surgeons had meticulously reattached his hands. And how one of his first uses of his hands had been to push a nurse down a flight of stairs. He'd only recently been diagnosed as schizophrenic, though there was still some dispute as to whether he'd ever been diagnosed at all.

Schizophrenics live in a world of external violence commensurate with their internal chaos. They assault, are assaulted, and commit suicide with greater frequency than the rest of the population. Little Peter's increasingly troubled street career hadn't contradicted this.

I peered ahead down the gray sidewalk, thinking I saw a figure coming toward me. Its shaggy shape reminded me of the terrifying gremlin on the wing of a jet plane in a particular episode of *The Twilight Zone*. The gremlin could only be seen by one man, a broken-down loser played by William Shatner. Each time that man, who'd apparently had a recent mental breakdown, called the other passengers over to look, the gremlin leaped in the night air and was blown backward off the wing. The figure I saw seemed to appear and disappear as it came closer. A shabby white plastic bag bobbled from each of its hands, which curled under like claws.

His walk was one that stray cats and homeless men develop unconsciously, an ambulatory cringe that says to the world, "Don't beat me, I'm moving on. I'm just taking this piece of sandwich, this container of moo shu pork, this spit-soaked cigarette butt. You don't want it. Now I've got it. I'll stop defiling your view in a minute."

The way I knew it was Little Peter, finally, was his eyes, his astonishing eyes, still as blue and clear as Paul Newman's. His nose had flattened and grown red and pulpy, and there was a crude long scar over his right eye that gave him a permanently worried look. His torn jeans and stained corduroy jacket had become too small for his thick and doughy body. The sleeves of his flannel shirt stuck out beyond his jacket sleeves, and over the flannel shirt was a long, untucked T-shirt. He was growing a beard, and his hair, once blond, was now orange, mixed with toffee brown, and was molded over his head like a bowl.

Before he reached me, he picked a white paper bag from a trash can, pried it open, and rattled the interior. The sound and motion were automatic and mechanical; they reminded me of the movements of a caged fox, returning again and again to its pan to check whether any specks of food remained.

"Peter?" I called out, through the darkness and the blowing snow.

He swung his two white plastic bags uncertainly this way and that, as if about to turn and run. With a furtive expression, he walked up to me.

"Big Peter?"

"Yes, it's me," I said. Carefully, I put my arms around my stepbrother's shoulders and gave him a hug. The hair on his face had bleached in tufts, over the rough, red skin of his cheeks. *He's gone feral,* I thought.

"It didn't look like you at all," he said, blinking. "I saw you standing there, and I thought you must have changed."

"Bullshit. I haven't changed a bit," I said. I turned and started to walk down Eighth Avenue. Little Peter began to scurry at my side, crablike, eagerly looking into my face.

"The last time I saw you, I was driving you to Choate. You must have been about seventeen."

"No," he said, "you're wrong—the last time you saw me was when I forgot to deliver the negatives of Tommy Tune."

How could I forget that? That was long after Little Peter left Choate in disgrace, in the mid-eighties. By then he'd also dropped out of the University of New Hampshire. Nothing was working for him then, and someone had thought to find him a job as a bicycle messenger in Manhattan. This turned out to be an extraordinarily fortunate choice—Little Peter loved to spin through the stone alleys of Wall Street with a bag slung over his shoulder, to wait breathlessly in a lobby for an important envelope to be brought down to him. He'd ride up the West Side Highway, smoking a cigarette, delirious with the hot sun beating down on the back of his neck and the fluffy clouds changing shape across the river in New Jersey. He always carried a bottle of Kahlua in his messenger bag and he'd reach for it now and then. Sometimes he forgot to deliver the envelope.

My father never formally adopted Little Peter, but at some point my stepbrother had taken our last name. That made two of us with the same name in the same family, both eldest sons. And since there are only twenty or so von Ziegesars left on the planet, it sometimes happened that our wires got crossed. It was always a case of mistaken identity. The postman delivered Little Peter's jury summonses and alumni notices to my door. This time it was an irate call. An enraged art director had rung me up, thinking I was my stepbrother, having somehow obtained my number.

"I'd like to wrap my hands around his throat, I swear I would," the guy from the ad agency said when I explained who I wasn't.

I could almost smell his cigar smoke coming in over the wire.

"Please don't kill my stepbrother," I said. "He's got a little thinking to do, maybe. But he'll figure things out." I asked the guy to give me his address and phone number and promised I'd call him right back.

Then I called Norwalk and got Erik on the phone, told him to get Little Peter up off the sofa and on the next train to New York City. "Stay with him," I said. "Call me from Grand Central when you get there. Bring the negatives. Got that? Don't let him out of your sight."

But that was years ago. Little Peter and I were still playing out our lives in opposition to each other. It always seemed that when he was on top, I was down, and the other way around. We were both a long way from where we started. Given the world of privilege in which Little Peter had been raised—the private schools, the music lessons, the European vacations—a lot of us who knew him had considered his fall from grace to have been caused by little less than a spectacular case of bad attitude. This is the boy whose Dalton music teacher once called "the next Paganini," the same angel-faced five-year-old I'd carried on my back on the green hills of Connecticut. Even just a few years ago in Idaho, a psychiatrist assigned by the state to assess his chances for involuntary commitment concluded that my stepbrother was just a "spoiled kid" who needed a swift kick in the pants.

"Peter, are you hungry?" I asked. "Come on, let's go home."

Chapter Two

Little Peter's sudden reappearance in my life threw a monkey wrench into what had been for me a prolonged and unaccustomed state of equilibrium. I'd gotten married, for one thing, which had surprised the hell out of my father, who'd always been skeptical about my ability to integrate vertically. My wife, Hali, was in her second year of social work school, and was pregnant, which was fine except that to keep from throwing up she had to constantly eat saltines and sniff the rinds of lemons.

She and I had met five years before in Kansas City, where I was working as a stringer for *The Kansas City Star*. It had happened that one afternoon, when deep in my usual fog, I walked into the local office of the ACLU, where I'd been invited to serve on the board on the strength of a flattering profile I'd written about a local constitutional lawyer. There, at the front desk, I was confronted by a bird of strange plumage. She looked about fourteen, with her old running shoes up on the desk and her jeans splattered with paint. Her jet-black hair, thick as a horse's mane, was clipped in a chaotic spray over her head. As she chatted away about the pro-choice march she was organizing in Kansas and Missouri, she gazed cheerfully at me through a pair of black cat's-eye glasses. So cheerful was she that I'd had the impression at first that she must belong to some kind of Christian sect that preached the power of positive thinking. She told me later that I, too, had appeared inexpressibly weird to her, in my jeans, Ray-Bans, and a

French striped fisherman's shirt that I'd borrowed from my girlfriend. But who thinks of these things ahead of time?

To be frank, I didn't get it, the whole picture. When she left the room I took a surreptitious peek into the Rolodex on the desk. Her name, a string of disconnected alliterative syllables, meant nothing to me. Nevertheless, small metal objects were beginning to click and fall into place inside my head like relays in an old-fashioned telephone exchange.

By our first date—to see an exhibition of mechanized dinosaurs in the lobby of the Westin Crown Center Hotel—I'd cautiously decided I wanted to see more of her. The dates we devised were deliberately improvised and random. A trip to Lawrence where I was supposed to give a lecture on writing, a late-night performance given by Kansas City artists that ended up with the usual en masse display of tantrum dancing by men in skirts. This girl—Hali was her name—was funny, post-minimalist, and thought I was completely full of shit. That in itself seemed like a good start.

One evening just at dusk we'd parked up on a hill in the center of town where the city fathers had erected a phallic sandstone monument to the war dead that glowed with a cherry-red light at its tip. For decades the dark roads that wound around this memorial had been a traditional meeting place for gay men in cars. Since Hali and I were meeting secretly, I didn't think anyone would look for us there. I chose the moment when the red sun dropped into the river bottoms to the west to tell Hali that I wanted her to have my children. She was surprised, but not terrified. She supposed I'd been around long enough to know what I wanted.

Eventually we climbed over the seats into the back of the Jeep. Perhaps we thought we would commence on that project of which we'd spoken earlier. Just then there came a loud cracking noise and powerful beams of light shining through the windows. We looked out to see a pair of white-faced Kansas City cops tapping on the glass with their flashlights, shouting for us to open the door. No doubt they were expecting to roust a couple of scared, skinny boys from their pimply—but fully protected under the Constitution—deeds. Instead when a proud, pretty, completely unafraid round-faced Korean woman in pigtails and a bang cut popped her head up over the backseat, the flatfoots couldn't have looked more surprised if an Eskimo fully decked out in a sealskin coat and a harpoon had suddenly walked into their basement den. The two backed away mumbling, jumped in their vehicle, and drove off.

Now that we were, at least to ourselves, "official," there came the terrifying process of disentangling ourselves from our respective mates. I would have sooner cut off an arm than do anything to hurt my girlfriend then. The next few weeks were not ones I was particularly proud of, nor did I execute the required tasks particularly well, but eventually they were over.

That Hali's almost infinitely extended Korean-American family of doctors and physicists were willing to accept me was in itself some miracle. The plan was for me to meet everyone in Boulder, Colorado, over Christmas. A few weeks before, I received a call from her mother's youngest brother, Uncle Chin. Hali had explained to me that his name had been Chul, but her ninety-year-old grandmother, the matriarch of the family, had learned recently that his name was unpropitious, and had changed it to Chin.

"Hi," he said. "This is Uncle Chin. You know me? Ha, ha. Good. We all looking forward to meeting you in Colorado this winter. Bring your skis. Just one thing. We love Hali, so if you hurt her, I kill you. Got that? Ha, ha, ha. Break you neck. Ha, ha. We gonna like you, I'm sure." It turned out that Uncle Chin had once had the longest hair in the family. He played guitar and harmonica, and had recently left the family optics business to design a small remote-controlled plastic boat that dropped a baited line for technical-minded fishermen. We got along fine. There was something about this big interconnected family headed by an impassioned matriarch that I instinctively understood from my own past. Hali's family was alive and moving, always searching. I found myself drawn into and instructed by her uncles' innumerable business schemes, as well as their Medici-class squabbles. Hali's mother, Priscilla, alternatively kidded me, "Peter, I hope you are taking notes! This is stranger than fiction!" and "Please, whatever you do, don't write about this. I don't want people to know what we're really like!" The unmediated zeal of her parents' generation, their intelligence, their love of education, their cuisine of salt and pickles, their sometimes goofy perspective on politics and war, their earthy humor, unwavering moral sense, and just plain love of each other taught me worlds. Sometimes I felt I'd never really started to grow up until I joined Hali's family.

Hali herself has said that we were not meant to meet, that we had knocked each other out of our normal orbits, that our two planets were meant to go flaming out into space instead of clinging to each other in a dizzying close dance, and I have to agree that this may also true.

Each day at three, if I were alone, I'd roll myself a cigarette, from a bag of fragrant imported Dutch tobacco, and smoke it by the window, with one foot up on the sill, listening to the plaintive *cree-awwk-eeee! cree-awwk-eeee!* of the swings in the playground below. Having finished the cigarette, I'd drown the repellent, foreskin-resembling butt end in the sink. That old familiar feeling, that the floor was about to open up and engulf me in clouds of black smoke, flames, and brimstone had retreated slightly, thanks to the steady flow of freelance work that had come my way recently, and the enduring, practical, mostly cheerful presence of my wife. I could now read of economic downturn, unusual prison practices, diminishing oil reserves, rising sea levels, melting polar ice caps, disoriented honeybees, emerging tropical viruses, and PCBs in the water supply without concluding that the floodwaters of doom were about to close over our city-pent heads. When my wife and I were debating the pros and cons of buying our apartment, and I was going through predictable convulsions of uncertainty and global darkness, Hali ended the discussion, with some irritation, by blurting out, "I can't plan for apocalypse!" And so, to please her, I learned simply to live with impending doom, and to try to give it a little less space in my day.

About to commence upon the enormously complex, economically indefensible, character-abrading enterprise called raising children, we had no idea what great slow grinding wheels we were setting loose. Our world was about to be broken apart, dissolved into its constituent molecules, and re-formed. For now, we lived in a high state of innocence and productivity.

It was into this temporary cocoon of nonchalance, this air pocket of prenatal haze, that my father had thrown a small hand grenade, a few nights before. My father is known as a great presager of events and is as hypersensitive to drops in the barometer as to the futures market. Once again I was at my desk.

I detected immediately that something was wrong by the sound of my father's voice. His normally rich baritone was tight and constrained. I waited out ten seconds or so of throat-clearing and raspy keening over several octaves.

My father's third wife, Liz, was vacuuming in the background, so the first thing I heard was Dad growling, "God damn it, Liz, you're about to knock over another stack of magazines . . . *ow-ow OW-AH-AH-aaah!*"

I pictured my father, in the reclining chair, glasses tipped down to the bottom of his nose, TV remote balanced on his stomach, which had grown as hard and round as a basketball. He added a few more anguished vocalizations to indicate the size and state of the mess in the living room and then to me he said, "I love my wife, but between you and me, she is an unbelievable slob! *AhhhGGGH!*"

I wished, not for the first time, that some ethnologist would study my father's more tonal communications, because there is something non-Western about them. I have some familiarity with tonal language through my wife's family. When Hali's aunts and uncles get together, for example, their talk contains rising and falling inflections that have little to do with anything you can look up in a Korean-American dictionary. As one recalls the perfidy of the last minister, the freeloading of relatives from the north, the moment when Big Uncle left the stone shelter to urinate and came back to find it blown up, each memory receives its quasi-operatic response from the others, ahhs of horror, disgust, amazement, and dismay—in other words, the full spectrum of emotion to be found in a typical Korean conversation.

I speculate that my father's own personal arpeggios of grunts, wheezes, and throat-clearings have come down to him from the Mongolian ancestors he's always claimed we have, descending from Batu Kahn's total rout of the Polish-German armies in the year 1241 and the subsequent rape of Mecklenburg-Vorpommern. Certainly, he says, ours is not a normal German last name. Its three syllables—"*EEE-AHH-Are*"—conform more readily to the Chinese system of surnames than to any found in Europe. But that may just be my father wheezing. He'd been spending more time on the family tree lately, translating old letters and sorting through scrapbooks.

"Dad," I said. "Is everything okay?"

Dad ignored this. "Your stepbrother is in town. Did you know that?"

I tried to think of whom he meant. After my mother had remarried, our many-times broken and re-glued family had grown to fourteen siblings. I knew at least four who would answer to the label, and one or two more who might laterally qualify. Erik was studying cartography in Idaho, though. Stephen was directing *The Ring Cycle* in Seattle, and David was running a bar in the West Village—he couldn't mean them.

"Little Peter?" I said.

"Yes, it's Little Peter. Who did you think I meant, you dummy!"

My father and I had improved our relationship in the past couple of years, mainly because he was so taken with Hali. But it was hard to tell that his opinion of his oldest son, i.e., myself, had risen much.

"Sorry, I was just being dim," I said.

"If that's your dad, say hi to him," Hali called from the kitchen.

"Hali says hi," I said.

"You tell your sweet wife that I love her dearly, and if she ever wants to find out what it's like to live with a real man, she should just let me know," he said.

"Dad says hi," I called out.

Liz grabbed the phone. "Listen, I know what it's like, and believe me it's not always what it's advertised to be."

At the time of their wedding, a year or so earlier, Liz was half my father's age and five years younger than myself. She was a scrappy, florid, Brooklyn blonde whose preferred cocktail was a splash of vodka stirred directly into a tall glass of reconstituted powdered diet lemonade drink.

"Liz says hi, too," I called out to Hali.

"God damn it, Liz!" my father sputtered. "I can't even have a decent conversation around here without some Irish Catholic floozy sticking her face into mine!"

"Okay, I'll get off the line," said Liz. "But tell your wife to keep cubes of cheddar cheese with her in a Ziploc bag. It works wonders for my cousin."

"Liz says to eat cheddar cheese cubes," I called.

"Tell her I'm already eating them," Hali called.

"Does it work?"

"Nothing works," said Hali.

"I'm sorry to hear that," said Liz. "Well, morning sickness doesn't last forever. I'll give you your father back. He really is upset. He was up all last night tossing and turning."

"What's up, Dad?" I asked.

"Your goddamn stepbrother called me from a telephone booth last night, that's what," he said.

He followed with what sounded like Navajo ululation: "*Oaaww—aww—aaww-ahh!* What I have to put up with! It's all his mother's fault! Who else would have given him our phone number in New Jersey?"

When Liz turned off the vacuum cleaner I heard waves breaking on the beach. They must have left their balcony door open, despite the cold.

"Where's he staying?" I asked.

"Staying? He's not staying anywhere. He's turned into a bum. He sleeps on the street and eats out of garbage cans."

"Wait a minute!" I said, still not fully taking this all in. "So, Little Peter called you? What'd he want?"

"He was drunk, that's what. He wanted to stay with us out here."

"What'd you tell him?"

"I said absolutely not! If you give him one thing he'll try to take it all. I have enough trouble with my brother Ulrich without adding another deadbeat to the roll. Ahh-*Ahhhgh-gh-ghh*!"

While my father lamented and grumbled, I put down the phone and looked out through the black windows of my apartment. Little Peter had found a way to live that I knew nothing about, slipped down the rabbit hole, and was slowly falling through the dark tunnel, plucking flowers from the sides as he fell.

"I'd like to see him," I said, suddenly, to my father, interrupting the bitter flow of his complaints.

"What?" he said.

"I'd like to see Peter," I said again, wondering what I was letting myself in for.

"Oh, no, you couldn't possibly want to see him," my father replied, aghast.

"I do," I said.

"You don't. You have a beautiful, pregnant wife and what you should be doing is protecting her from people like your brother."

"Hali can take care of herself, even without me," I said, which was more than true. "I want to meet him."

"But why?" asked my father, at a loss for words for the first time I could remember.

"I want to ask him what it's like to be a homeless person."

"Oh, for Christ's sake!"

"I'm serious."

As my father took a long pull on his gin and tonic, I heard ice cubes clinking in the glass. He came back to the receiver with his mellow baritone fitted into place like a pair of dentures.

"Okay, if you're so goddamn curious, why don't you go out to look for him?" he said. "He used to have an apartment downtown, and you know he always returns to the places he's lived—the dummy!"

Chapter Three

Back on Fourteenth Street, Little Peter scurried by my side in half-rotted clothing. What would his mother, Olivia, think if she saw him, I wondered. She probably thought by now she'd be showing off her diamonds under the twinkling chandeliers of the New York Philharmonic. While the dark hall echoed with coughs and metallic chair-scrapings, up on stage, attired in a flawless black tuxedo, my stepbrother would stand poised and prescient, lighting the room with his brilliant blue eyes. He would stare over the top of his violin with planetary intensity for a few seconds, while the audience hushed, place his Stradivarius up to his chin, and proceed casually to dismember a Bach concerto with deft, surgical flicks of his bow. Afterward the sophisticated crowd would break into unprecedented applause. Instead there was this broken bum in a clown suit that smelled of roach spray and vomit.

I studied the man lurching along beside me. His peculiar way of worrying his lip with his teeth gave the impression he was talking to himself. Or perhaps he *was* talking to himself. In the dim light I couldn't tell.

Perhaps I should be more careful of the errands my father sends me on, I told myself. Although my father had never directly *asked* me to adventure out here on the sidewalk, I suspected he'd engineered all the possibilities so that I wouldn't refuse. His errands always served a dual purpose. They made some inescapable task more convenient for him, of course, but more important they assuaged deeply hidden pangs of guilt in his mind that he hadn't spent enough time, or done enough for me in my life. Right enough on both counts, I thought, though it was too late to go back and start over. Dad always was an adept manager of personnel. "I am no genius at all, but very pragmatic," he wrote about himself once, ". . . and have always been able to recognize that others can do certain things much better than I. Therefore it seemed easy to accomplish a lot simply by relying on reasonably able subordinates who prided themselves on their work." And of course he made sure there were always enough people around who were ready to jump when he said, "Boo."

"Do you talk to your mother anymore?" I asked Little Peter, as we crossed Fourteenth Street and began to descend through the Village toward my apartment.

"She doesn't want to hear the truth, that I'm living like a rat on the street and licking the crumbs off my frozen whiskers."

"Where have you been sleeping?"

"Somewhere, man. Anywhere."

"Anywhere is not a place."

"It is for me, man."

Little Peter fished out a pair of dark glasses and then tamped down earphones over his ears.

"What's with the shades?" I asked. "It's almost dark."

"It's not the light, it's people's eyes. They're like lasers scouring into my soul," he said. "If we can just make it to Chinatown, I'll be all right." He pulled out several books on Eastern thought, each one curled and thumbed— Alan Watts, the *I Ching*, and *Zen and the Art of Motorcycle Maintenance*.

"Nothing's been the same since I went through Central Booking," Little Peter went on. "That was back in 'ninety-two, the first winter I was homeless.

"Some cop got me for sleeping on the subway, and I mouthed off to him. That was a mistake. They took me to a room where the walls and the ceiling were painted blue. Even the chairs where you were supposed to sleep were blue. You couldn't get away from that color.

"The whole room was full of silly black teenagers who wouldn't leave me alone even in the bathroom. The only way I got through the night was by being very submissive."

"*Submissive?*"

"Never mind that. You don't want to get hung up on a single word."

I thought about this for a moment.

"The important thing is the video cameras mounted on the ceiling burned their way right into the bottom of my brain. Like corrosive acid. By morning, I'd lost whatever soul I had. I was not even a person," Little Peter said.

"Incarceration," he said after a while. "That's an ugly word, isn't it? It sounds like a combination of *incineration* and *carcinogen*. But the thing it stands for is even uglier. They take away everything that makes you human and put you in a box that closes off all your senses. If you need to move around outside, they stop you from doing that. If you want to warm yourself in the sun, they stop that. If you absolutely have to be alone and quiet with your thoughts, they stop that too. And if you need to taste something with some flavor to make you feel like you are alive, that's against the rules too. I promise you I never did anything that warranted that they treat me this way."

As we hurried down Eighth Avenue, I saw that the tenor of the afternoon had changed. When I'd come up to meet Little Peter, the air had been chaotic, filled with the harsh rush of soot and the bark of traffic. Now a soft sprinkling of crystalline flakes caught the light from the streetlights and floated down to settle on our hair. As we walked, cameras on tall lampposts spun and tilted on oiled gimbals, panning slowly to follow our progress. Angry-eyed suburban ladies, their hair glazed into sharp points, punched the lock buttons on their car doors, and hordes of small furry mice streamed almost invisibly around the edges of our sight and disappeared down holes in the sidewalk.

Little Peter ducked his head between his shoulders, and shivered. "I never felt comfortable in the Village," he said. "There's too much money here. I always feel that people are watching and passing judgment on the way I look. This isn't a place for someone like me."

I explained to Little Peter how the neighborhood was changing. The walk-up hovels of artists were being taken over by young hedge-fund managers, and the old men in black leather vests, with their shriveled nipples, their chains and pit bulls, were being chased off the sidewalks by chic young matrons with baby carriages. The abandoned warehouses on the Hudson River were being replaced by enormous glass palaces filled with celebrities and the superrich.

Little Peter cackled and did a little jig on the sidewalk.

"Wouldn't it be funny if all this wealth was based on some mistake that somebody made, on money they thought was there, but through some miscalculation really wasn't?" he asked.

"Get out of here," I said. "You're a madman."

I had no desire to let my stepbrother know our address, so as we got closer to my apartment, I pushed him faster and faster, so that he kept looking around bewildered, asking, "What street is this? Where am I?" We spun around the corner, and I slipped him through the door before he could note the street number inscribed over the entrance.

Little Peter came through the door to our apartment. He looked around, blinking. The living room was littered with the usual assortment of books and clothes. It certainly was nothing compared to the place Little Peter had grown up in.

"How do you get an apartment like this? Do you have to be rich? Do you have to have a job?" he asked.

"Something like that," I answered.

Hali came out of the bedroom, smiling. She'd piled her hair over her head with a tortoise-shell clip. Her hands were folded over her stomach, which was just beginning to swell.

"How about introducing us?" she said.

I'd been worried about how my stepbrother would react when he met my wife. His relationship with the opposite sex had always been iffy to say the least. In the past few years he'd committed half a dozen assaults against women that I knew about, including the two times he'd attacked his mother and been arrested. Would he freak out, would he run amok?

In the hallway darkness, Little Peter said a few polite words, though as Hali later noted he didn't try to look her in the eye.

I went into the bathroom and started the water running, while Hali hunted in my closet for a pair of jeans, a T-shirt, cotton socks, and a worn plaid shirt.

Little Peter spent an exceptionally long time in the bathroom. A skilled homeless person makes use of indoor plumbing wherever it becomes available, I suppose.

"How does he seem to you?" Hali asked.

"Fine," I said. "Philosophical. Nonviolent."

"What does he want?"

"He wants to go to Chinatown to drink tea."

"What about afterwards?"

"Not sure."

For a while Hali had worked at a battered women's shelter in Independence, Missouri, where many of the clients were indigent. From the shelter, she'd learned the three rules of social work the hard way. They are: First, never bring a client home. Second, never give him money. Third, never (ever) drink or do drugs with him. With Little Peter, we were about to violate at least the first two. But he was not a client, so I wasn't sure how the rules applied.

Hali and I tend to pick up strays, both of the animal and the human variety. It's a trait her mother, Priscilla, often notes with disapproval. Yet, now and then I think I detect a grudging note of respect in my mother-in-law's voice as well, and recognition of inevitability, for it's in the blood.

Priscilla's mother had been perhaps the biggest stray picker-upper in the history of the modern Korean peninsula. Her fierce and impromptu acts of philanthropy ultimately played a part in her family's coming through the Korean War intact, and could almost have been called a survival strategy. Priscilla tells the story of how, eighteen hours after the North Korean army overran Seoul, she and her mother and her three younger siblings found themselves huddled under blankets in the parking lot of the train station in Pusan, hundreds of miles from home, hungry, desperate, and without shelter. They were surrounded by thousands of refugees in the same situation. Hali's grandmother sniffed the air, wrapped a scarf around her head, and disappeared, leaving Priscilla in charge. She returned just before dark to lead her hungry chicks on a meandering path through the brick alleyways of that strange and increasingly hostile city. She was looking for a banker whom she had rescued from starvation when he was a child. She found him, and he quickly cleared room for them in his mansion. Thus it had happened countless times, that the complex and sticky web of obligation woven by their mother had pulled them out of desperate situations.

"We can't let Little Peter stay in this house," Hali said.

"Don't worry, I wasn't considering that," I said.

"What are you going to tell him if he asks?"

"Unclear," I said.

Hali shivered. "It seems so cruel."

"He's a grown-up," I said. "A self-centered, irrational, unwashed, work-shirking grown-up."

"So, what are you?" Hali said sweetly.

We heard the tub faucet shriek shut inside the bathroom and the cessation of water tumbling into the tub.

"What should we do with these," Hali said, pointing to the pile of clothes Peter had left outside the bathroom door.

"Burn them!" I said. Hali went down the hallway to our bedroom to change.

I waited until she was around the corner, then slipped into my office—a closet lined with bookshelves. I felt around on a high shelf until I found what I was looking for, an old CD of The Bands *Music from Big Pink.*

My stepbrother was smoking crack, according to my father—a hazard of the road. I couldn't come down on my stepbrother too much for that. My old prep school friend Lester Bergamot, a trust-fund junkie, had started turning me on to heroin in the late eighties. As a teenager, he'd had a habit, whenever he'd visited my parents' house, of ransacking the medicine cabinet for prescription drugs. Lester's father, a medic in World War II, had returned home from the battlefield with a suitcase full of morphine ampoules, spoils of war. Lester had taken to those army surplus opium derivatives early and had never looked back; he was now a happy, if somewhat shopworn, powderhead in the East Village, still pretending to be an artist at age thirty-five.

When I opened the CD case, three small green rectangles of translucent plastic fell out onto my desk. From one that was already sliced open I slid out a small glassine packet, unfolded it, and tapped one end, until a small sprinkle of grayish powder fell on the smooth CD back. Then I took a business card from my desk, scraped the powder into a tiny line about the size of a mealworm, and sniffed it up through a Bic ballpoint pen whose innards I'd removed.

The crude stuff burned the back of my sinuses. I hastily sprinkled another line, then stuffed the plastic envelopes back into the CD and put it up on the shelf.

By the time I returned to the living room, a warm glow had begun to uncurl like a saucer-eyed octopus from the hard cold crannies of coral that were permanently cemented at the back of my brain. As the strain of the past few hours washed away, I inadvertently gave out a loud sigh—then looked around quickly to see if anyone had heard me.

A minute later Little Peter came out of the bathroom fully dressed, rubbing his hair with a towel. "You'd better swish some water around the tub before you take a bath," he said. "It's pretty gnarly in there."

I handed him a blue parka I hadn't worn in a couple of years. "Are you sure you want to give this to me, man?" he asked.

"Of course!" I said, feeling guilty, because it was just an old jacket I probably would have thrown away anyway. Hali came out from the bedroom; she'd put on dark red lipstick and little beaded bangles in her ears. She looked great. We headed for the elevator and into, I was sure, unknown galaxies.

Chapter Four

I looked up as we were standing on the sidewalk outside our building. The sky had frozen to a pointillist hardness. It was so cold that if you spat, your spit would hit the ground as a glassy marble. If you pissed, your piss would break up into icicles and fall to the sidewalk with a tinkling sound. Overhead the stars twinkled like tiny LED lights in the black, faraway quiet of space.

As we crossed Carmine Street, the bells of Our Lady of Pompeii Church began to peal over our heads, pure and clamorous. Arrested by the sound of the bells, we halted on the pavement in front of the white tile-fronted church. For a few moments we completely lost ourselves. There were no separate entities, Hali and I and my stepbrother standing there, just a river of liquid notes filling our heads and erasing our bodies, ringing louder and fuller than anything we'd ever heard before, until we had no knowledge of anything else but their ringing.

Then, as the long sweet savor of the big brass bells died away in our ears, the air grew as still as a Christmas Eve in the country.

Little Peter took a breath of cold air and blew it out. "Something big is about to happen," he said.

"What are you talking about?" Hali asked, frowning.

"Shhhh!" said Little Peter. "Can't you hear it?"

"I can't hear anything," said Hali. "It's incredibly quiet."

Little Peter's blue eyes glinted with excitement. "I don't know what it is, but it's probably something enormous. Maybe bigger than anything we know. Like two planets passing in space. Like some huge spaceship hissing down through the atmosphere to pick us all up. Or like a grand piano quietly falling through the air, just before it squashes us flat. Or it could be something tiny, like two ants fighting on the sidewalk."

We stared at each other, listening to the silence for a full minute. Then the light changed on Sixth Avenue and with it came again the rushing of tires, the heel-clicking step-step of pedestrians crossing the street, the harried drivers tapping out notes of warning and outrage on their horns, the babble and rush and relentless scrimmage of city life.

Little Peter started pulling ahead like an eager dog, hot on the track of something. We stumbled on slush frozen into hard ruts. As we paused outside of the Bowery Mission to look at the stained-glass windows, now suffused with a soft warm glow from the inside, showing the return of the prodigal son, a tall man in front of us slowly began to list over. His face was covered with tiny black moles like bricks fallen in a city lot. He had a blonde with him, and he was grappling at her shoulders, while she tried to hold him up.

"Danny!" the blonde said. "Danny!"

As we watched this paltry drama unfold, a tan Oldsmobile sedan of seventies vintage rolled up to the curb. It was obviously an unmarked police car. The driver's window slid down and a reedy voice over a thin tie shouted out, "Man, you ready for the Fourth Floor?"

The man, Danny, looked back, his arms flying akimbo above his shoulders and said, "Fourth Floor? No, man, I'm not ready."

But the cop knew different. He pulled over the car, and got out, his face narrow and serious, with a complete set of broken veins on his nose; he was Irish Catholic, no doubt, and he knew his drink.

Hali and I stood back with wonder, as Little Peter stepped in to help the blonde and the cop lever the tall drunk into the car's backseat. There were already quite a few men back there, piled on top of each other, looking out through the windshield like captured owls.

"What about *her*?" asked the man Danny from the car, his head already starting to roll.

"She can come, too," said the cop.

"No, not me," said the blonde, "I've still got some money left in the till at the Four Gold Coins."

She went to the window of the car and snapped her fingers, until the man handed her his pack of cigarettes. Then he slumped back, and we didn't see him anymore.

When the tan car pulled away, the blonde sat on the sidewalk, with her back to the wall under a plate-glass window, and lit a cigarette. We saw that she was no girl, either; her face was torn in two by drink like a piece of paper, one side written on, the other one blank.

"Phew!" she said, and seemed to mean it.

"What was that all about?" I asked Little Peter, as we walked away.

"The Fourth Floor?" he asked. "I thought everyone knew about the Fourth Floor."

"Not me," I said.

"A place of rehabilitation and detoxification. The city provides it to the indigent. You go in for four days, get a hospital bed, and they feed you."

"You ever been there?"

"No, I haven't. That's for the old guys, the real hard-core alcoholics. The only purpose I can see for the Fourth Floor is that after a few days in a hospital bed, your first drink is going to taste a whole lot sweeter."

After Houston Street, signs with the squiggles and dabs of Chinese writing started turning up. We passed chairs, tables, stools, stainless steel sinks and counters taken from failed restaurants, and the giant bowls of commercial mixing machines, all chained together on the sidewalk outside of restaurant supply stores.

As we descended toward Chinatown, Little Peter's face visibly relaxed.

The windows were steamed up in the Wo Hop Restaurant, scene of many late-night and early-morning refuelings for me. The air inside smelled of steam and grease and soy sauce and garlic and noodles and men's sweat. We took a table under the stairs, and Little Peter stowed the ratty plastic bags he carried his belongings in against the wall. The waiter, a skinny, middle-aged man with thick lips who thumbed his greasy pad incessantly, came over right away with warm, tasteless tea.

We had no sooner settled into our seats and brought the tea up to our lips when Little Peter said, in a loud voice, "I didn't know that we were going to have the honor of New York's Finest visiting us today!" Little Peter's voice was a cracked and cigarette-scarred bray. You could hear it in a four-block radius.

I looked over, and, sure enough, two female cops stood at the counter, picking up a bag of takeout. One was Hispanic, and the other a white woman with ears that had grown bright red from the cold.

"Couldn't you talk a little louder?" I asked Little Peter. "I don't think they heard you."

"Why don't we just ask our ladies in blue to have a seat with us!" Little Peter said. "I know they're getting paid to watch me. Why don't we make it that much easier!"

I tried to quiet him again. "I can talk, this is a free country. The First Amendment and all that!" he replied.

The two cops looked at each other uneasily. They'd probably just ducked in here from their car for a quiet bite to eat. The Hispanic cop whispered a comment in her partner's ear and they both laughed. I figured they were discussing whether they had time in their busy schedule to break a few heads. In a minute, though, they'd paid up and left, shoving their wallets, pads, and flashlights into the pockets of their uniforms, which were spread by broad girl butts.

"You know," said Little Peter, "I've always been responsible for whatever I've done. Anything that's happened to me, it's been because of something I've done that I meant to do. But there's one thing I've never asked for and it's this constant police scrutiny of everything that I do and say. I've never done anything to harass the cops. I've never robbed anyone or hurt anyone. There's a war on here. A real war."

The waiter returned. "Regular customers," he said to me. "They ask me to tell you that your friend talk too loud."

"What the hell, I'm not talking at all now," said Little Peter.

"Talk too loud. Better not next time," the waiter said.

"Got you," I said. I picked up the menu. I wasn't that hungry because of the powder, but I thought I'd better have something. "Peter, what do you want?"

We ordered our food, which took awhile, as Little Peter had to study every item on the menu, hemming and hawing, and there were hundreds.

"Do you remember when you used to saw away at that violin of yours?" I asked Little Peter when we were done. "We all thought you were going to play in the symphony. You played the piano, too. What ever became of all that?"

Little Peter pulled his hat low over his scarred forehead. "That was a long time ago," he replied. His huge, scarred right arm lay on the tabletop like a beached whale. The surgeon in Salt Lake City had been able to reattach the nerves of his left hand, but the right hand remained little more than a club.

"But you still listen to classical music?"

Little Peter scowled. He'd shown me the tapes in his bag; they ran more toward heavy metal than baroque.

"I hear Bach in my head," he said at last, slowly. "I hear it every night when I'm alone. Mostly Bach. Sometimes it's Mozart. Sometimes it's others."

"Other composers? Classical composers?"

"I hear the notes playing in my head, but they are notes no one has ever heard before."

"Music you've composed yourself?"

"I guess." He seemed wary.

"Could you write them down?"

"I would if I had the time," Little Peter said, looking ill-at-ease. "But I never have enough time."

Just then the waiter set down plates of steaming tofu, ginger chicken, and something brown piled high that looked like eels.

"What's this?" asked Little Peter.

"Tree fungus. You order," said the waiter.

"Oh, yes, I did," Little Peter said. He took a fork with his ruined hand and began carefully to push the shiny brown banners of food around in circles.

"I hear you called your dad," said Hali, looking at Little Peter with compassionate eyes.

"Yeah, I called him," Little Peter admitted. He held his teacup up to his eyes and peered over it.

"How'd it go?"

"Hali, there is an opposite magnetic polarity between me and Franz. Has been since I was a kid. When I was a kid, just the sound of his voice used to disrupt my peace of mind. And he used to say I had a voice that could shatter glass. I guess he just drove me crazy and I just drove him crazy and that was all there was to it."

"So, why were you calling him?" she asked.

Little Peter put down his teacup. "Man, you don't know what it's like to want something so bad it hurts and have to give it up because you're just not good enough. And whether you're good enough or not, that's something you're going to have to find out for yourself, and you might not want to know the answer. Because most of us aren't."

"I think my Peter knows," Hali said, looking at me.

I did know. I'd once tried to explain to an old girlfriend, with all sincerity, how I sometimes came away feeling, after a conversation with my father, even a short one, as though someone had injected a toxic fluid into my veins, a cold, dark liquid that quietly rose up through my body, paralyzing my limbs one by one, poisoning everything I thought was happy, or could exist in the future. After a few seconds, she cut me off. "I'd sooner hear about a case of child molestation," she said, and she got off the phone.

But my wife is in for the long term. She has a theory about why I am the way I am. When she sees me frozen with my hand on the doorknob between one room and another; when she sees my face portraying, like a tiny movie screen, the Max Fleischer characters of my life, raging in conflict; when she finds me stopped in mid-sentence, staring at the wall with a kind of fascination and horror, she says to me, "I hate your father for what he did to you—" even though she loves him, for the colorful, profane, self-centered, larger-than-life, Macy's Day Parade character he has become in her life.

"He took away your self-confidence," she says. "He destroyed your purpose. He belittled you as a child. He ignored and abandoned you. He made you helpless. He made you so afraid."

"How do you know this?" I ask, in fascination and dread. I'm not sure I want to know the answer.

"I know it because he still does it to you. I know it because . . ."

And here she stops, and continues to gaze at me with an unsettling mixture of indignation and thoughtfulness. Nothing I can say will get her to go on and finish her sentence.

Little Peter was looking at us, his blue eyes somewhat unfocused.

"This is not to take anything away from Franz," he said, "who's an incredible person, as you and I both know. Maybe neither one of us will ever live to be anything like him. He can be whatever he wants to be, and he's probably earned the right to that, living with my mother for as long as he did. But if you happen to be a boy, and if you happen to be his son, and you happen to be me, he can be a coldhearted son-of-a-bitch."

"What are you talking about?" I asked.

"I'm talking about Franz," he said. "I'm talking about my family tossing me aside like a piece of Kleenex."

Something was rising in me. I wasn't sure what it was, but I decided to let it out. "Do you want to start over?" I said. "Do you want to make it a blank slate?"

Little Peter jerked. "What do you mean?"

"Could be a hell of a lot worse. He never came at you with a tire iron. He never burned you with cigarettes."

"Peter, stop," said Hali.

"He didn't carve his initials in your chest with a fork."

"He didn't do any of those things to you, either," said Little Peter.

"No, he didn't."

"Sometimes maybe it just felt like that," said Hali, helpfully.

"That's what other dads do," I said, ignoring her. "Our dad didn't do that."

"Other dads were not that cruel," Little Peter said. "What our dad did was worse."

"Where are you going to go when you leave here, Peter?" Hali asked. Little Peter looked at us, and I saw that he was deciding that now was as good a time as any to make his pitch.

"Can I please stay with you?" he asked. "I don't take up much space, and I don't need a lot to eat."

I looked at my wife. No help there. Hali looked like she was ready to cry.

"Sorry, Peter," I said.

"I mean, just for one night."

"Not even for one night."

"Why not?"

"Well, first of all, the doormen of our building are a mean bunch, kid. They're not going to understand."

"What's the other reason?"

"My wife," I said. "We're going to have a baby."

"Congratulations," Little Peter said. His smile seemed genuine.

"Thanks. The problem is you're a street person, Peter. You hang around in the street. You buy drugs in the street. Your friends are in the street. I can't take a chance of your bringing any of that into our house."

"You're right," said Little Peter. His great shaggy brown head nodded. "That's what I'd say, too, if I were you."

"You would?" said Hali.

"Yes," he said.

"Then this is it, then." I reached across the table and handed Little Peter a subway token. I was determined to pull the Band-Aid off fast.

"Wait!" he said.

We waited while he poured another cup of tea and drank it down slowly.

He stood up. "Now, it's okay. I'm ready to go," he said.

Outside the Wo Hop, I bought Little Peter a blue Chinese daypack from a small outdoor shop. Nearby a man in a stained white apron was making a wall of green garbage bags. The wind had picked up and streams of snow blew sideways across Canal Street. We were standing by the black cast-iron railing of the subway entrance. Little Peter shouldered the daypack.

The heroin was wearing off, leaving a headache in the back of my eyes. For the umpteenth time I asked myself, what was the point? It hadn't even been that good, except in the first few minutes.

Snow was building up on Little Peter's thick eyebrows. As usual, the raised scar on his brow made him look worried and quizzical. Hali hugged him. "Take care of yourself, Peter."

"There's just one thing."

"What's that?"

"Promise you'll call me if you ever come to the end of the line," I said.

"What do you mean?"

"I don't want to hear about you jumping out of a window, or dousing yourself with gasoline."

"Okay," he said.

"Promise."

"I promise."

"All right," I said. "Take care." It was such a stupid, useless admonition to give to anyone under those circumstances.

Little Peter started to descend the steps into the subway. He seemed to be pulling against every atom of his being. On the third step, he turned back.

"You have to remember all of this," he said to me. His blazing eyes stared directly into mine.

"What do you mean?" I gulped.

"Not only what happened here in this restaurant right now, but everything that happened from the time you were born, right up to this minute. It's your job. You have to take out all the pieces and see how they all fit together, because I can't anymore. I've lost that. That's the only way we're going to untangle this terrible mess we're in.

"I used to be able to do that," he said. "I used to lie in bed, and see the whole thing at once, all the pieces of the puzzle falling into place. But I can't anymore. It's all gone, since I went down to Central Booking."

"What is it exactly that you want me to do?"

"Just take it from the beginning," he said. "That's all I ask."

Little Peter turned and went down the steps and was gone.

The following day I called my father to tell him what had transpired. He listened carefully, punctuating his questions with his usual array of throat-clearings, snorts, and vocalizations.

Ow-ow OW-AH-AH-aaah! What had Little Peter looked like? How had he been dressed? Did you give him any money? "Yeah, right! He really skinned you!" Where has he been staying? Was he drunk? Did he talk about his mother?

"Aha! Aho! *Aeeee-IIII-eieieiei-OOOOohohoh!* What a scam artist! *Heh-heh-heh!*" Where did he go? "He'll be back. He always comes back!"

Finally he said, "Congratulations. You have just acquired a thirty-one-year-old son."

I protested, saying nothing could be farther from the truth. I hadn't really done anything, and in fact I'd ditched Little Peter as soon as I could. I was about to have a kid of my own, was awed by that eventuality, and wasn't about to take on any new responsibilities. But Dad had said all he had to say and he stuck to it.

Then Liz got on the line and said I was a saint, and that made me feel even worse. She might as well have said "sucker."

Part Two

The whole temple of Man's achievement must inevitably be
buried beneath the debris of a universe in ruins.

—Bertrand Russell

Chapter Five

July 4, 1961
Long Island, New York

My father drove our Ford station wagon through the sunny bedroom communities of Locust Valley and Glen Cove with my mother at his side, while my two sisters and I, lolling in the backseat, were still making loud throat-clearing sounds after crossing what we laughingly dubbed the "Frog's Neck" Bridge.

A shady tree-lined road wound through the wealthy unincorporated town of Lattingtown. Every quarter mile or so we passed the imposing iron gates of some fallen robber baron's estate. Most were subdivided, had been turned into tree nurseries, or had been carved up by Robert Moses in his obsessive quest to weave a net of roaring motorways around New York City. Compared to these, the gates marking the entrance of Peacock Point were relatively unassuming, a pair of brick towers topped with bronze peacocks. Once inside, a private paved roadway curled under tall locust trees. Almost immediately my sisters and I began to hear cicadas rasping their monotonous summer love songs. These, the skittering blades of the hand-pushed lawn mowers, and the enthused *swoosh-swoosh! Click-clack! Swish, swish, swish, swish!* of the sprinklers, being towed gradually across the lawns on long wires, were the background music of our summers here. We passed several stately, shingled houses on the left, half hidden by bowing leafy branches. Scattered across Peacock Point's seventy-seven acres were the homes of my great-aunts and -uncles, Dot and Trubee Davison and Alice and Di Gates, as well as of my mother's cousin, Harry Davison, and his wife.

The drive to Peacock Point had become a summer ritual for our family. If our pale work-and-school existence in suburban Connecticut during the winter months formed one pole of our lives, then Peacock Point formed the other more extravagant and colorful pole. There we could look forward to sharing days of drowsy summer indolence with our many cousins, barely cognizant of the darkly tanned and sweating gardeners who toiled in the hazy distance.

My mother, Anne, sometimes expressed qualms about exposing her children to Peacock Point's insular luxury and reactionary politics from such an early age. "Do you feel sometimes as though you are living in a glass bubble?" she'd ask me anxiously, gripping my arms just below the elbows with hands grown tan and strong from tennis playing. She searched my eyes. "Do you feel as though everything outside is unreal and dangerous?" She fought an inner conviction that each month at Peacock Point meant an additional month on the analyst's couch for myself and my sisters in later life. Still, for my mother, the return to her childhood home remained a guilty pleasure, a respite from her steady efforts to escape its magnetic pull. With her mother, Frances, slipping into alcoholism and her father, Ward, increasingly distant, spending July and August at her parents' home was a way she could continue to see herself as a dutiful daughter. She continued to hate the assumptions that seemed to pervade the estate, however, that God had created the earth to serve the Davison family and that there was no other place on the planet so fit to live in as Peacock Point.

My father, on the other hand, adored Peacock Point. Its fantastic appointments matched some inner need for pomp and finery he had perhaps inherited from his mother, Mimia, who'd always been something of a snob. He looked forward with fondness to Sunday's formal meals at the Big House, when the long dining room table would be laid out for anywhere from twenty to forty guests, and the pink slices of roast beef and long French beans were served from silver trays by a tuxedo-clad Bedford, the mild, balding English butler. It was a deeply satisfying experience for my father to lounge afterward in the Trophy Room with my great uncles, smoking cigars and drinking brandy, as the talk turned to bagging pheasant in Georgia and the correct methods of steering a yacht in the Bay of Fundy. Around the walls, paneled in dark wood, jutted the stuffed corpses of wild animals shot on African safaris—a black wildebeest; a slavering jackal; a half lion about to spring, its paws poised on a half rock; rows of antelope horns and boar tusks; a full tiger skin stretched over the library table. He took strong pleasure in the company of my mother's cousin Danny as they commuted together on the Long Island Railroad from Glen Cove during the summer months to their respective jobs in New York City.

My mother's grandfather, Henry P. Davison, a loyal banking lieutenant of J. P. Morgan, had purchased Peacock Point in the early 1900s. The family, including my grandmother, Frances—whom we all called Froggie— still spoke of "Harry Dear" in hushed tones, as if he was standing just behind the florid, oversized portrait of him that dominated the main hall of my great-grandmother's three-story Georgian mansion, which we called the Big House.

Harry Dear had been a fantastically gregarious man, apparently, but the men who warmed their hands on the bright flame of his personality both loved and feared him. His story had a fairytale quality, as the newspapers were fond of noting. As a youth, he'd left the hardscrabble town in the Pennsylvania hills in which he'd been raised and went through some years of wandering. Landing somehow in the industrial port town of Bridgeport, Connecticut, he attached himself to the legendary sideshow impresario, P. T. Barnum, whose motto was "There's a sucker born every minute." Barnum introduced the young man to his future wife, Kate Trubee, daughter of a prominent Bridgeport family, and to his first job in a New York bank. There, after Harry foiled a madman's stickup, he came to the attention of the megabanker J. P. Morgan. Morgan admired young Harry's ruthlessness, boundless energy, and unquestioning loyalty and soon made him a henchman. Harry's rise after that was meteoric—wags in the press called him "Morgannapoleon." Under Morgan, he worked round the clock deciding which companies to save and which to allow to crack open and sink. He'd been instrumental in starting both Banker's Trust and the Federal Reserve. After World War I, he had restructured China's debt, then that of the tottering European nations, and when a banking scare threatened the nation's economy, he'd helped J. P. Morgan gather the banks to shore it up.

My great-grandfather died of a brain tumor in 1922, but by some miracle of preservation, his wife, my great-grandmother, Kate Trubee Davison, lived on. She was short and plump, yet ramrod straight, a woman of impeccable morals and few audible words. Famously, she was known to boil the toothbrushes left behind by guests in order to reuse them. Everyone called her "Goggie," after some grandchild's lisping mispronunciation. As her children grew up, and even as some of their children grew up, instead of moving away and starting lives of their own, they'd built houses on the estate and continued to live there, many of them until they died.

Goggie herself seemed to epitomize the New England Protestant matron, though she was, in fact, a direct descendant of Andris Trubee, a Jewish merchant who'd settled near Bridgeport in the early 1700s. Now in her nineties, Goggie wore strange, shapeless hats decorated with artificial flowers and flounced dresses that had gone out of style with the abdication of Edward VIII. While we, a brainless flock of platinum-haired children, ran barefoot from one end of the estate to another, she drove herself in stately fashion around its paved roads in an ancient, black, hearselike electric car with the words NO SKID carved into its tires in lieu of treads.

My father eased the wheel of the station wagon to one side. As we rounded a long descending curve, we passed over $W \ldots O \ldots L \ldots S$, painted large and white on the pavement, no doubt warning of a species of predacious animal that had been common hereabouts long ago, but was extinct now, and turned left at a small willow-shaded pond.

Here, the road continued on in a kidney-shaped circle for a lazy half mile, enclosing the fishpond, a formal English croquet court, some outstanding trees, and one or two small guest cottages.

Steering with his knees, my father tilted his head sideways in order to light a cigarette, showing a lean, lupine jaw.

"Don't ever go to Wall Street!" he said, as he struck the match and then smoothly cupped it in his half-closed fist to protect the flame from the wind—a patented method he'd picked up during the war, or, perhaps, sailing on Long Island Sound.

His match flared once, twice, three times, throwing a red glare over the stubble of his cheek. Then after the butt was lit, the wonderful fragrance of burning tobacco filled the car, and he shook the match and threw it out the window.

I looked up from the book in my lap. "Why?" I asked, semi-innocently, wanting to prolong the conversation.

"Why, because it's a bunch of crap, that's why!" my father replied, with scorn.

This was interesting information to an alert ten-year-old, since I knew (because he'd often told me) that Wall Street was the warm teat at which my father sucked every day, and that stocks and bonds were the milk upon which we grew fat. But as he puffed his potent, unfiltered Camel cigarette, his thoughts became tangled in a web of nicotine musings and he refused to illuminate further.

"You take after your mother," he said instead, turning his face half toward me. "It's true, you have the same build. And you're sensitive. You never really say what you are thinking. You hang back."

I detected an edge of warning in his voice. He hadn't meant this description as a compliment. Last night at dinner, his eyes had suddenly gone tiny and black. I forget what the subject was. There was a moment when I think he wondered whether he wanted to let *that* particular genie out of the bottle. Then my father reached across the table and landed a slap on the side of my temple with the palm of his hand.

I stood up immediately. I probably should have said something witty and biting, but there's nothing like a slap to scoot all the relevant thoughts out of your head. I couldn't even remember what we had been talking about. My mother turned away. Dad was standing now, too, with an expression of cold fury on his face. I threw the chair back, ducked through the kitchen, clattered up the back stairs to my room, where I slammed the door and threw myself down on the bed. As I lay staring at the gray crack under my door, I began to dream of ways I could get out on my own and live away from my family. Thomas Edison had worked on a train when he was about ten; he'd set up a chemistry lab in the mail car for his experiments. Ehrich Weiss was touring and escaping from handcuffs and cabinets when he was my age, way before he became Houdini.

I switched on the bed light and took a book at random from the shelves, a paperback with a lurid red cover, H. G. Wells's *War of the Worlds*. I read for an hour, listening for my father's step in the hallway outside my room. I knew he'd come—he always did after a blowout like that. Eventually I saw the pale line of shadow under the door darken with his shoes, and his knock sounded lightly.

"Hello, it's your dad. Might I come in?" he asked, with a bumptiousness that, from my current frosty position of emancipation, I thought rather pathetic.

"Yeah, come in," I said, immediately unsure if I had adopted the right tone. Perhaps a plain "Enter!" would have been better.

The door opened and closed as my father slipped inside. He took a pull from his cigarette—which made his face glow as red as a Martian—and tapped the ash into his hand.

"Your mother thinks I treat you too harshly," he said at last. "I don't think so. I came to find out what you think."

"What do you mean?" I asked. My voice didn't come out quite right. I'd meant to sound commanding and stern, but instead I sounded shaky and unsure of myself.

"I mean what happened at dinner," he said.

I tried to think. When I tried to remember, my thoughts just slipped away.

"I think it's time you acknowledge that you bear some responsibility for what happens in this house," he said. He blew a stream of smoke to one side. "I'm just a human being and I'm vulnerable like anyone else."

"Yeah, Dad, that's okay," I said. "I mean, I understand."

"You can forgive your old man, can't you? Even your old man deserves a break sometimes." I smelled tobacco and whiskey as he leaned in to ruffle my hair and felt his stubble scrape across my cheek.

"Get it?" he asked. "Got it? Good!"

As our station wagon passed the white strand of beach on our left, with its large, old-fashioned changing house, which we called the Tea House, its tall metal maypole and grass tennis courts, my sisters craned their necks to see if any of our cousins were playing there. Two of the tennis courts had recently metamorphosed into a swimming pool as a concession to the burgeoning number of great-grandchildren running about the estate.

There was a slight wind up, and sunlight sparkled on the tips of the waves beyond the curved breakwater of the cove, just as it had when an entire village of Matinecock Indians had lived here, cutting thatch for their huts and collecting oysters for food. Every now and then, the breeze broke off the top of a wave, and turned out a spoonful of surf roiling inside, like the white of an egg. Through the car window my sisters and I watched the seagulls slide across the air currents, the slate gray of the water and the brilliant puffs of white cloud inlaid like stones in a lapis sky. My father also cast a discerning eye over the wind, noting its direction and velocity, its temperature and potential for bringing foul weather and for dragging a small skiff off course.

Within the closed precincts of Peacock Point the grass barely quivered, however, and the air remained sultry and immovable. Sweat made the vinyl of the car seat cling to my back through my cotton knit shirt, and the tires of our station wagon rolled stickily over the asphalt road, at the edges of which small puddles of black tar oozed.

I studied the back of my father's neck over the car seat. I always thought he looked a bit like Humphrey Bogart. Like Bogey, he had thinning, dark, slightly curly hair, and an oval, expressive, at times even clownish face. Like Bogey, he faced the world and all of its inhabitants with a studied slouch and a cigarette always stuck in his jaw. Most of the time, he wore worn army khakis and a leather jacket when he was home. He was an avid sailor, the owner of a thirty-five-foot, fiberglass-hulled sailboat, *The Frances*— named after my grandmother—which he kept moored in Norwalk Harbor, and long days out on the water kept him clear-eyed, tanned, and wiry. He was perhaps an inch or two below average height, which made him shorter than my mother, Anne, and for this reason, perhaps, he maintained a small-guy's unimpressed stance toward his fellow man, his razor sharp mind always feeding him the words he needed to cut away a taller man's pretensions.

I went back to my book, hoping for one or two minutes of uninterrupted reading before we arrived at my grandmother's house and I had to stop and be sociable. My sisters returned to their happy chitchat about horses and clothes and friends at school. I tried to shut out the sound.

My sisters Olga and Lisa were nine and seven, pretty blond girls with bangs and long hair behind that hung down below their shoulders. Olga was the confident one, athletic at field hockey, with frank, blue eyes. Lisa was the cute one, with the slight lisp, who didn't always quite catch on to things, and wore glasses to correct a wandering eye. The tight little orbit they made around each other was almost impenetrable. At night I went to sleep listening to their garbled giggling through the walls of my bedroom, wondering what in the world they were talking about, and I woke up hearing the same thing. My mother and her only sibling, Alessandra, had formed just such a bond when they were young, and she understood what my sisters were about. But of boys she hadn't a clue, and she left me alone. As for my father, he didn't understand a boy who preferred to read rather than go out to play. His world consisted of making other people like him and bending them to his will.

Photographs of me at the time show a typical boy of the early sixties, with an egg-shaped head covered with a blond buzz cut, and a toothy grin, but I felt myself to be invisible, a fog, made of air and moisture. My father told me in a moment of frankness that, growing up, I'd never been the kind of boy he'd ever considered as a son. This kind of candor was typical of my father, the kind that cut deeply. I'd given up trying to do the things I thought he wanted, because they were just met with scorn. Though I could climb trees like a monkey, I was puny and awkward for my age, and no good at team sports. Nor was I much help on my father's sailboat. I knew the basic points of sailing, but being on deck made me queasy, and I preferred staying below with a book to having my father toss me a line and swear when I didn't react quickly enough. My friends tended to be the ones who built airplane models and took piano lessons. I couldn't make any headway with the large, brutish, sporty, blond preppy boys— among whom was my cousin, Chipper Davison—who dominated my class, though I'd been in school with them since we were all three. I was an outsider, and even at ten I knew the brand on my forehead would never lift.

At home, I retreated further and further into my own world. The corridor that connected my room to my parents' room was so long that I lived, literally, across a border and in another town. To avoid contact with bipeds with whom I felt only a marginal connection, I often climbed down the tree outside my window instead of taking the stairs. In the second grade I'd discovered the school library and was still burning through its contents three years later.

A patient omnivore, I read about Hiroshima victims, escapees from German prison camps, beloved cocker spaniels, and famed inventors. I read interplanetary science fiction and earthbound memoirs by authors whose names had barely escaped the gravity of the nineteenth century. By now I'd started to make inroads in the books my parents left lying about the house—*Franny and Zooey, Rabbit Run, To Kill a Mockingbird, Trustee from the Toolroom, Catch-22*, and Richard Fariña's prototypical hipster novel, *Been Down So Long It Looks Like Up to Me*, a creased copy of which I'd found on my father's dresser. Dangerous stuff. Each time I read a book that reached ungodly heights, I closed its covers, and with a feeling of awe and self-importance placed it on a shelf in my room reserved for the sacred canon, alongside *The Colditz Story*, Jules Verne's *The Mysterious Island*, and *Houdini's Escapes and Magic*. Both of my parents were hungry readers. I often heard my father declare that there were no writers in the English language who could compare to Nabokov or Capote. I cautiously started to browse within Nabokov's early translations and Capote's *Other Voices, Other Rooms* and *Breakfast at Tiffany's*. I never mentioned these books to kids at school, however, not even to my so-called best friends. My friends' interest in books started and stopped with *Homer Price* and *The Adventures of Freddy the Detective*. Most of them didn't read at all.

The book in my lap was *Call It Sleep*, by Henry Roth. I'd picked it up by chance from my father's wardrobe. It was probably due to books like this that I thought I could fend for myself whether I was dropped into a sled on the polar ice pack, a jungle trail, or a packed ghetto street in New York's Lower East Side. In my mind I spoke every language easily, including obscure criminal cant. In my own immature way, I was just lurching toward awareness that there was more to these pages than just the story of a lonely boy rising up in the slums of New York. I began to hear in Henry Roth's keening voice something like the notes in a jazz trumpet solo coming out of the recordings that my parents occasionally put on the record player. As I nodded my head to Roth's lush overtones and contrapuntal rhythms, I was startled, at times, to notice the author's own silhouette pacing restlessly just behind the page in half light, as if in a window, a man in a wife-beater T-shirt, I thought, smoking a cigar.

Our station wagon slid smoothly around another curve. We waved at my Uncle Di (whose name was short for Artemis), a tall, white-haired figure standing absently in flannels at the edge of the croquet court with his two black Labradors. Next to him sat my great-uncle Trubee in his wheelchair. The *pock, pock* of wooden balls colliding arrived at my ears like the snap of a hypnotist's fingers that instantly puts you to sleep. The sound was followed by a strange awakening call, as my great-aunt Alice shouted, "No, you're dead on me!" I glanced up to see a rusty thatch of hair move through a screen of leaves. It was my mother's first cousin, Jack. He laughed and placed his heel on a red-colored ball and gave it a whack with a long stem of polished wood, making the second ball next to it, a yellow one, dart away past the tall weeping locust we called the "House Tree." Under the voluminous skirts of this tree, it was said, the grand lady of the house, my great-grandmother Goggie, would sometimes disappear to take a ladylike pee when a croquet game went on too long.

"Oh, darn you, Jack! Why must you always pick me?" asked Alice as she marched after the ball into the rough grass.

"Because I love you so much," said Jack, red-haired, florid, laughing his low hyena laugh.

When Uncle Di didn't wave back at us, my dad took a puff of his cigarette and muttered, "Stuffed shirt!"

The croquet players fell away behind us. Soon the eight chimneys of the Big House rose out of the oaks and maples, a squat brick building that climbed higher and higher as we got closer. Four white columns reached to the third-floor balustrade, where they were topped by large concrete Grecian urns. The wings of the mansion on either side begat further wings, which begat further wings, servants' quarters, enclosed porches, verandas, and sitting rooms, so the whole building seemed to stretch its arms wider and wider and then swoop to envelop us.

My father drank water from the canteen he always kept on the front seat of the car since his kidney stone, and wiped his mouth with the back of his hand. As we approached this seat of wealth and power connected to my mother's family, he may have told himself that he had little reason to be intimidated. He was a Yale man, after all, like my grandfather, Ward Cheney, and all of my mother's cousins and uncles (though he'd never been tapped to join Yale's secret society, Skull and Bones, as they had). The Davisons traditionally sent their sons to the Groton School, north of Boston, but my father had spent his boarding school days at the equally prestigious Choate school in Connecticut. And while the Davison men were hereditary bankers, my father had recently been promoted to Vice President in Charge of Planning at the respected financial printing firm Bowne & Company, founded in 1776 and the oldest continually operating company in America.

My father was proud to have entered Bowne as a salesman. Never mind that his first cousin Ted Stanley owned the company; he'd worked his way up on his own merits, and everyone knew it. Being an executive at Bowne automatically made him a stock market insider. Although he might have been put in jail if he'd revealed them, my father knew secrets about American corporations that no one else knew, simply because that information had to pass through Bowne to be printed before it was disseminated to the world, in the form of quarterly reports to stockholders and filings with the SEC. It occasionally happened that a minor Bowne executive, or even one of its typesetters, tried to cash in on advance knowledge of a merger, gleaned from the printing plant trash bins, and invariably he was caught and imprisoned, or made to pay a large fine.

Our Ford station wagon rolled by the white-painted Casino, a partially roofed summer pavilion upon whose red-tiled terrace my parents had been married, and slowed at the Big House. Seeing my great-grandmother's black electric car parked out front reminded my mother to look over the backseat and say, "Kids, even if she invites you, you are not allowed to ride in the car with Goggie. Do you understand?"

"Why not?" asked my sister Olga, knowing why, but just wanting to hear the answer.

"The old bag can't even see," scoffed my father. "One of these days she's going to wrap that thing around a tree."

"Franz!" reproved my mother, stretching a long, tanned arm over the back of the seat to play with my father's hair. Dad chuckled, and crossed his right hand over his shoulder to flick his cigarette out the window.

My mother was young then, almost a girl herself. She was tall, with an athlete's lank and a dark brown off-the-shoulder bob. Her hair had been so fair when she was a girl that she still referred to herself as a blonde, though her thoroughly unpretentious mind would have never thought to bleach her hair to bring that youthful shade back. Nor would she have deigned to soften the beakish shape of her nose, an inheritance from her father's family, the Cheneys of Manchester, Connecticut, though plastic surgery was the rage in the early sixties. Her nose fit aptly with her high cheekbones, and she looked easily five years younger than her age. Her curves weren't the kind that made liquor salesmen, stockbrokers, or golfers in our Connecticut township lust after her, but my mother's rare, unassuming beauty and quiet honesty caused many of their wives to fall in love with her. My earliest memory is of my mother standing at the phone in the pantry by the kitchen saying patiently, over and over, "Yes . . . yes . . . yes . . . yes . . . yes . . ." as some bosom friend poured out her troubles to her.

A wooden sign on one of the trees coyly spelled out the letters w.c. in black enamel, along with an elegant arrow pointing ahead, as if showing the way to the bathroom. But "W.C." actually stood for my grandfather's name, Ward Cheney.

Here my father cut the engine and got out, stretching out his arms over the sun-dappled drive. My sisters, too, pushed open the doors and began to run back and forth on the asphalt, which radiated heat. I stayed in the backseat with the novel open in my lap. I'd just finished the book, and now I was feeling a familiar sense of awe. It had been almost perfect and I couldn't wait to put it on the shelf in my room with the others.

"Hey, kiddo, going to help with your bag?" my mother said, peering over the backseat at me through her sunglasses. I looked up. My sisters were already tugging their bags from the back of the wagon.

"Never mind, he's useless," said my father, starting for the screen doors of the foyer. But my mother said something in his ear, and he put my bag down on the ground. I picked it up and followed after.

As we stumbled from the sun into the dark foyer of my grandmother's house, we were rescued from the insane barking of an ancient black miniature poodle who lurked in the shadows of our grandmother's coat closet by gray-haired, smiling Dorothy, who greeted us in a starched maid's uniform.

"So pleasant to see you all!" she said, as she led us through the living room, her voice soft and English-accented. "Oh my gosh! *Look* at you kids, look at how tall you've grown! Your grandmother is in a great mood, I can tell you, just thinking about you coming today."

As Dorothy led us farther into the cool shadows of the house, my father ruminated out loud as to whether my grandmother's happy state was caused *merely* by our sudden appearance. He knew ever well that by this time in the afternoon she'd be well into her second pitcher of martinis.

"Franz," said my mother, reprovingly. "Franz!"

My grandmother grew up in an age when the daughters of the rich, especially those with wit and style, could achieve a certain fame of their own. Newspapers carried gushing articles about her boat christenings, her movements to East Hampton and back. When she and my grandfather left for Europe on their honeymoon (accompanied by my great-grandmother and a large black dog), the pulps were so avid for details that one news story used generic photo models to stand in for my grandparents.

Only one of the four children of my great-grandfather, Harry Dear, had ever had the slightest desire to leave home, apparently. The others built their houses on the estate. My grandmother, "Froggie," constructed a modernist deco octagon on the shore of Long Island Sound by her mother's place. Her white-painted cinderblock palace was so plainly visible to sailors out on the water that it was marked on nautical charts. The house had two wings: the one on the left housed the original children's quarters, quite out of earshot, or view, of parents, and now adapted as guest rooms (where we stayed), and the wing on the right held the kitchen and the servants' quarters. Anticipating the cavernous lofts that would become fashionable fifty years in the future, Froggie caused the middle of the building to be taken up entirely by its living room, an enormous open eight-sided space perhaps eighty feet in diameter, whose ceiling sprung twenty-five feet above its plush brown carpet. Servants passed discreetly from the kitchen into the living room from a door hidden behind a black lacquered screen inlaid with mother-of-pearl. Guests were invited to drift from one social island to another. Afternoons, they joined Froggie and Ward for drinks around a low, black Chinese table in the shape of a lily pad. From there they looked out through tall French doors to the Sound. At dinnertime, they grouped around a formal table set in the exact center of the octagon, under a pendulous crystal chandelier. Afterward, they smoked and drank on Louis XIV furniture, around a small marble fireplace.

Ward and Froggie's bedroom was a glass outpost on the roof, reached by a curving staircase from the living room. The stairway's entrance was obscured by a velvet curtain, through which we grandchildren staged hastily concocted plays. When equipping her bathroom, my grandmother had found no bathtub suitable to her imagination, and so had one created out of beveled mirrors. The toilet, too, rested within a silver reflective throne. Each morning, lulled by her air conditioner's athletic whirl, Froggie would sleep until noon, while my grandfather, a tall, self-contained, balding man who read Homer and Thucydides in the original and collected first editions of Joyce, Pound, Eliot, and Hemingway, would read in his small study. During this time, the living room was deserted; we kids dragged our shoes to make designs in the brown carpet, played board games, or hung long, tanned legs over the arms of the chairs, reading.

My grandparents' house was just a cottage compared to the Big House next door, of course, a nod to quaint Bohemianism, to freedom, and to a daughter's willful ways. In the marbled entrance at the Big House was a sculpture in black stone, by Houdon, of a naked girl wrapped in rags; above it curled a massive staircase with a brass rail; and above that hung a life-sized portrait of my grandmother, beloved daughter, as a young woman upon her equally life-sized, equally beloved horse.

My grandmother Froggie was conscious of her position as a fashion trendsetter. Her walls were decorated with works of Picasso, Rouault, Dufy,

Gauguin, Klee, Rodin, all, I think, picked up relatively cheaply on trips to Europe after the war. To promote her "novel" idea that paintings could hang in homes rather than just museums, Froggie joined forces with her sister, Alice Gates, to start the Decorator's Picture Gallery, about which she had two thick, crumbling scrapbooks of reviews from the New York press.

A portrait of Froggie painted in the 1930s, which now hangs in my living room, shows a confident, handsome woman standing in a summer blouse by the beach with a martini in one hand and a cigarette in the other. She didn't know that these two symbols of womanly liberation would eventually become relentless instruments of her own downfall. In the stylish 1934 movie comedy *The Thin Man*, the actress Myrna Loy might line up five martinis on a tray and gaily wolf them down, one after another, but in real life one cannot do that—at least not indefinitely, or not without incurring terrible consequences to oneself and one's family—as we were all to discover soon enough.

Chapter Six

The maid, Dorothy, took us straight out to the flagstone terrace, where Froggie was having a martini. My grandfather, "Big" Ward, sat across from her in a cast-iron lawn chair, silently sipping a glass of wine. He probably would have preferred to be back in his small study. Why did a man who read avant-garde literature, copied Rodin and Renoir paintings in charcoal, and translated classical Greek drama hang around Peacock Point, where for most residents the highest form of aesthetic was the taxidermied rhinoceros? My mother screwed up the courage to ask her father that question one day, and he'd replied, "I'm just here to be with your grandmother during her golden years," an answer that had struck my mother as so fatuous that it took her breath away.

My grandmother was a world-class raconteur, and so my father immediately took the chair next to her so that he could begin tossing her straight man's lines. She had the most outrageous way of observing her friends and family and reciting the incidents that happened to them. She could be loud, intentionally crude, and also very funny.

"You wouldn't *believe*," she'd say, launching into yet another ribald story about some supposed affair between the servants. Most of her stories took place along the broad highway of the here and now, but tonight she was reminiscing about the late night on the campaign trail with the liberal Republican presidential hopeful Wendell Wilkie, when the candidate walked into her train compartment naked. My grandmother, a young woman with a husband away in the navy, had no intention of succumbing to the candidate's rather dubious physical charms. She'd drawn her blanket up to her chin and said the first thing that came into her head, which in my grandmother's case was always the right thing. "What's on your mind, Mr. Wilkie?" she'd asked with mock innocence. And then of course had burst into giggles.

Tonight Froggie's silk pantsuit vibrated like a magician's handkerchief with shards of purple, yellow, orange, red, green, and blue outlined in black. No one else could dream of wearing Froggie's clothes; a dress that on another woman would simply have looked bizarre, Froggie carried off without effort. As she chattered on, she waved a cigarette with bright lipstick stains in her narrow fingers, making her gold charm bracelet swing and rattle; a gold-plated Greek drachma coin the size of a silver dollar was perhaps the smallest charm on its oversized links. The flawed pale amethyst on her ring was as big as a walnut. Red lipstick shouted from the pale, ravaged mask of a face whose lips moved so animatedly. Her black hair, dry and obviously dyed, was swept up and back in the Jackie Kennedy style fashionable then. I went over to the rolling bar and mixed myself a ginger ale with a sprig of mint and went to sit down at her feet.

With my grandmother, the conversation always raced ahead with the pace of a runaway train. I had the feeling that if the talk ever did halt, even for a moment, she'd pull her head back and stare at us all in horror. Anticipating a silence, even a second's lapse, far ahead of time, she was poised to throw in a nugget, an observation, a joke, a non sequitur, anything to keep the raw engines of conversation burning. You couldn't say she was manic; she simply was richly within her element, riding not just the crosscurrents of her imagination, dipping here and there into her stock of gossipy tidbits, but riding also the buoyant down-swirls of her martini as it coursed through her veins.

I looked over at my mother. I could tell by the crinkling around her eyes that the regular hiss of the black plastic device filled with Freon that my grandmother used to frost her martini glass before she refilled it from a thermos jug was getting on her nerves. My father was gazing into my mother's face uneasily. I thought it was interesting that my father, the forceful and confident one, was always looking at my mother for clues as to how to go on. The air had grown sticky and filled with electricity. I glanced around for my sisters, but they'd disappeared, most likely playing in the Appleby house next door, where our cousins lived. Dark purple clouds spread tentacles of rain over the water in the distance. A tentative burst of green-and-white fireworks flew up from Rye Beach across the Sound, making a faint popping noise.

My father seemed tense. He was staring off at the water, where wavering threads of steel-white lightning were silently breaking from a bruised elbow of sky. He appeared to be listening to my uncle Danny telling a story on the veranda of the Big House, separated from us by low hedges and a stretch of lawn, where the tinkling of silverware told us that a small gathering was taking place.

The person I was then couldn't have conjectured what my father was thinking about because he was very good at hiding his thoughts. Keeping secrets was part of his job, after all. But with the distance I have now I can venture a guess: he was thinking about leaving my mother. Another filled his thoughts, a soft creature who curled behind the blue smoke of his cigarette that streamed around his temples. A creature, sure and ravishing, wily in an innocent kind of way, and half his age. He'd met someone, or someone had met him; it had happened many times before, and each time he'd been on the verge of jumping off a cliff, and then had pulled back.

Of course, my mother would have known nothing of the affair. Whoever the girl was this time, she was a smart girl, and fantastic in the sack, and now my father was wondering if it was time to make a clean break—it would be fantastically liberating, he thought, to ditch the scene in Connecticut, no longer to have to endure the morning commute, the tense conversations over the dinner table. Anne would be decent about it, he was sure. No threats. No scenes.

My grandmother's gravelly voice broke into my father's thoughts. "Franz, my favorite son-in-law, if I'm going to pretend to have a conversation with you, the least you can do is pretend to listen."

"Veddy sorry," he said, in the fake British accent he sometimes employed to be funny. "You were saying?"

She ignored him. "Peter, you were listening, weren't you?"

"Yes," I said. "I was listening."

"Good. It's nice to see you without your face buried in a book, for a change. I've been waiting so long for you children to grow up so I can have a decent conversation with you. You can't *imagine* how boring it's been."

"It's too dark to read now," I pointed out.

"That's irrelevant. Anyway, I can't think *what* about my stories lately makes people go right to sleep. I spent ten minutes last night telling my doting nephew Gates about our trip to Greece, and when I looked over he was out cold."

"How veddy, veddy curious," said my father. "What was the matter?"

"Well, jet lag, *he* says," said Froggie. "But you and I know Gates never goes *anywhere*. Which reminds me. When we go over to the Big House on Sunday I want you all to check Bedford's breath. I'm the only one that drinks gin, and yesterday at dinner Bedford had the nerve to tell me they were all out. Someone must be drinking it and I'm sure it's not *Mother!*" Gleefully, my grandmother commenced a story about my great-grandmother, Goggie, trying to hide that she'd taken a shot of whiskey just before bed to stop a cough.

As the sky darkened, whips of silent lightning began to show across the lawn, appearing not much taller than my father's height, though in reality I knew they were far away across the Sound. I looked over at my grandmother. She was making that goofy smile she was famous for, the one that curled up on one side and down at the other. I had the strange feeling I'd remember this moment forever—my grandfather Ward telling my mother with elegant calm that there were no wars anywhere in the world and therefore nothing more to be afraid of; my father fixing his full attention on Froggie and laughing a hearty guffaw.

I knew suddenly what my grandmother was afraid of: not the conversation dying and not even the closing of the book and the ensuing darkness, but the time when you know you can't back out, when death sucks at your feet like the backwash of a wave, and knocks you down. No one dies in peace, I thought. Something awful always happens to you before you go. You strangled, or were crushed flat, or bled out on the kitchen floor, or faced an animal's hungry smile, or choked trying to breathe water, or had your face smashed through the windshield of a car.

During the Gatsby era, my great-grandmother's children had been beautiful and young and without conscience, and the fetes at Peacock Point had been legendary. Now Death was closing in on the party. Like the tolling of the great brass bell at Lattingtown Church, his visits came regularly, and then with increasing frequency as if his concern was to clear out the whole tottering nest. My mother often quoted Dylan Thomas's lines to us:

Do not go gentle into that good night,
Old age should burn and rave at close of day;
Rage, rage against the dying of the light.

Yeah, sure, I thought, "Rage, rage against the dying of the light!"—that was something to be admired, I suppose, an alcoholic poet's last stand, taken while rolling and staggering with his back against the bar at the White Horse Tavern, but I had to disagree. There was no point in raging against something you were just going to have to go through anyway. Every one of us was going to have to get through that last little bit, and death was going to be the good part. Death was the reward.

Chapter Seven

When they married and moved to Connecticut in 1953, my mother and father vowed to give their children the normal American upbringing they'd never had themselves. As the location for this ambitious experiment, they'd chosen New Canaan, a unselfconsciously moneyed suburb about fifty minutes' commute by train from Grand Central Station. Dad had lived in nearby Greenwich as a teenager, and although those had been grim years for him, the terrain was familiar. For my mother, though, New Canaan had been a leap into unknown territory. Possibly she thought her experience would resemble the comfortable television banalities of Rob and Laura Petrie's life in New Rochelle—though, in truth, the series wouldn't debut for another decade.

Ah, the incomparable blandness of a suburban New England upbringing! Everything conspired toward monochromatism, the trees in winter, the endless white sky, the perpetual layer of snow on the ground, the slicked black of the wet roads, the muddy tracks in our driveway, the television in the living room. The peas were frozen, the shoes were laceless, the clothes were practical cotton with collars and belt loops that originated in a store in the center of town called Bob's Sports. Our vacations in winter were spent in rented A-frames in the ski hills in Vermont where more starkly black trees reached for the sky and more snow dusted the ground. Our family did not eat out at restaurants. I came across my first slice of pizza, a thin, crusty, Parmesan-dusted concoction, at the 1965

World's Fair in Flushing, New York, where it was presented as a curious foreign edible along with the Belgian waffle. Jukeboxes and pinball machines were forbidden by law in the ice-cream parlors and coffee shops that clung like lice eggs along the hair shaft of Route One, which was known variously by its ancient colonial names of King's Highway and the Boston Post Road. You could easily think you were living inside of a photographic negative.

On the weekends, my mother and father gardened together, mowing, trimming, cutting and piling branches. No matter how hard they worked, the formal English garden that was quite a wonder when they bought the house from a diligent retired couple gradually declined, grew less formal and more plainly American, as the roses died and the flagstones lifted and anthills formed between the stones, the rhododendrons expired, the forsythia grew unruly, the tulip tree blew down in the tail of a hurricane, and moles tore long swaths in the lawn. Dad and I worked in the woodshop, or went on long hikes to find nuggets of garnet and jasper that we polished on a tumbler that endlessly turned over in our garage. On Sundays our family read Bible stories together, not because we believed, but because the stories were great, enlightening "myths."

The house, built in the 1920s, was the kind of white elephant that young couples love to take on. The original boxy oil furnace that skulked in the basement was almost as large as the van that delivered milk bottles to our back door. Radiators hissed and sputtered under the windows. The stove in our kitchen with its yellow linoleum floor still burned oil as its fuel.

My mother, Anne, ruled our kitchen more by force of self-will than natural inclination or ability. Each night, from my bedroom at the top of the back stairs, I listened to her clang about the old-fashioned sink, washing dishes and putting dinner things away. After she was done and had gone up to bed, there would be, perhaps, fifteen minutes of suspenseful quiet, before an enormous crash, as all of the pots she had piled up in the drainer collapsed and hurled themselves to the floor.

In her role as housekeeper, my mother dutifully studied cookbooks, made lists, and produced a weekly menu, which she taped to the refrigerator door. My father made fun of the invariability of Monday's hamburgers, Tuesday's chicken and gravy with rice and French-cut green beans, Wednesday's chicken liver casserole, and Thursday's pot pie, but today as a parent I can fully appreciate the discipline and planning it took to get those simple meals on the table every day. Although our family would have expired without the occasional application of Swanson's TV dinners, my mother was a rapt follower of Adelle Davis, the nutritionist, and Coca-Cola was banned from our house. We ate Dannon yogurt and Pepperidge Farm whole-wheat bread. For snacks we stirred together a sticky goo of molasses and brewer's yeast. My sisters and I were each allowed a single bar of candy per week. When the news came out that clear glass milk bottles allowed the sun to penetrate and destroy vitamin D, my mother ended her ten-year relationship with our Sealtest driver, despite his vehement protests, and switched to Borden, which came in brown glass bottles.

In truth, being a suburban housewife in the fifties seemed a grand adventure to my mother. She loved its toil and solitude, its television clichés, its casseroles and amorphous carved serving platters; it was magic, because it was all hers. As a girl, growing up in a wealthy family, surrounded by servants, she'd never had to lift a finger, and now she was enchanted to be living the Cinderella story in reverse. It was as if, at the stroke of midnight, she'd escaped from the royal ball, taken a taxi home to her mop and her scrub brush, her stacks of dishes, dirty floors, and endless bins of laundry, and simply tossed her glass slipper out the window.

Dad in those days was playing the family man—though the effort did not come naturally to him. Each morning, he rose at six thirty to begin his exercises, designed to keep the blood flowing in his legs, since his job kept him stationary; he'd already suffered attacks of phlebitis in both legs. His exercises shook the house. I listened from my bedroom perhaps fifty feet away, as he jumped from foot to foot: *Thump! Thump! Thump! Thump!* Then he dusted his feet with antifungal powder, leaving a fine sheen on the water in the toilet.

Each night, as he undressed, he hung his gray flannel suit on the mahogany silent butler in the bathroom, so that the steam from his morning shower would erase the wrinkles. He carefully placed his change, his keys, and his rosary in shallow depressions made for that purpose in the wooden tray, and hung his gray fedora on the rack above. Now, dressing for work, he went through the same process in reverse. By seven, he was sipping his coffee at the kitchen table and scanning the stock market tables in the morning *New York Times.* By seven fifteen, he was speeding down leafy suburban capillaries in a cutthroat race with other fathers in their Oldsmobiles and Pontiacs for choice slots in the Darien train station parking lot. My father drove fast, took chances on corners, and passed everyone he could on the two-lane road. His silver Cutlass Supreme, a massive vehicle, lunged like a powerboat.

By seven thirty-five, the station platform was dark with the milling shadows of a hundred pinstriped suits. When the New Haven Railroad commuter train squealed to a halt, five minutes later, my father joined a stampede of gasping, snorting businessmen, each vying for a seat in one of the forward cars. Claiming such a seat guaranteed him a decent game of bridge and a chance at the head of the pack in the sprint to the Times Square shuttle when the train arrived. From the shuttle, my father transferred to the Independent Line and got off at Varick Street, a block or two from his place of business, on the tenth floor of an Arts and Crafts building at 345 Hudson.

It was in Connecticut that my father learned to sail. Sailing seemed to satisfy and soothe him. He spent hours in the basement knocking together furniture for the boat of rich varnished mahogany, shelves with luscious curves, a mess table with a red Formica top, a stand for the radio direction finder. He read and reread Joshua Slocum's *Sailing Alone Around the World* and *Endurance,* the story of Shackleton's escape from the Antarctic ice. He taught us, his children, to whistle, to tie knots, and to whip a rope end with stiff brown twine that smelled of tar.

Sailing lore is full of randy metaphors: a ship is a woman, the seafaring life is a seductive mistress, and the sea herself is a bitch goddess, unpredictable, proud, and vengeful. In high weather, a boat shudders and slams like two people engaged in coition. In the evening, when the bright sun grows small as it drops into the vast circle of the horizon, it resembles a sperm cell entering the ovum; there is, even, a nautical joining of two ropes that is called a cunt splice. He spent years exploring the nooks and inlets of the New England coastline. He also, with a boyish enthusiasm we didn't see much when he was at home, gave himself the task of exploring the crannies, the low-lying bogs, the intoxicating hills, the long craggy vistas of any and all available females he ran across.

He was a young executive, brash and full of gab; it never took much effort for him to lure a lush receptionist into having a few drinks with him at the Minetta Street Tavern. The string of his conquests stretched back to his honeymoon, he boasted, when he'd slipped out the window of their Venice hotel room to enact some tryst, but had gotten caught on the way back into the bedroom when his arms weren't strong enough to lift him over the windowsill. Ah, the adventures! The present was a thin skin over the unthinkable, but the future stretched ahead with hope and excitement; the future was a young woman taking off her bra for the first time, her breasts soft and bright as the starry dawn.

At home his movements were masterly and mysterious. When I look back I see that many of the important passages of my life had taken place under the darkening pull of a faraway stranger's influence. There was the blonde in North Carolina when I was six, for example. The recorder-playing female in Providence when I was nine. *She* was unusual in that my father left home for a time to live with her, until my mother's cousin Danny was sent as an emissary to bring him back. When I was ten, there was the mysterious sojourner in a Greenwich Village apartment, a reclusive young queen of the Mardi Gras. When I was twelve, and my father and I began to drive around the East Coast checking out boarding schools, there was already in his life a California blonde, a computer programmer in the San Francisco branch of his company. The dark matter in our universe had begun to pull our family apart long before this, of course.

In the afternoons while my father was at work, Mom retreated to a glassed-in porch off her bedroom that must have once been used to pot plants. Amid the smell of hot sun, cracking paint, and empty suitcases, she pecked on the keys of a sleek portable typewriter that her father had given to her, an Olivetti. She set about writing a magical novel about a boy who rode with dolphins. She named the book and its hero "Peter," the same as her firstborn son. She typed her manuscript in triplicate, with three layers of paper and two of carbon paper, so that the sentences on the last sheet were ghostly and gray. These pale pages she mailed out to friends, publishers, friends of friends, and agents, and they would come back to her with suggestions written in lightly penciled curlicues on the margins—that was how it was done in those days.

My mother loved her life in New Canaan, the porch off her bedroom, the companionship of other mothers and their kids, the school bus coming to take us every morning and leaving her alone with her thoughts in the sunlit, friendly old house, but I wonder if it wasn't hard for her sometimes. I wonder if there weren't times when she cried for the hopelessness of it all.

Often I was allowed to accompany my father in the back of the car in my pajamas, as he drove to buy a pack of Camels after dinner. This was for us an evening ritual, a way of getting together, man to man, away from a house overrun by women.

Feeling grown up, and up well past my bedtime, I'd tiptoe over the cold gravel of our driveway in bare feet, and slide into the backseat. My father would come in from the other side, a dark ovular shape, slam the door shut with a *cu-clunk*, and the tires would gently begin to crunch up the driveway. A lamp-lit image of my mother reading to my sisters in bed would grow small behind us in my imagination as we pulled into the road.

My father tapped his cigarette on the edge of the window, causing an orange shower of sparks to fan out into the darkness of the Connecticut night behind our car. He talked of the incredible deal he'd gotten with our mortgage, and how at 4 percent he never wanted to pay it off, and how my mother would never understand that, coming from the kind of world she came from, and how funny it was that my sister Lisa could hold court for hours on the toilet with the door open as if it were her throne.

The latter drew a shrill, appreciative laugh from me, an eager presence leaning over the backseat.

"I never really got to know your mother before we married," he said. "We met on a skiing trip, and shacked up together right away. You know what 'shacked up' means?"

"Yes," I said, picturing the whitewashed shack built onto the end of a pier, its porch rail decorated with fishnets and strings of buoys, the seagulls crying and swooping overhead.

"I didn't know she was going to cry every day, or be scared to talk to the butcher"—he imitated my mother's voice—"'Franz, I'm scared to talk to the butcher!'" It was not only the butcher whom my mother approached with timidity, but the dry cleaner, the liquor salesman, the guy who filled her car at the gas station.

I thought to myself with shame that I, too, was afraid to talk to the butcher.

"I've tried to make her understand over and over that her mood changes like crazy with the month, but she never does."

We bounced from the road, through a stand of pines to the lot behind the gas station. Years ago my father had found this way to go in without entering the parkway. A low brick building stood in yellow puddles of light. A lone teenager in a plaid shirt smoked a butt out by the pumps, filling the tank of a wooden-sided station wagon.

While Dad went inside to the cigarette machine, I waited in the back of the car. The Connecticut night air throbbed with the calls of crickets and peeping tree frogs.

The car lurched as my father slid into the front seat. He guided the car out through the pine trees.

"Forty-five cents for a pack of cigarettes. It's highway robbery!" he said, winding the cellophane off with one hand and pounding the end of the pack on the dashboard to settle the tobacco. He tore a bit off the top and shook the pack until a couple of pale sticks popped their heads up. Then he took one in his mouth, and lit a match. "It's taxation, you see. The cost of the cigarettes is probably only about seven cents. Another eight for the package and marketing, five cents for the retailer, and the government adds twenty-five cents in taxes."

"How can they do that?" I demanded.

"Just because they can. They need the money to build roads and fight wars and buy uniforms for cops. Where did you think the money came from? And they figure the extra quarter might make an idiot like me quit smoking."

Dad laughed. Our drive had put him in a good mood, as it always did. "When a pack of cigarettes reaches a dollar, I'll give them up," he promised.

The car bucked as we turned down the driveway, the tires grinding over the gravel. "You go to bed now," my father said, slapping me on the back. "Upstairs, now!" He stayed in the car, finishing his cigarette.

I stopped as I opened the basement door. The basement was completely dark. The stairway coming down divided the pale light falling from the hallway into ghostly slices. There was a presence in the dark shape of the furnace. Something old that had evolved before our planet had formed. When I looked back at the car I saw my father's cigarette, a tiny red dot aglow in the blackness.

"Go!" my father shouted hoarsely. "Go!"

Chapter Eight

In the next few days, a great uncovering of snow liberated the pent-up odors of the winter. Hali suffered immensely from her heightened sense of smell and the constant nausea caused by her pregnancy. She kept her pockets stuffed with tiny fragrant red clementines, which she broke open and held under her nose in moments of panic, when the urge to vomit overwhelmed her in public places, at a bus stop, or in school.

From the look on his face as he left us after our dinner in Chinatown, I never thought I'd see my stepbrother again. Arms flailing, he'd slipped away into darkness and a kind of finality, like a creature in a horror movie. But one sunny afternoon there came a phone call, and there he was, Little Peter, sitting on a stone bench, hair sticking out every which way like a junior Wizard of Oz, his pale, half-demented face grimacing out of his too-small brown corduroy jacket—my ragged boss. Only now it was spring-time, and the green buds were popping out on the crooked branches of the dogwood trees, the snow was melting around the scattered calligraphy of dog shit on the sidewalk, and for me, there was the awful feeling of sadness and loss that always comes with the sweetening of the air.

I soon discovered just how hard it was to "help" Little Peter. His present way of life had its own codes and values, and they were not to be lightly broken. For example, when I took him into an army-navy store on Eighth Avenue to try on a new jacket and boots, to replace his torn, filthy ones, he fidgeted, complained about feeling conspicuous in the store, and wouldn't try on any of the shoes. Finally he lost his temper.

"I'm a street person," he cried out, tearing at his mouldering jacket. "Don't you understand? Look at me! I don't *want* to look any different than I do!"

With the exception of his night in jail (which had happened after our dinner in Chinatown), Little Peter had been sleeping on a flattened cardboard carton since I saw him last, so I imagined the first thing on his list of needs would be shelter. I led him down Jane Street to the Jane West Hotel, a tall Victorian brick building with an impressive hexagonal tower and views of the Hudson River. I'd visited the hotel once before while filming a documentary about the graduates of a Bowery drunk tank. It was the place where the survivors of the *Titanic* had first been brought after their rescue, and I had a hunch that Little Peter would like it.

The marble lobby was dingy, and smelled like Mr. Clean. The clerk, a pleasant, polite, grizzled Palestinian with a scrub-broom mustache, who reminded me of begrizzled Officer Pupp in the Krazy Kat comic strip, kept a sharp eye on the door, allowing only residents to get in. Upstairs the hotel had a rummy look, with a long sagging hallway lit by bare lightbulbs and gray-painted floorboards. One or two open doorways gave us a peep at the narrow seven-foot-by-seven-foot coffins most of the permanent residents lived in, with barely enough floor space to squeeze by their beds. In contrast to these, Little Peter's $206-per-week "double" was luxurious, with a chair and a table, a view of the Hudson River through slit windows, an iron bed, a threadbare towel, and a television with a snowy image on its screen, brought in by an aerial made from a coat hanger.

Having settled on the room, I took Little Peter out for a meal at the Baby Buddha, a small Chinese restaurant in my neighborhood. Little Peter ordered six courses including squid. He tried to finish it all off, since, "You never know when you are going to eat again," he said.

"The doctors have been treating me the wrong way," he told me earnestly—shoving a jellied mass of squid into his mouth. "Trying to fix my head first, then the body later. That's the exact opposite of the way it should be: the body gets fixed first and then the mind just follows. That's what Rajneesh says and that's the way it is in most Eastern religions."

"Look, Peter, I don't know anything about that. I just know I want to stay in touch," I said.

Little Peter scrutinized me from under a furled brow. "The telephone is a powerful instrument," he said at last. "It can be used for great good and great evil."

"Fine," I said. "The hotel room is paid up. Call me when anything comes up. Or call me if you just want something to eat."

Before he shambled off in search of shade and shadows, Little Peter put in a touch for twenty dollars. "It's so hard to budget your money in New York City," he confided. I left thinking that I'd helped my stepbrother out, but the truth is, as I learned later, the crack dealers on Fourteenth Street skimmed the money from him within minutes.

I called my father that night to tell him about my meeting with Little Peter—I described how he always carried his possessions with him wherever he went, and how his back and shoulder muscles had become hugely developed as a result.

"His mother dropped him on the head when he was a baby," my father said. "If you want to know why he is the way he is."

Each morning, those first few days, I walked down the polished cobblestones of Jane Street almost to the Hudson River to leave something for Little Peter, first a small bag of toiletries, next a pair of blue jeans, then white socks and a used copy of *The Bourne Identity*. Each day the friendly hotel clerk told me that my stepbrother had just left.

"Your brother is in possession of an enigmatic soul," he said. "No, he did not reveal to me where he was going. But he seemed to have a positive outlook." Each morning I left my stepbrother a note asking him to call.

At night when I looked through my cold windowpanes and heard a prowler rattling the garbage cans near my building, I wondered if it was him. Was that Little Peter howling in the park across the street, where homeless men drank, fought, and banged conga drums all night?

I had to admit I was fascinated with the very idea. I felt as though I'd caught a thrumming, green, iridescent June bug under a glass. I wanted to take him out and study him. I wasn't so worried about Little Peter's physical well-being. He'd always been a skier and a camper, a great overall outdoor athlete, who'd proven himself to be almost impervious to the cold. What I did worry about, the image I couldn't shake from my head, was of him alone in the hotel room. Alone with the faucet, the bed, and the snowy television set. Alone with his thoughts, alone with his past, and about to come, perhaps, to some terrible final solution.

The next time I ran into my stepbrother, it was by chance at a deli on Eighth Avenue. We sat down at a table.

"The rest of my family is really good at saying that they care about me, but their actions say just the opposite," he complained. "That's why I've been so angry with them in the past.

"You can say that I've only asked my mother for *this* much help," he went on. He tore off a bit of his coffee lid, and put a small curl of plastic on the table between us. Then he tore off another bit of the lid, even smaller, a tiny wedge. "But she only wanted to give me *this* much.

"But if she would only give me *this* much more, it'd mean so much to me," he said, tearing off another wedge of plastic and placing it between us. "Just this much."

Impressed by his graphic demonstration, I said, "Olivia would probably free up some of your bank account if you got an apartment, and maybe even a part-time job."

"Oh, yeah, sure. When I've asked her before, she always says, 'You need money like a hole in the head!'"

"I think she's afraid if she gave you all the money in your bank account at once, you'd end up hurting yourself."

"What she doesn't realize is I'm smarter than that."

As long as he remained nearby at the hotel on Jane Street, I tried, without much conviction, to spend a few minutes at my desk each day calling half-way houses, dual programs, SROs, residential care centers for adults, state hospital out-clinics, interim housing. If Little Peter was anything like me, I knew he wasn't going to like the structure. But who knows? One of the bad habits I was trying to break myself of was thinking that everyone was like me. Maybe my stepbrother would find a niche for himself in some sober little society of beings I knew nothing about.

I had a surreal telephone conversation with an elderly volunteer at the national desk for NAMI, the National Alliance for the Mentally Ill. Her querulous Southern accent reminded me of Opie's Aunt Bee in *The Andy Griffith Show*.

"I'd like to see about obtaining services for my stepbrother, who's schizo-phrenic and homeless," I said.

"Well, if he's homeless, would you mind my asking which city is he homeless in?"

It seemed an odd question, but I answered as best I could.

"Almost every city," I said. "Whatever city he arrives in."

Her voice crackled. "Could you tell me specifically, what cities are those?" She seemed to be reading from a script.

I listed the ones I knew. "Albuquerque. Miami. Twin Falls. San Francisco. Salt Lake City. Denver. And currently, New York City."

"He's in New York now?"

"Yes."

"And he's living in the streets?"

"Well, he's in a hotel."

"So, he's not really homeless."

"Temporarily not," I agreed.

"You know, it's really such a crying shame," she said. "I've heard that so many of these men are alcoholics. Does your brother drink?"

"Yes, he does," I admitted.

"But I suppose he prefers drugs."

"Yes, ma'am. Crack cocaine, marijuana, and heroin. That may not be a complete list, but those are the ones I know about."

"Oh, my! Well, you must tell him to stop right away! Those are all very dangerous chemicals!"

I promised that I would tell my stepbrother the earliest chance I got.

"We really can't help a man like that," she said. She seemed relieved to be able to wash her hands of us. "He really must learn to help himself."

A few days later an envelope arrived from Little Peter's mother, Olivia. The return address was the river rafting company in Sun Valley, Idaho, that she'd bought with her divorce settlement after splitting up with my father. She enclosed a check to cover two weeks' stay for Peter at the hotel. In her typed letter she asked me to get hold of Peter's old piano teacher, Glenn Jacobson, on West Seventy-ninth Street, so that Peter could resume his study of music. "He could make a performing career out of left-hand-only pieces," she wrote. "Since you are in a nonthreatening position vis-à-vis Peter, I'll leave it up to you to bring these things up to him, when you think the timing is right."

The idea made me laugh out loud, though, as I pictured my stepbrother dressed in black tie and tails with one sleeve pinned to his chest, sitting down to a sleek, black Steinway in Carnegie Hall to hushed applause. It was a bizarre idea only a mother blinded by love could have thought up.

From her letter, it appeared that Olivia desired to make friends. My sisters and I had first met Little Peter in the unmediated opulence of my father's West End Avenue apartment, which in the early, more optimistic years of my father's second marriage, we'd visited fairly often. The elevator opened to a small foyer inhabited by an enormous, black, expensive-looking English perambulator. There was only one door in the foyer, and through it we could hear my father braying, "Here they are! Here they are! *Oh, my Go-ah-ah-d! Wife*, where are you? Come here, I need you!"

"Holy shit, is this where they live?" asked my younger sister, Lisa.

Olga simply looked around and said, "Wow!"

My father opened the front door in the middle of his own sentence, making the ice in his gin and tonic swirl dizzily. He was dressed in a pin-striped suit with wide lapels and flared pant legs, a wide floral tie, patent leather shoes, and a narrow belt. It was the costume of an arriviste, though as far as I had known my father had already arrived decades ago.

"*Aagghhhh-eee!*" my father said, holding his drink high to protect it from a presumed stampede. "Children, come in, come in!"

"Dad, you look like a gangster!" Lisa said.

The new apartment was enormous, consisting of half of the entire floor of a West End Avenue building (in which Harry Belafonte also lived). It had been redecorated by a professional in yellows and mauves. On the living room wall was an enormous abstract painting in pink, egg yolk, and cream that also sported a realistic painting of a cow's head—perhaps in homage to Andy Warhol. Everything seemed over-colored and partially inflated. There was a puffy cream-colored sofa and an oversized wire-wrought chess set upon a glass coffee table. The library shelves held heavy sets of "classics," bound in red and green leather. The kitchen could have served the breakfast room at the Plaza Hotel, with its professional stove and stations for chopping and preparing food. There was a grand piano. I'd recently been kicked out of boarding school and had spent the past year wallowing in the newfound debaucheries of suburban youth culture, still, it came as a shock to realize that here, in my father's new apartment, I'd truly entered Babylon.

In that moment, two small tow-headed boys catapulted out of nowhere, clinging to the legs of my sisters and me as if we were the tall stuffed giraffes at F.A.O. Schwarz. The oldest, an angelic five-year-old with a platinum bowl-cut, shouted, "Big Peter! Big Peter!" as he wrapped his arms around my knees.

Then he searched my face with quizzical, yearning eyes, as if looking for the secret of the universe there. He was dressed in a miniature navy blue blazer over an Oxford shirt, khaki pants, and penny loafers. I, in contrast, was wearing torn jeans, a T-shirt, and a plaid shirt, with long, greasy, untrained hair.

"Big Peter, meet Little Peter," said my father. "And this is Erik," indicating a roly-poly boy of three, endowed with a cute layer of baby fat.

Little Peter dug his nails into my knees. Wincing, I glanced again down into his brilliant blue eyes and was startled to see something so inchoate and desperate forming there that without thinking, I turned to my father. "Those are the eyes of a killer," I said. "You're going to have real trouble with this kid later on."

I hadn't meant my remark to be especially prophetic or revelatory. Nevertheless, my father remembered what I'd said, and in light of what happened later, often repeated it back to me.

Olivia was "Marilyn" then, a name from her childhood with bad associations, which she eventually jettisoned. She came out of the kitchen wiping her hands on a dish towel. With her frilled white peasant blouse, her long Germanic cheekbones, and her blond hair pulled back in a tight ponytail, she looked as though she'd just swung down from a branch of our family tree.

"Well, I'm glad you can feel so relaxed in your father's house," she said, eyeing my ripped sneakers. "Would you mind taking off your shoes and leaving them in the elevator lobby? The carpet shows every little mark."

Then she looked me up and down. "Well, Franz told me about your hair, but I must say, I thought he was kidding. I know it's considered okay these days for a boy to be effeminate, but doesn't it bother you to be mistaken for a girl?"

I stood there frozen, until my sister Lisa guffawed and said, "No, he usually gets mistaken for a horse!"

Olivia did something twiddly and unpleasant with her fingers and said, "Well, I have an extremely demanding soufflé to attend to. I'll leave it to Franz to show you around."

"Come on, let me show you the digs," Dad said. The boys galloped ahead of us.

"Wait up!" said my father. "God damn it, will you kids wait up!"

Later, to impress us, Olivia whipped up a meal on her commercial-grade stove, then served us in her new dining room. The table could hold, perhaps, sixteen guests, though I imagine more could have been accommodated.

She brewed thick, pungent French coffee in a scientific-looking glass plunger pot. "Your parents spoiled you rotten," she said, "though your father can hardly be blamed for that, since he obviously received no guidance from your mother."

It was obvious that in her opinion our trajectories were crossing. Little Peter was on his way up—to Yale, Julliard, MIT, or perhaps all three, and then a brilliant career as a concert violinist—while I was on my way down. There was to be no floor under my feet, no mediocrity to which I would not eventually drop. It was a shame, wasn't it? The way I was throwing my life away.

Though she knew I was a vegetarian, each dish had its hidden component of flesh: blades of bacon stirred in with the string beans, gravel chunks of pork in the pasta. I pushed each plate aside until she shouted at my father, "Your son is beyond belief! I can't be expected to cook like this!" and ran from the room.

Worse, when my sister Olga presented Dad and his new wife with a housewarming present of pottery she'd made herself, Olivia refused to accept the gift. She'd read somewhere that "Mexican" pottery couldn't be trusted—that the glaze was full of lead. My sisters retreated, shattered and weeping, from the apartment with my smirking visage in tow.

In the letter Olivia had sent me, besides the check for Little Peter's hotel, she also enclosed a brochure for her river rafting company in Idaho and invited me to come up for a visit. She wrote of her third husband, Erasmo, portraying him as an itinerant musician who'd been living in a six-by-twelve-foot trailer pulled by a 1969 Buick when she first met him, and went on to describe how as one of her first acts of marriage she had asked him to change his last name to Paulo. "The fact that I prefer vegetarian fare [now] should amuse you!" she quipped.

It did amuse me, as did several other things about her letter. I could tolerate being in touch with Olivia, since getting Little Peter off the streets seemed a common and worthy cause. But I could never forget the way my stepmother had treated my sisters and myself when we were young and vulnerable, how she'd disparaged us openly, and kept us from my father. There would be so much largess each Christmas that Olivia would hide it from us, the earlier set of my father's children: skateboards, skis, surfboards, keyboards, and windsurf boards, so that we would not know how favored her children were among us. One Christmas I recall, when we arrived at the apartment before my father, Olivia had taken us aside and unearthed a few boxes, stuff obviously gotten on sale, including an iridescent pink acrylic sweater for my sister Lisa.

Cecily, even though just a few years old, spoke up, "That's not a very nice present!"

"Sure it is. This sweater is very much in style. It's a *perfect* present!"

"Maybe," Cecily said doubtfully, "but not for a *girl*."

My sisters and I had had no tolerance for Olivia, or her ways, of course, but for some reason, we loved her kids, who'd arrived with her from a previous marriage to a Silicon Valley electrical engineer named Raymond Sluis. From the moment we laid eyes on Little Peter and Erik, we plotted to steal them away from the rigid, pretentious, utterly mistaken and valueless (if opulent) life that was being set out for them in the Upper West Side—to hide them in a tree house, feed them brown rice and stir-fried vegetables, and teach them all the things we knew to be true, the foremost truth being that parents lie and that one cannot trust a word that comes out of their mouths. (I guess we were willing to abandon my baby half sister on the theory that she was already too compromised.) But there wasn't to be much opportunity to cast our favorable Aquarian influence on our two tousle-headed stepbrothers, since my father was in the process of sloughing us off, as a snake sheds its skin.

Because of her blond self-assurance, my sisters and I assumed Olivia had walked into our lives straight from some haute middle-class enclave in Northern California, Palm Springs, Bel Air, or Santa Barbara. In truth, however, she grew up in a small, depressed, aluminum siding–covered town in rural upstate New York. We didn't know that Olivia's dreams of society life on the Upper West Side came straight out of magazines, or were improvised on the spot, and were wired together with white-knuckled will.

———

Now Olivia wrote, "I always adored Olga; I saw less of you and Lisa, but never thought of you in a disapproving way. What I did hate was the way Franz behaved when you kids were around. When he was with us he was a maniac; carrying on, screaming, throwing things, chasing after Peter, often abusive. When you, Olga, and Lisa were around, he was like a lamb—tolerant and sweet; the kind of behavior seldom seen during the years I spent with him. This personality change was what I found objectionable."

Aside from Olivia's occasional attempt to rewrite history, what I found disturbing about the letter was the glimpse it afforded into the chaos and pain of her relationship with my father. I'd never had much reason to question the image that my father had put forth that with his second marriage he'd made a more perfect union. Sure, I knew firsthand that Olivia was a difficult and maddening woman and I'd sympathized with his decision to divorce her, but my father had always presented himself as a passive recipient of Olivia's unreasonableness—her untrammeled credit card use, her supposed buying of a string of expensive thoroughbred horses for Cecily. What Olivia was talking about were the scars left by her divorce, deep scars that in her words "keep interfering on a regular basis." If there was one thing I'd learned from being around the shelter for battered women in Kansas City where Hali worked, it was that scars are made by wounds that hurt and penetrate, and wounds are made by psychic and physical violence.

Chapter Nine

Every month or two, while all of this was going on, I'd find my way down through the East Village, passing the ancient Puritan cemetery, to Lester Bergamot's black-painted tenement building, with its two boarded-over storefronts standing like gouged-out eyes on the block and its wobbly creaking flight of stairs. Since I didn't have a phone number for Lester, I relied on luck to bring us together. But Lester was almost always home.

Lester's apartment existed in a space and gradient all of its own. Once I guess he had cared enough to fix up the place, probably when he was still married and in graduate school. He'd assembled bookshelves, hand-cut a swirling op art pattern into the linoleum floor, and encased his bathtub in a tile mosaic. But now an upright drill press stood in the kitchen, the bathtub faucet poured a permanent stream of hot water, a wasteful leak, and his floor was barely visible beneath rank piles of jeans, torn books, record covers, and sleeping bags.

A box of brown sugar with a spoon in it sat by the bed: Lester's dinner. On the table, spread out, were all the accessories of a genuine dopehead—plastic hypodermic needles; razor blades; bits of cotton; squares of glassine that had been cut open, turned inside out, and many times scraped and licked; crumbs of marijuana; mechanical pencils; a spoon; and a candle. Lester's walls were covered with crude oil portraits of his friends.

"Ah, my art critic!" Lester said, carrying over a small maquette of bent aluminum, probably something he'd made in art school. He showed it to me every time I came. Lester wore his stained old thrift-shop bowling shirt untucked, and paced with the nervous energy of a commodities trader. It sometimes shocked me to look into his face, though, a pale, desiccated sweat-soaked dough-gray skull incised with parallel lines that ran from his scalp line to his chin, like the Mummy (containing the "look of borrowed flesh" as William Burroughs had so succinctly put it). But his pale gray eyes remained animated and cheery.

"I want you to look at this—getting ready for a show, man, this November," Lester said with enthusiasm, opening a black-covered notebook for me. He'd hand-drawn cutouts of Dick and Jane in S & M poses, and added hypodermic needle pop-ups, wallpaper samples, and scribbled rants about his daily life in scratchy pen. There were pages and pages of the stuff. At first glance it looked like the notebook of a madman, but an artist's notebook is supposed to be a bit crazy, and I took this to be part of Lester's aesthetic.

"What do you think?"

"Lester, if you have a show, I'll write a review of it," I promised.

"Thanks, man. How many artists can say they have their own personal art critic?"

A knock came, followed by a key turning in the lock. When the door opened it was Arnie. Arnie was an actual Australian who worked as a lower-level VP at Chase bank, and who seemed to spend every one of his nonwork hours with Lester and sometimes stayed with him when he wasn't getting along with his wife, which was often. He must have just gotten off of work, because he was still wearing a suit.

"Arnie," I said, nodding.

"How're you doing?" he said. Then he repeated the phrase, aiming for a more American accent: "How're ya do-ang?" He went up to Lester and sniffed loudly. "God, you stink," he said. "Can't you pay more attention to your personal hygiene?"

"I take a bath on St. Patrick's Day and the first day of Lent," Lester said with dignity.

"Well, will you do me a favor and hose yourself down a bit. At least under the armpits. And do you mind if I pick up some of these clothes. It smells like a hamster cage in here."

Arnie spread some fresh pages of The Wall Street Journal over the seat of a grimy upholstered chair, flipped back his suit jacket, and sat down carefully.

"Actually why don't you let us clean up this place?" Arnie went on.

"You're going to die in here and no one will find your body until the flies start buzzing in the hallway."

"What do you want?" Lester asked me, ignoring this. "You must be here for something."

I thrust a hundred dollars in his hand. He fanned out the twenty-dollar notes before his prematurely wizened face. "This is a lot of money." I could see that he was higher than he looked. Sometimes when I went to visit him at his apartment to score, he'd ask me helplessly, "Hey man, tell me how much it is—you wouldn't fool a friend, would you?"

Elated by the possession of so much cash, Lester headed for the door. We heard him take the wobbly stairs three at a time.

Arnie walked over and locked the apartment door.

"Don't touch *anything* in here," he advised. "It'd be better if we both wore gloves."

For some reason, no matter what time of day I went over to Lester's apartment, old episodes of *Star Trek* were playing on the television. That was one reason I felt so comfortable there. Time just hadn't happened yet. I got a glimpse of why you sometimes see a well-dressed businessman sitting in the back row of a topless bar. Not to goggle at the wobbling tits, or have some blond-dyed, part-time Pratt student punish his lap with her bicycle machine–tightened buttocks, but just to be in a place where none of his business partners would be likely to find him, where no cell phone could reach him. Lester's flat was an insulated limbo where the hypothalamus could unwind and stretch itself out like a snake on a warm rock.

I turned down the volume on the TV, blew the ash from the top of the turntable, and put on a Dexter Gordon vinyl, *Our Man in Paris*. Arnie busied himself rolling a couple of cigarettes, using Lester's cheap Top shag.

"We should call a crew up here while Lester's out," he said, handing me one. "Clear out all of these filthy clothes. Throw them in a Dumpster. And then wipe all the surfaces down with rubbing alcohol."

"What do you think of his notebook?" I asked.

"God, what crap!"

"You think he'll ever have a show?"

"Well, he's got to actually make some artwork first, doesn't he?"

After a few minutes Lester came tromping back up the stairs, his sallow face glistening with sweat. Whenever he did a powder run for me, he tried to show how hard he was working to earn his cut. "Humping to please," as the sign used to say on the side of the trucks going cross-country.

He got right down to business, flipping off the rubber band that held the ten-pack of powder, peeling off the two little green rectangles that were his cut, squinting as he sliced open the plastic with a razor. "Man, it's tighter than a virgin's asshole out there," he said. "Almost got popped just now."

He vigilantly scraped the sides of the waxed paper with his razor blade, tapped powder into a spoon and dripped a few drops of water into it, then heated the solution over a candle flame.

"Here's what the cop said to me just now on Sixth Street: 'Show me the money!'"

"What's that mean?" asked Arnie.

"If you've got a wad of cash in your pocket, then he knows you haven't scored yet, so he lets you go. But if you can't show him money, then he knows you're holding, so he hauls you in."

Lester pulled the liquid up into a thin plastic syringe and held it up to the light.

"Man, that's just not right," said Arnie, his Australian accent making him sound somehow more outraged. "How does that cop know you're even a junkie? What happened to the good old American presumption of innocence? What about your constitutional right not to incriminate yourself?"

While he was saying this, he picked up one of the green plastic rectangles. "I'm taking this out of *your* cut, since I treated you last time," he said to me as an aside, as he snipped it open.

"What about my constitutional right not to be called a douche bag?" asked Lester. "Just the way it is on Sixth Street these days, thanks to the mayor. If you don't have money in your pocket, then you've got to go to Central Booking."

Arnie tapped out a couple of match head–sized lines on a small hand mirror for the two of us.

"By the way, how is this stuff, Lester, my friend?" he asked casually.

Lester shook his head as he tightened a length of yellow rubber tube around his upper arm.

"You shithead, you said this was going to be the good!"

"It's the best there is right now."

Then Lester stung himself in the soft part of his elbow with the tiniest and narrowest of silver needles, and immediately popped the tourniquet off his arm.

"Ahh!" he said, closing his eyes.

Arnie tipped the small mirror toward me. I leaned my nose close, smelled

harsh dust, and felt the back of my nostrils burn. I looked at my watch. I
knew that in a few minutes, everything was going to seem different.

Lester was sitting back on the mattress with a silly smile on his face.
There was no helping that expression. It was caused perhaps by an involuntary loosening of the facial muscles, combined with the stimulation of
the pleasure factors.

Way back, I'd made the mistake of bringing Hali to meet Lester in his pad.
No one else but me would have thought to do such a stupid thing as intro-
duce his wife to such a sordid scene, but I was in love and wanted to share
everything with her. Besides, Lester was an old boarding school friend.
We'd been looking at stoves at Gringer's, a kitchen appliance store on First
Avenue, when we stopped by in the late morning. Lester was just stirring.
As it happened Arnie was there too. His wife must have kicked him out
again.

"Are you *sure*, man?" Lester asked me, a look of exaggerated concern
crossing his wizened face. Dust motes moved through the brilliant shards
of morning sun that fell through the windows of his front room, as he and
Arnie tied each other off and pricked each other's arms.

Eventually Hali and I left. As we were walking away into the sunshine,
my true love turned her dark eyes to me and remarked, "Well, you popped
my cherry."

"What do you mean?" I asked, shocked. She usually didn't speak this
crudely.

"I was a virgin. But I'm not one anymore. Not after seeing that."

"Oh, God, I'm sorry!" I said, instantly plunging into a dark canyon of
regret.

"It's all right," she said. "I'll live. You don't have to worry about me, or
anything. It's just something that happened."

Four minutes later, the powder had kicked in and I was sitting on a Greyhound bus, looking out the window at the bare fields, with bare branches
of trees flashing by, icy air falling down over my face. Then the bus must
have stopped, I guess, because suddenly I was walking through one of the
fields, stepping over rows of dry frozen corn stubble, all lit by the slanting
rays of a cheerless December sun. A distant rifle shot sounded hollowly,

causing a flock of crows to fly up, cawing. I started to pick my way over the furrows. Up ahead, I saw, was an oblong shape, jammed into one of the rows, looking like a dark cocoon. As I got closer, the shape began to move, and I saw who it was.

"I'm afraid," I said. My heart was hammering in my chest.

"What's that?" blustered Arnie, picking at a shred of tobacco hanging off his lips. "You're afraid? What are you afraid of?"

"Nothing," I said. "I'm just afraid."

Lester started coming out of his nowhere haze.

"You like to breathe, don't you?" he asked me.

"What?" I asked.

"Hey, is this going to be one of your impenetrable haikus?" asked Arnie, picking crumbs of ash off of his sleeve.

"No-o-o-o . . ." said Lester.

"Well, I sense one coming on."

"Don't forget, my art critic and I go back a long way," Lester said, keeping his bloodshot gray eyes fixed on me. "All the way to the frozen wastelands of New Hampshire. I know where all the bodies are buried. So, I'm asking you again. You like to breathe, don't you?"

"I guess," I said. I knew that sticky alkaloid poisons were short-circuiting the reward circuits of my brain, filling the slots reserved for natural brain chemicals, but right then I didn't care.

"When your head's been held underwater all your life, heroin can be like oxygen," he said. "It can be like sitting next to the open window and letting a fresh breeze blow over your face."

"Oh, Jesus Christ, do we have to listen to this crap!" howled Arnie. He began twitching spastically, trying to brush a spark off of his knee.

"I'm serious," Lester said. He held one of Arnie's ultra-slim hand-rolled cigarettes over his head and contemplated the narrow stream of smoke tumbling up toward the ceiling.

"Anyway, what good does it do to know this stuff, or even understand it?" I asked.

"Never mind," Lester said, giving me a quick sad smile before he stubbed his cigarette end out in an empty film can. "It's good."

Part Three

Innumerable confusions and a profound feeling of despair invariably emerge in periods of great technological and cultural transitions.

—Marshall McLuhan

Chapter Ten

It was at Peacock Point that I first developed the feeling that something was pursuing me, something morbid and deadly. I recently asked one of my cousins about this sense of blurred darkness, where it might have come from, and she thought for a moment and said, "Well, um, you know, people *died* there."

The dread was strangely mixed with sweetness, the sweetness of the peppermint candies that my grandmother served after dinner, which we would climb up on the counter to steal from her pantry cupboard, the taste of the honey sap oozing from the red poinsettias at Christmastime, the rank cloying smell of the dried flowers in the black electric phaeton that my great-grandmother Goggie drove.

Goggie herself seemed half mummified. Her flesh hung in long loose gray wrinkles down her face and under her chin, and the eyes that looked out on her world were pale and lifeless if still a brilliant blue. During long Sunday afternoons, I often sat listless in seersucker shorts, watching Goggie play canasta with her beloved coterie of exiled Russian aristocrats in the shadows of the Trophy Room, the murk around the card table cut by shafts of pale sunlight.

The Russians had shown up in the 1920s, and had never left. Their heavily accented speech remained hilarious and scabrous. The Russians added the smell of leather and cigars to the stultified air of Peacock Point, and even a bit of sex appeal. My mother's cousin Danny had married the blond, aristocratic Katusha Sheremetyev—whose grandfather, a count in the Russian court, had owned 250,000 serfs—when she had arrived at Peacock Point as an au pair. Sandra Loris-Melikov, whose own grandfather had been prime minister under Czar Alexander II, had been working as a children's nanny when my grandmother had run across her in a Colorado resort. Ishka, as we called her, had been struck by multiple sclerosis, and was confined to a wheelchair. Ishka's brother, Count Vasya Loris-Melikov, a former White Russian officer, escaped to Paris, where he'd worked as a cabdriver. He was now a motorcycle messenger with my father's company.

Vasya, a short, balding man with a hatchet face and thick scrub mustache, always in a dark suit and tie, would lift his cigar in a wide, all-encompassing gesture that surrounded us in swirls of fragrant smoke as he began to tell his favorite joke. The joke was vulgar, certainly, yet he told it over and over, perhaps because it was so redolent of the cruel fall from grace that fate had visited upon himself and his fellow aristocrats.

"A *turd* is floating down the Volga River!" he'd announce to the room. "You know how wide is the Volga River just outside of Moscow? Very wide. So the turd is getting extremely tired, and he is looking for someplace to rest. Ahead he sees a lily pad, so beautiful, with skirts of green and yellow. He swims over, hoping that he can hold on for just a minute. But this lily pad, she pulls her dress away and says, 'Excuse me, sir, Mr. Turd, kindly remove your disgusting self from my presence!' 'Oh, madam!' says the turd. 'Please let me stay. I know I'm not much to look at now, but would you believe it? Last night I was a *peche melba!*' "

Roaring his enormous Cossack laugh, Vasya would wipe a tear from the corner of his eye. "And that's the way it is, my dear friends," he'd say. "One day you are a delightful person, a treat to everyone who knows you, the next you are just another turd floating down the Volga River!"

The first deadly occurrence, as I recall, happened when my great-grandmother's secretary, Grace Mann, hurled herself off the end of the pier. Grace was a fascinating and spectral presence who slipped my sisters and me small wrapped toffees when our mother wasn't looking. She was a rail-thin woman with a British accent, dyed gingery hair, and a heavily rouged and powdered face. Her polished red fingernails were so long that she had once picked up a live firecracker, using her fingernails as tongs. The firecracker exploded without causing injury. Suddenly, Grace Mann was gone. We were informed that she had been sick for a long time. By stealthily listening in, I learned that the secretary's chief symptom, apparently, had been stinginess. "Well, *really*, you would *not* have believed those last dinners!" I heard my grandmother complain at cocktails. "If this had gone on for one week longer, we'd all be eating gruel, like Oliver Twist!" This made an odd kind of sense to us. We all knew that Grace had been starving herself and refusing to cut her nails. Now, we learned, she'd also stopped getting out of bed, brushing her teeth, taking baths, putting her shoes on, as well as paying bills. The idea of throwing oneself off the pier to avoid doing annoying chores had a certain stark beauty.

My aunt Allie's dying took several years. The cause was breast cancer, and although doctors brought experimental medicines into play, her death was excruciatingly painful and drawn out. As she was my mother's only sibling, my mother was inconsolable, and for many months, her sobs marked the long hours of our afternoons, whether we were napping or playing. There were many nights when my father steered along the East River Drive after visits to the hospital, the rain pelting in rough sheets over our windshield. Later on the Merritt Parkway the red lights of the cars ahead would rise in a column all the way up to heaven. I'd wake up the next morning in pressed sheets, having inevitably fallen asleep in the car, and been magically transported to my own bed, by what agency I didn't know.

Allie and her dapper and somewhat nervous husband, Edgar Appleby, had built their home on the shore down from my grandmother, just as Froggie had long ago built a house next to *her* mother. Edgar, a tall, pale, and curiously youthful man, had always cut an odd figure at Peacock Point, wading in the shallows of the beach with the pants of his light-colored seersucker suit rolled over his knees. Their four children were my first cousins, and our closest companions at Peacock Point when my sisters and I were growing up.

After Allie's death, apparently the strain of raising his four children by himself caused my uncle to become strange and exacting. He recited off-color limericks at dinnertime—that is, if my mother wasn't present. When I wandered over to his house to play with my cousins, I found copies of *Playboy*—a novelty then—lined up absolutely pin-straight with the folios of Beethoven and Brahms on the music rest of the white grand piano. Noticing one day that the so-called "fitted" sheets in his linen closet were loosely and imperfectly folded, Edgar summoned the household staff and ordered all of the bottom sheets thrown away, then had the beds in the house remade with tight hospital corners, using only flat sheets that could be stacked with precision upon the closet shelves.

Perceiving looseness and imperfection in his children as well, he hired a wiry French mountain climber whom we knew only as *Mam'sel* to be their nanny. Mam'sel walked among us with a suspicious squint as if on a tour of inspection; she wore shiny black lederhosen and tapped a braided leather rider's quirt against her bare thigh. She quickly took my grandmother's fat, cheerful nurse and companion, "Mac" Macintosh, as her lover, and soon had my cousins washing their own clothes in the bathtub, taking long naps in the afternoons, and climbing the trellis on the Tea House in order to strengthen their arm muscles.

Having seemingly brought things at home under control, my uncle wedded a wispy, soft-spoken society woman named Marjory, who brought three of her own children to the marriage. The middle of these was Eric, a handsome, dark-haired, and somewhat demonic boy a couple of years older than I was. There was darkness in Eric; he was the son and the grandson of suicides. But he had laughter, too, and was fairly obstreperous. He looked around at Peacock Point and its pretentious furnishings and said, "What a worm show!" Although I admired him, Eric always seemed a little too alive for Peacock Point; his references were beyond its borders, and he lacked essential passivity. Starting when he was thirteen, he began to drink on the shore with a group of gangly boys whose fathers worked on the grounds. One night, he pushed off into the cove in a skiff by himself, and his body was found the next morning tangled in ropes under the pier.

Eric's death was a loss for me in a family where the girls outnumbered the boys two to one, indeed where boys seemed to be a diminishing race. For several years after his drowning my cousins continued to hear footsteps in the rooms upstairs. Eric, or his specter, would rummage in the closet and then begin to step down the curved marble staircase, *clack . . . clip . . . clack . . . clip*, as if coming down to show his stepbrother Ward a magic trick or a fishing rod. The footsteps would die away just before they entered the dining room. Sometimes late at night, when my cousins were alone in the house, Eric's ghost would march briskly down the hall to knock on one or another of his stepsister's doors. "I've got something to show you!" he would shout. And though my cousins looked at each other in terror, they half hoped Eric would actually come through the door, even if covered with barnacles and oozing worms and seawater from his nose. Mam'sel's petty tyrannies were becoming too harsh to bear, and Eric was the only sibling who'd been able to stand up to her. But Eric never became much more than a noisy nuisance, and eventually even his poltergeist faded away.

After Eric's death, the Lattington Church bell began to toll more regularly for those at Peacock Point. First my great-grandmother Goggie succumbed to old age and a kind of withering. Soon afterward my grandfather, Big Ward, was silenced by a brain tumor. During Ward's illness, an old friend, the artist and socialite Gerald Murphy, came to pay his respects. Gerald had been a friend of Picasso and Hemingway, and was said to be the model for Dick Diver in F. Scott Fitzgerald's *Tender Is the Night*. Words were of no more use to my grandfather, so Gerald gave him a red rose from his garden to hold in his hand. Looking through the door my mother saw her father, silhouetted against the sound, turning the flower in a kind of wonder. The rose spoke more elegantly of the two men's love for each other than any words could have. Following Big Ward, Froggie herself, with great unwillingness, was led by her sticklike arms down the long hospital corridor. "Please don't tell me!" she begged, but the cause was colon cancer exacerbated by her daily diet of gin.

I never returned to Peacock Point after my grandmother's funeral, nor did I talk about it much. Having a background like that was the kind of thing that marked you off as different from other people, made them angry and patronizing or unpleasantly curious. I sealed the memory of my summers on the estate in a glass ball, complete in miniature detail: the crescent yellow beach and curling tar roadways; its rocky breakwater, gleaned from the construction of the New York City subway tunnels; its enormous weeping House Tree enfolding in its branches' shadows a kind of autumnal chill; its Georgian mansion and croquet green, where my great-aunt Alice in a long skirt still stood swinging her polished mallet and shouting, "I'm dead on you!" As years and even decades passed, I would sometimes take this odd keepsake out from the pocket in which I held it to look at, in my mind's eye, like some well-crafted music box from another century, and wonder at its strangeness, its perfection and obsolescence.

Chapter Eleven

Due to arcane city laws about hotel residency, Little Peter was forced to check out of the Jane West for one night every three weeks. On the last day of the third week, a Sunday morning, I arrived early so as to catch him before he went out. I found my stepbrother standing on the steps of the hotel, staring balefully up at the sky and holding up to his chest with both hands an enormous pale blue vinyl suitcase, into which, apparently, he'd put everything he owned.

On the ride across town, he was subdued.

"What's the matter?" I asked.

Finally he came out with his story. He'd tried to buy a vial of crack from a group of toughs on Fourteenth Street the night before. They used an old street ploy to get him to hand over the money: "Hey, man! Hey, man, don't you trust me?" As soon as he gave them the money—boom—the kids ran away laughing down the sidewalk.

"Peter, no one past third grade should fall for that trick!"

"I know it, man. You want to rub it in?"

The cabdriver offered us cigarettes and told us how he'd gotten his hack license by attending school, and what a great job it was because you didn't have a boss and could just show up any time, at any cab company, plop down a hundred-dollar deposit, and get a car and a lease for the day. At this, Little Peter immediately perked up. It sounded like the perfect job for him. And it might have been . . .

The cab let us off at Canal and the Bowery. Although it was still April, it was as hot and crowded and dirty an intersection as any in Bangkok. As we muscled our way along the sidewalk, Little Peter renewed his disconcerting habit of walking a few feet behind me, like a squaw or a servant. His corduroy jacket was soiled and the sleeves were ripped and open and the whole thing looked too tight. He was wearing one of my T-shirts out at the waist, and he was unshaved. It went without saying that he looked like a bum. He began to walk with a peculiar bum walk, hunched over as if with humility, taking quick steps. His face, from drinking, lack of sleep, and Dumpster food heavy on oil and carbohydrates, looked bloated and rummy. His eyes still retained their famous Paul Newman blueness, incredibly bright, or was it, I wondered, the blue, manic tinge of a John Wayne Gacy?

Lately I'd started to carry around in my wallet the scowling visage of an irascible old hermit monk named Dalma. (That's the Korean version of his name. In India he was known as Bodhidharma and in Japan as Daruma Daishi.) Dalma was a strange outsider who traveled through the Himalayas and into the mountains of western China in the sixth century; most people assumed that he was South Indian, because of his big nose, his pop eyes, dark skin, and thick beard. He founded the Zen Buddhist sect and is also supposed to be the father of kung fu and martial arts. These days in Korea, where the influence of the Christian missionaries is gradually fading, half the people you meet carry pictures of Dalma around with them. Having Dalma's face in your pocket brings good luck and safe passage, sort of like a Saint Christopher medal used to do. Dalma was the epitome of the mountain monk, the original Yoda, dressed in rags, spewing out incomprehensible sayings, camping deep in the mountains and preferring his own society to anyone else's. He was, in short, uncompromisingly weird. After being refused admittance into the Shaolin Monastery, it's said, he sat in a nearby cave facing the wall for nine years and refused to speak. In brush paintings Dalma is usually depicted as downcast, worried, folded in upon himself, with a haunted expression, a look that reminds me strongly of that often worn by my stepbrother Peter. As the founder of Zen, the wordless religion devoted to flashes of insight, Dalma inspired thousands of artists and writers to eloquence over the centuries. But sometimes his sayings went beyond mystery and were not only tantalizing but simply odd.

For example, when Dalma encountered the emperor of China, Emperor Wu of Liang, the emperor said to him, "Tell me, pious monk, how much merit have I built up in heaven for the hundreds of temples I've built, the thousands of monks I've supported, and the millions of ceremonies I've paid for?"

"None at all," Dalma replied.

"Well then," the emperor wanted to know, "what are the first principles of Buddhism?"

"First, vast emptiness. Second, nothing holy!" Dalma returned.

The emperor finally demanded, "Who are you?"

"I don't know!" Dalma howled, and ran away.

My feeling, looking at Dalma's distracted face in the picture I keep in my wallet, is that someday, when the schizophrenic community gets it together (if it ever does), it will make a claim for him as one of their own, the way the autistic community has now taken to counting Einstein, Mozart, and the pianist Glenn Gould among its numbers. How many other schizophrenics have shaped history? Joan of Arc; Napoleon Bonaparte; Hitler; Stalin, who drew a thousand pictures of wolf heads each day with a red pencil; Churchill, who greeted visitors naked; even Jesus Christ, who had strong messianic tendencies, perhaps?

Personally it gave me a strong sense of comfort to look into the Dalma's face whenever I felt like a misfit and an outcast. Here was a man far more strange than I will ever be, whose influence lasted almost fifteen hundred years and brought millions to satori. Was it simply that he told the unvarnished truth wherever he went (even if the truth didn't always make the best sense)? Or was it his example of uncompromising cantankerousness, carried to us by word of mouth and the fanciful drawings of brush artists? Most of what's known about this saint is apocryphal. One sniff of his spiritual pheromones convinces us, though, that Dalma's the real thing without our exactly knowing why.

A pensive blonde sat in the metal cage of the Pioneer Hotel's ancient, marble lobby, a captured bird. Her accent was Slavic. Very reluctantly, since it was against hotel rules, she agreed to let Little Peter and me pass upstairs to check out the room. We promised to report back in a minute or two. The room was small, but clean, with a black vinyl tile floor, a tiny sink, and a TV chained to a table. I turned to leave, but Little Peter called me back.

He'd already settled himself on the bed, his hands behind his head. He took out a stick of incense, stuck it into the edge of the bed, and lit it with a lighter. The intense smell of cherry smoke filled the room.

"Peter, what are you doing?" I asked. "We haven't paid for the room yet. We have to go!"

His eyes grew angry and black, simmering. "No one in our whole fractured family will listen to me, except for you," he said.

"Yeah, I know, but . . ."

"You gotta hear me out."

The woman was probably calling the cops downstairs, but Little Peter wouldn't budge. He had things he had to get off his chest right now.

"Do you know what my mother said when the cops came to get me in Idaho last summer? 'Take him away and kill him!' "

"Look, Peter, you haven't actually rented this place yet," I said. "All we have to do is go downstairs and tell the lady we like the room. Then we can talk all you want."

"Fuck that," he said. "I'm sick of all this jacking around. It has to be right here and right now."

The room across the light well had some kind of children's birthday party going on. Little Peter was half watching the camera flashes out of the side of his face and apparently thought something apocalyptic was going on. His head jerked with each intense burst of light.

"Sit down!" he ordered.

"No, I'd rather stand," I said.

"This world is such an interfering place," he said. "Here we are, two brothers just having a conversation, but you just know someone's going to come along and tell us to stop."

"Look, Peter, what do you want to say?"

He growled. "It's not so much *what* I want to say, but how I want to say it."

"How you want to say what?"

"Ninety percent of the people I talk to tell me these things are all in my head," Little Peter said, as a conversation opener. "But they're not. They're heavy, life-and-death things I have to deal with and they are real."

It appeared what Little Peter was burning to tell me about was his biological father, Ray Sluis. After his accident, when his hands were severed, then reattached, he'd gone to live for a time with Ray, but things hadn't gone well from the start.

"The one thing I don't do well is get up early in the morning," my stepbrother complained. "My father is a retired old codger who gets up at the first light of day. Just during the most important and soundest part of my sleep cycle, at six A.M., the time when the finest dreams are made, that's when Ray would get up and start stomping around, getting ready for his morning run. That drove me nuts.

"Plus we argued all the time about his sailboat. I thought we should go on an extended cruise to South America. I mean what was the boat for, anyway? Ray thought I should just shut up and get a job. Typical parental bullshit.

"The one good thing I can say about Ray is that he did fulfill his promise and get me a couple of tickets to an Ozzy Osbourne concert that was taking place somewhere outside of L.A. We made the three-hundred-mile drive together, sharing bad feelings all the way," Little Peter said.

"Ray also drove me back to Utah for the second operation on my hands. I had a screaming fight with him in the halls of the hospital, just before the operation began.

"The one person I liked and trusted was my doctor, but while I was under, White House operatives gave me drugs that changed my mind forever. A microchip was surgically embedded in my brain. The microchip controls my thoughts, and records everything I have to say. That's how people can follow me, but when I look there's nobody there.

"About the only thing I have control of is my own body," Little Peter said.

There was a knock at the door. The Russian blonde, her hair in a ponytail, pushed the door open. Her eyes were hurt and angry.

"You know you have to go right now," she said. "This is not acceptable behavior for here."

I apologized, and tamely followed her down the stairs.

When we reached the lobby we both turned and listened in amazement as Little Peter thundered down behind us, taking the steps two at a time. He stuck his face into the barred window and yelled at the girl, "You got a problem with me?"

A balding man in a sweater had come out of a back room to examine my stepbrother. "It's no problem with you, sir. It's the way that you are acting now that is not good."

"Well, I say the way I *act* is none of your business. What do you think of that?"

"Fine," the man said calmly. "You're out of here. Gone. Permanently barred."

Muttering darkly, Little Peter climbed back up the stairs to the room to retrieve his suitcase. I apologized to the floor clerk and the manager.

"Your boy had better change his attitude if he wants to get a hotel room," said the man.

I told him a bit about Little Peter's background, and almost thought I had him coming around, but then Little Peter appeared with the suitcase and said he wasn't sorry at all and fuck all of them and the box they came in.

So there we were out on the sidewalk, on the Bowery. All morning, we trudged up and down that misbegotten avenue, dragging Little Peter's enormous blue vinyl suitcase behind us, as the pitiless sun glittered off the broken glass on the sidewalk, to all of the classic flophouses that had lined the Bowery from time immemorial, to the Palace Hotel, and then the Grand, the World, the Andrews, the Providence, and the Sunshine, but there must have been a convention for the homeless, misshapen, and hapless in town, because every blessed one was full.

Bowery teemed with big-haired Italian women from Jersey shopping for lamps and chandeliers and Chinese old ladies feeling enormous durian fruits and powdered white slabs of dried fish. Once a bright blue and red crab ran away down the sidewalk away from us, to escape its cookpot fate.

We crossed Houston Street and tried the old Prince Hotel, climbed two flights of stairs, lugging that impossible suitcase—you always have to climb stairs in these places, I was to find out—but a thin Chinese man behind a metal grille said he had no vacancies.

Little Peter held his great shaggy head in both hands, to contain the angry thoughts buzzing inside like a bee swarm.

Finally we were down to our last hotel, the White House, a local institution, apparently. Everyone knew about it, but the way to get there was unclear. When I asked about the White House, a gnarled black rummy walking by us, pushing a shopping cart full of junk, waved me away and said, "I ain't holding your hand, bud."

I slipped into a deli to order a couple of sandwiches and coffee. "The White House?" The white-coated counterman told me, in surprise, "It's just two doors down!"

The White House had a wide front room with square-paned windows that opened up right onto the street. In the windows we saw old shaggy men chatting and reading at card tables set up for that purpose in the slanting rays of the sun. There was no sign on the door, and although I'd seen the place many times before, I'd thought it was a mission of some kind.

As we walked in, I joked to Little Peter that he would be staying with the Clintons that night, but he scowled and didn't get my joke. At the metal grille was a pleasant-looking old man with a bald head. He told me there were no vacancies at the White House either. Above the cage was a hand-lettered sign with the rates:

ROOMS $8.79 + $1.21 TAX = $10.00.

"How come your rooms are so cheap?" I asked the clerk before we left.

"Because this here's your typical Bowery-type flophouse," he answered, perfectly deadpan.

By the way, except for my stepbrother, I'd never met such a bunch of nice guys and straight shooters as I did on the Bowery that day. There seemed to be a code of conduct (no doubt enforced by violence) that at least on this avenue you must respect your fellow man and treat him right. Even the two who'd thrown us out of the Pioneer Hotel had seemed more hurt than anything else that Little Peter had broken the code, and I guess he had.

Little Peter and I shared a cigarette out on the sidewalk, balancing our cups of coffee on a fire hydrant.

Little Peter still wanted to talk, talk, talk. The urgency of his need was starting to burn dangerously. A violet flame kindled in his eyes.

"It's killing me," he said. "We *got* to get a room somewhere where they allow visitors, so we can talk. But first we have to get out of this danger zone."

I looked around. The three guys sitting on the hood of the car in front of us, basically ignoring us, in truth did seem a bit sketchy, if not life-threatening.

"Sometimes you just have to break out and yell at somebody, or else they'll just run your life," Little Peter said.

"Well, don't do it to me," I said.

"I won't," he said.

"I'm a peaceful man and I don't like yelling or violence," I said.

"I've got to bust out every once in a while, because if I don't it might add up and then I'll have to kill someone," he said.

"What's that, street bullshit wisdom?" I asked.

"No, it's just me," he said.

I was tempted to give him a twenty and leave him there on the Bowery outside of the deli. The stress of constantly having to pound reason into my stepbrother's poor bedraggled head, and of waiting for his next verbal breakout, was getting to me.

Little Peter resumed his complaining. He needed more space; his drink was poisoned; he had a terrific pain in the back of his head. He began to knuckle his eyeballs with his balled-up hands. It didn't do any good when I offered to switch coffees with him; the poison was already swirling inside his head, sending tentacles deep into the soft center of his brain.

A couple of years later, I might have passed on to myself a bit of wisdom I picked up from having children that could have helped me under those circumstances. That is, no matter how bad things get—and they can get pretty bad when you have kids—in the end they will turn out all right. There is simply no other option. Even let's say, to give a typical example, you are on the Number 4 train during evening rush hour, and your one-year-old begins to have a meltdown in your arms while you struggle to hold the folded stroller, and the kid is strong—stronger than you can believe—and he beshits your pants, and people pressing on all sides shriek and press back in horror, alerted by the sour smell of diarrhea, and just then the stroller opens up and the wheels fling themselves out into some lady's stomach. No matter; sometime soon, in an hour or two at the most, you will be sitting at home, and you will be safe, drinking a glass of whiskey, drawing a bath, and if God is watching, the baby will be asleep. There is no alternative to that outcome. You will endure because you must. I could have used that knowledge then, but that was a few months in the future.

Right now I waited for my stepbrother to notice the broken piece of two-by-four I saw on the sidewalk near us. I was going to die with a nail in my brain from a board wielded by my sick brother, who would regret what he did almost the moment he had done it.

I decided to go back inside the deli and give it another shot. I asked if anyone knew of a vacant hotel room around, and threw the question open to everyone in the store. A thin, worm-pale young man in a checkered shirt spoke up. "How about the St. Mark's?" he asked. "It's a nice place if you can afford it. It's fifty bucks a night."

I said, "Okay," and made the call. The guy on the phone told me they had no vacancies either, but hinted that it would be fine for us to come in person.

I had a cozy thought as we trudged up the Bowery. Screw this expensive hotel room—twice as much as Little Peter's crib at the Riverview! How about introducing Little Peter to my trusted trust fund junkie, Lester Bergamot? There was always a guy or two camped out on the floor at Lester's sordid walk-up apartment. Lester seemed to have infinite patience with their scratching and endless street rap all day long. But I answered myself, "That's just what Little Peter needs right now, a reliable drug connection!" Maybe it was best that he was getting burned almost every time he tried to buy drugs on the street, thus limiting his intake. He could always rely on his forty-ounce bottles of malt liquor.

There were, thank God!, no visitors allowed at the St. Mark's. I let Little Peter go upstairs to see the room, while the clerk and I watched his progress on the bank of security cameras overhead. Here again, I marveled at the politeness and respect with which we were treated. Little Peter was an obvious deadbeat, and I myself didn't look so great at that point. I'd missed my shower that morning, along with other necessary ablutions, had a two-day stubble, and had also had a couple of meals yanked away from me before I could eat them.

Little Peter came down the steps smiling. "You know there is one thing you can do that will help me no end. It will erase all difficulties, make me happy, and help me pull together the shattered parts of my mind."

"What's that?" I asked.

"Buy me a Walkman for twelve dollars and two Ozzy Osbourne tapes."

Easily done. We walked back to Canal Street, leaving the giant blue suitcase behind, and I bought Little Peter the stereo player. Then I gave him a twenty and he went down into the subway, on his way up to Seventy-second Street to buy his tapes. His gloom was completely gone, replaced by the happy thought at being once again able to listen to his beloved Ozzy. Before he left, I asked what he was planning to do tomorrow. I dearly wanted him to tell me he'd return to the Jane West Hotel by himself.

"Tomorrow?" he asked. "Tomorrow?"

He furled up his forehead as if tomorrow was the hardest thing to think about ever, harder than spooky action at a distance, harder than monogamy, harder than a cure for world hunger or AIDS, harder than the decision of which format to buy music in. There were times when my stepbrother could be almost endearing.

"That's okay," I said gently, after a moment. "Why don't we just let tomorrow take care of itself?"

Little Peter stayed in New York for a month or two, until the electronic demons returned to scribble messages on his naked skull, then he boarded the Greyhound bus for nowhere, anywhere.

Chapter Twelve

Eventually, my stepbrother found his way to San Francisco, which still had the reputation of being the end of the interstate, the dock of the bay, a place of mists and gulls, where gold nuggets could still be found among the pebbles of the beach. There Little Peter lived under Pier 41 for several weeks, mixing with slackers and bikers and tourists. He called his biological father, Ray Sluis, the software engineer, who'd retired and now lived in Sausalito, on the other side of the Golden Gate Bridge. Raymond responded with unusual alacrity by placing Little Peter in a halfway house in San Rafael. And there Little Peter seemed to run out of energy and willpower.

From there, apparently overcome by wistfulness, and a sense of regret, Little Peter left another telephone message for me:

"You know, I remembered what it was I wanted to tell you. Here it is. As far as I've come, I really haven't gotten anywhere. That's my message for the day."

After Little Peter had been in the halfway house for two or three months, I decided that the time was ripe for me to pay my stepbrother a visit, now that he was, apparently, staying put. Hali and I were visiting a college friend of hers in the affluent town of Piedmont, near Oakland. The drive to San Rafael in my rental car took me north, through huge fields adorned by giant rusting pipes, and across the bay on the Oakland Bridge. San

Rafael turned out to be a beachy, palm-lined suburb, a small city mature enough to have blight of its own. In the city center was B Street, a two-block strip devoted to homelessness and sleaze, into which a hopeful sprinkling of architecture offices, interior design stores, and a Starbucks were trying to insinuate themselves. There was a Vietnamese barbershop, a unisex beauty parlor, and a rowdy corner bar open early Sunday morning. A line of bantering down-on-their-luck couples clustered around the free lunch center run by the Catholic church.

The place Little Peter had given me as his address, the Carmel Hotel, was locked up tight and no one answered my knock. A young girl with black hair in braids and a backpack sat on the steps, chewing gum.

I was about to walk away, when one of the B Street residents pattered up to me—a man with a sun-fried face peppered with red bursts of capillaries—to tell me that the only way to get into the hotel was by calling from a pay phone. When I asked where the nearest pay phone might be, he pointed to a 7-Eleven several blocks away. Convenience is not an issue for the homeless.

When I returned, a kindly female employee let me in. I walked silently in sneakers into enameled eggshell whiteness. The place was clean and odorless and quiet as a rectory. There was a living room with several sofas for meetings, and a kitchen with a long eating table. No one was around. Eventually a second employee named Dave, wearing a white T-shirt and an earring, led me to an empty office, and bade me to sit. After I'd spent about twenty minutes in that hushed chamber, a doorway to the outside suddenly opened, the light nearly blinding me, and Little Peter emerged, his curls haloed in brilliant sunlight.

Little Peter looked the same: he wore a faded blue nylon jacket and jeans, and his shoulders were huge, hunching under a clean white T-shirt. The deep indentation in his gnarled forehead, the beard of two or three weeks without a razor, the hair a tangle of frayed rope-end.

I jumped up, took his dead rubber hand in mine, and shook it. "How are you, Peter?" I asked. "What have you been doing?"

It was one too many questions, I saw. A look of confusion and deep ponder crossed his red, weathered face.

"Well, now that I'm here, what would you like to do?" I asked.

"Drive," he said. "Just drive. If that's okay."

The previous night, Little Peter had hiked up into the hills behind the hotel, he told me. He'd climbed up a jogging trail until it branched into other trails and then more trails, each leading to a little camp where a homeless man could sleep and no one would bother him. On the way he stooped to pick up a blanket—one of the easily discarded conveniences of the possession-challenged. He'd learned this much: don't carry with you what you can easily find again—blankets, old clothes, pots and frying pans, grills, mattress springs, shopping carts, all waiting for you in the next hobo jungle.

In the morning he woke as early risers tripped down the trail by his bedroll, going to breakfast. He left his blanket and followed them to B Street. He stood in the parking lot for forty-five minutes looking at the hotel. Then he went up to his room and took a Risperidone, the first he'd taken of a stash his mother had left during a recent visit.

That was at 8:00 A.M. When he met me at 11:00 A.M. he was a tentative, staggering presence.

As we drove on California's Route 1, we passed a Zen farm that Little Peter said he'd ridden by once on his bike—and wound around through yellow grassy hills that suddenly opened up to views of the misty ocean. Meanwhile, my stepbrother slumped in the passenger seat almost comatose.

"Bad things are happening in my head. I feel really terrible."

"How so?"

"Like I'm going to burst."

"Are you nauseous?" I said, alarmed.

"No, it's not like that."

"Does it make you feel bad to see me, a person out of your past?"

"No, not at all. Just the opposite."

"It's the drug," I said. "It'll wear off. You'll feel better as the day goes on."

"I hope you're right," he said. "I don't understand—when I take that drug in prison, it makes me feel good. When I take it alone, it makes me feel crazy."

On B Street men wandered up and down all day with nothing to do but eat, he explained, which causes their blood to heat up and their eyes to become more sensitive to the light. Our first order of business, therefore, was to buy him a new pair of sunglasses, as usual the darkest ones possible. We stopped at a mall, found a head shop festooned with Bob Marley posters, and got the sunglasses he needed for six dollars.

"What about your job interview?" I asked when we were back on the road. Keeper Dave had earlier told me that Little Peter had an important job interview to attend to that day.

"Keep driving," Little Peter said. "I already *have* that job. But I missed work on Saturday because they changed the time. Now we have to schedule a meeting to discuss whether I can handle working at all."

"Sounds 'complicated,'" I said, hooking my fingers into quotation marks.

"It is," he said, then smiled slyly in boyish acknowledgment that, just between himself and me, it was all bullshit. He's not a dumb guy, wherever his head is at.

"I don't really want the job," he confided after a few miles. "I already have the money—thirty-seven fifty. I can use that to make my life easier."

I tried to be responsible. "You should go to that meeting, because even if the job seems like a drag now, you might want it later on."

Little Peter had already worked for three days and found the restaurant job dirty and difficult. But he agreed with me without hesitating. "Yes, I guess you're right," he said, with perhaps too-easy deference. I was the one with money in my pocket, after all.

It was the summer before the 1996 election, and Little Peter had been following the candidates closely. "If Clinton wins," he said, "I'll have to leave the country."

"Well, you've managed to survive four years of Clinton so far," I observed.

Little Peter's eyes shifted back and forth slowly, as if recoiling from an internal explosion, walls of yellow flame lighting up the screen on the six o'clock news.

"But I haven't survived," he said.

Twenty minutes later, I halted the car at Little Peter's gruff insistence.

"I liked the view before, but you wouldn't stop," he complained, and he got out to sit alone in the yellow scrub, looking at the valley and the distant hills. I took a picture of him through licorice-smelling leaves.

"Nice view," I said.

"Doesn't it ever occur to you that all of this—THIS!—exists merely because we are thinking of it, that it's all manifested in our minds?"

I took a handful of anise seeds from the plant near me.

"It's hard to imagine all of this detail just coming out of our heads," I said.

We drove on, to a beach of screaming children and pregnant mothers. Blond daughters in red-and-white-checkered bikinis threw us slant-eyed glances, and beery fathers in knee-length shorts threw balls back and forth, and dragged boogie boards across the surf with enormous energy. Out beyond the surf a few skinny windsurfers slid and swooped. A cold breeze blew, despite the strong sun, and the waves came in low short rollers.

Little Peter stretched out on the sand in his dark glasses with his fingers entwined over his stomach, staring straight up at the sky.

I took several snapshots, including one of Little Peter curled up on the beach with his blue nylon jacket over his head. His ruined right arm lay under him, crooked at the elbow. He was hiding; hiding from me, hiding from the camera, hiding from the world.

When he saw me taking the picture, my stepbrother looked up bashfully, but he didn't ask me to stop.

In the second snapshot, he was standing with his back to me facing the dazzling ocean, and by a trick of the camera the gulls standing in the sand around him, which were closer to the lens, appeared as giants towering over his head. He was Gulliver just landed in the land of the Brobdingnagians, a stranded scientist, bemused, enthralled by the majesty of his own fate.

"Wish I had my windsurf board," he said. "I'd be far and away the best windsurfer around. These guys . . ." He waved his hand to indicate the four or five slim figures wobbling through the surf, the sun shining through bright sails.

"They look pretty good to me."

"Ach . . . I don't know, there's an art to it . . . a language and maybe even a science. You can tell they don't have a clue. As far as windsurfing goes, they're still speaking baby talk. That's my professional opinion."

He watched them intently for a few more moments. "Well, maybe I'll jump in and have a swim," he said.

We decided to walk back to the car to pick up Little Peter's bathing suit. The wind blew strongly against us, and he started slowing down, complaining about his low energy and how out of shape he was. I worried that, under the influence of the drugs he'd taken that morning, my stepbrother would simply sit down and refuse to go on, like Ferdinand the Bull in the children's book.

When we reached the car, however, Little Peter decided that he didn't want to swim after all. I was delighted, secretly.

Instead we drove south into a set of low hills. It was a beautiful day, the air cold and thin just like in the mountains.

Soon we entered Sausalito, a yachting harbor and suburb where Little Peter had lived with his father, Ray, in the hazy past before everything went blooey, before his mother met my father and moved with him to New York, taking the young boys, Peter and Erik, with her.

We drove faster and faster, through eucalyptus and acacia, jacaranda, California buckeye, red flowering gum, and Grecian laurel, on twisting dusty roads. Little Peter grew more enthusiastic with each turn, as if grasping a lost vision. "Here! No, up here! Turn left! Now right and right again!" he shouted.

We were searching for Peter's old house. He was convinced that he could find it on instinct alone, from truncated memories of twenty-five years before. In the yellowing afternoon we whipped through pockets of shade and blinding light, up and down gullied hills like fleeing bootleggers in some early Hammett novel. *Caledonia, Cazneau, Girard, Bulkley, Filbert, Santa Rosa*—the street signs flew by us. At last, we drove up a winding lane, came over the peak of a ridge, and arrived to the front of a redwood porch set into the side of a small red-painted ranch house, which by its flat, unassuming style I judged to have been built in the early sixties.

"Stop!" Little Peter bellowed. "Stop right here!"

I pulled the car over with a rude skid of tires on gravel.

"Here it is," my stepbrother said. "Here is the porch where I spent many happy hours in play."

The place looked like a starter home for a young college professor, a house in which, having grasped tenure, he might dare to start a small family. A few colorful plastic toys were strewn around the front door.

"Are you sure this is it?" I asked.

"Absolutely sure," Little Peter said, with the kind of conviction only an ex-preppy can express. He stared through the car window at the sandy deck as if seeing himself, at four, with his two-year-old brother Erik still in diapers, noodling around the golden sandals of a young blond mother.

"Shall we get out of the car?" I asked after a minute.

"Yes, let's," Little Peter said.

Oblivious as to whether the owners were home or not, we shoved ourselves out of the rental car, two scuffed young men in T-shirts, and sat
down on the cracked redwood benches of the porch.

Since the house stood on the ridge of one of Sausalito's steep dusty hills,
we were surrounded by the branches of trees whose thick twisted trunks
rose up from the yards below. Beyond us were purple roof squares and the
bright needles of swaying masts in the wide slate of Sausalito Harbor.

I snapped another photograph of Little Peter leaning on a rail. He
looked like a successful Silicon Valley entrepreneur, scruffy, self-composed,
and sure of himself.

"What do you remember about this place?" I asked him. I was skeptical
that this porch was the real location of his childhood memories; perhaps
that place lay a few houses down, or in a completely different neighborhood. But the effect on Little Peter was real enough.

"Plenty!" he said, but did not elaborate.

Instead he leaned back and closed his eyes and let the sun wash over
him. After a moment I closed my eyes too. As the wind eased through the
jacaranda leaves, I could feel air molecules hitting my face by the thousands, perhaps billions.

"What are you seeing?" I asked.

"Nothing," Little Peter said. "How about you?"

"Nothing," I said. "Do you think anyone's home?"

"Nah."

After a minute or two he opened his remarkable cobalt eyes and blinked
a few times at me.

"Things got pretty fucked up, didn't they?" he said.

"Yes," I said. "They did."

Later, after depositing Little Peter at the group home in San Rafael, I drove
back over the burned yellow hills and through long beautiful wooded
landscapes and twisting shaded roadways, feeling the abiding sadness of
summer, the years of my all too prolonged youth piling up and crumpling
like the leaves on the hills, like the miles on my speedometer . . .

Each time I thought about my stepbrother alone in that strangely mo-
nastic white hotel, surrounded by bland social workers, hiking up to sleep
in the hills by night, coming down to scrape dishes at a restaurant by day,
I felt a sharp pang of guilt. He was trying, I thought, but the setup was so

vacant and incomplete. When I'd left him that afternoon, he'd given me a despairing look, like a kid being dropped off at boarding school after a nice meal at the inn with his mother and father. A look that said, "Why me, and why this place? And when did you stop loving me, and don't tell me that you didn't, because it's obvious, or you wouldn't be leaving me here." A look I'd been on the inside of many times myself.

Two days later I made the same half-hour drive up from Piedmont. This time I stood on the porch of the white hotel for ten minutes before Dave came out in his white T-shirt and his gold earring to tell me that Little Peter had flown the coop. The note about my phone call from the previous night was still taped to his door, unread.

I wasn't surprised, then, when my stepbrother called a few weeks later from Sacramento to say he'd left the auspices of the halfway house on B Street permanently. He'd made his way mostly by walking, and now from a phone booth begged me to buy him a bus ticket to Albuquerque, his next stop on the freedom tour.

My first and abiding instinct was to say yes, but within hours I was in-volved in a long-distance tussle with Little Peter's mother, Olivia, who in-sisted that he had unfinished business in San Rafael and should go back.

I'd tried not to interfere in the relationship between Little Peter and his mother—and certainly not to take sides, and even more certainly not to play them both down the middle.

So when he called me again, I said, "Peter, I don't know what to do, your mother is saying one thing and you are saying another, and my brain is hurting, I'm in a genuine quandary and I don't know which way to go."

Little Peter, ever practical, said, "Well, I don't want either you or me to get a headache." And so he rang off.

My hardheaded stepbrother never made it to Albuquerque, but instead rode the rails to Leadville, Colorado. There he moved into an old miner's cabin up in the hills provided to him by a mountain mystic named Jamie. For thirty days, at 3:30 A.M., he was visited by a tall accusing wraith, a ma-lignant spirit, who came out of the darkest part of the night to watch him without speaking. Perhaps it was the spirit of his thwarted future, come to point a bent and cadaverous finger at him. Perhaps it was Bach himself, warning him to bend back to his scales. Rattled, he got into a drunken tavern brawl with some locals who used his head to bash the door down, the better to propel the rest of his body outside. He was arrested, fined, ordered to pay for the damage to the door, and spent Thanksgiving of that autumn in jail.

Hearing all of this, I thought many times about what a mistake it had been to promise my stepbrother a bus ticket and then withdraw that promise. All I had done was send him down the dangerous path of tramping, hitching, and freighting across the cruel unmediated West, and perhaps ruin his faith in me as a friend. His mother and I had not—in actuality—come anywhere close to our stated "goal" of getting Little Peter safely into a medicated opportunity cocoon in San Rafael, California. I should have followed my own instincts and just said, "Go!"

Part Four

For my thoughts are not your thoughts,

neither are your ways my ways.

—Isaiah 55:8

Chapter Thirteen

When my father took off in the spring of my junior year in high school, my mother wrapped her arms around my stiff teenage shoulders and said, "Daddy's left us!" in exactly the same words she'd used a year or so earlier to tell me that my grandfather, Big Ward, had died.

For a while my mother and I lived in unhappy tolerance of each other, the last forlorn inhabitants of a big cold house in Connecticut. My mother seemed to me to be a kind of sad, left-behind jailer, and I was in sympathy with my father's having gone off to look for freedom and to have time to think things over.

One Saturday afternoon, though, I looked from the kitchen and saw my father's gray Oldsmobile parked in front of our house, steam coming out of its tailpipe.

My sister Lisa was doing dishes. She looked out the window with a sponge in her hand and said, "I'm not getting into that car."

I said, "Why not?"

"I don't know," she said. "I'm just not."

Instead, it was I who walked out to the sleek side of the Oldsmobile. Except for the rumbling of the car, all was quiet. Just as I got there, though, the car erupted with noise, as if a violent dogfight had suddenly broken out inside, although the sound was encased and made tinny by the closed car windows. Suddenly the passenger-side door flew open and my mother tumbled out. Skidding in the gravel, she ran into the house and slammed the door.

Curious, I bent and looked through the door. My father was sitting in the driver's seat in a dun cardigan, smoking a cigarette. He motioned to me to get in, and I did. He expertly slid the stick on the steering column and got the car going forward.

Gravel raked the rear window as the car began to pick up speed, and when I looked out, there was my mother again, standing in the place left by the car, her face distorted and red with tears. "You're not going off with that woman! You . . . lied . . . to . . . me!" she shouted. As the car pulled away she grew smaller and smaller.

"Your mother doesn't hate me. I know it may look like she does. But in the end, she has to realize that we all just need to get along," my father said evenly. He drove until we got to the parking lot behind the Merritt Parkway gas station. Then he stopped the car and went inside the station to buy cigarettes.

Returning, he spoke soberly, as if talking about the terms of his will. He told me he was going to be married to a woman, whom I was going to like, who had two boys. There was a baby sister on the way. He had purchased an apartment in Manhattan, which I and my sisters were welcome to visit anytime we wished. The car filled with the smell of his burning cigarette.

Gradually I realized that there was to be no reprieve for me. It wasn't freedom my father had been looking for after all—there was no log cabin in Canada he was going to build, as he'd said. He'd just gotten tired of our family and found a new one he liked better. What I had now was what I'd get until the end of high school, the dinners of grilled-cheese sandwiches and tomato soup with my mother, the unbearable stretches of time in the classrooms, the sneering lettermen with their combs and red and white letter jackets lined up on Senior Row. The long hours smoking in my car in the high school parking lot, listening to FM radio. The endless hovering of high school authorities, getting on my back over missed homework, missed classes, missed days, missed opportunities.

That spring was so wet that the walls of our house dripped with moisture. Through the window the bare trees reached their branches toward the leaden sky, looking like parched roots. I felt that I'd entered an inverse planet. Somehow below in a world I couldn't reach, no doubt, trees still produced green leaves, birds were flying and darting around, and children were playing and shouting in warm sunlight. But that was all happening somewhere else, not here.

I felt completely alone. My friends at the high school were all involved in their own lives, my sister Lisa had returned from an aborted year abroad and was busy listening to soul music and hanging out with kids like Roland Gross and Shine in Fudge Town, my other sister was at boarding school in California. Late at night sometimes I'd climb into the blue Datsun truck my father had left behind and drive along the twisting Connecticut roads, always hemmed in by walls of gray stones piled up like eggs, but as I had no destination and no one to visit, I would end up coming home to find my mother sitting at the kitchen table picking at a frozen dinner, crying.

Of course it hadn't occurred to me that an unspoiled woman like my mother (though she was forty) was not going to remain single for long. As it turned out, a great many men thought her a not-to-be-hoped-for prize. Although it seemed like an age, probably less than two years passed before she remarried to a gentle, book-loving man named John Zinsser. Johnny was slightly gaunt and bore a remarkable resemblance to (we thought) Abraham Lincoln. As an editor at Reader's Digest Books, Johnny felt that his mission lay in keeping the veins of the reading public open as long as possible, on the chance that someday there should be something worthwhile to inject into them. He was an opera lover, an exceptional tennis player, a collector of histories of the British royal family and of small antique teacups with sentimental sayings printed on them. He brought four hyper-precocious children into the arrangement from a former marriage, two boys and two girls.

Well before the wedding, Johnny's kids had already moved into our New Canaan house. They joined my Appleby cousins, the four children of my mother's dead sister, Alessandra, whom we had come to consider siblings. The house that had once snugly held a family of five—Mom, Dad, and three small percolations—now held eleven full-sized teenagers and two adults. Add to that mixture the innumerable friends and runaways (there was always at least one runaway staying over with us) and you can get the idea of what it was like then, a heady mixture of camaraderie and chaos.

We had an open house. My room was skimmed of its valuable contents—books, stereo albums, clothes—within days. The walls thumped with discordant strains of music: Tosca from one window, Alice Cooper from another. I threw out all the furniture from my room and slept on a bare Tibetan rug.

It was during this time that I gave up reading books. I guess you could say, since I was a teenager and given to dramatic gestures, that I made a "solemn vow" to give up reading. In this I was probably influenced by one of older brother Buddy's interminable letters to his younger siblings in *Franny and Zooey*, or some such thing. If you want to become a productive member of society, an early reading of *Franny and Zooey*, or indeed *any* of Salinger's books, is probably not recommended. If I remember correctly, and I probably haven't, Buddy had foresworn reading in favor of chainsawing firewood as kind of a Buddhist penance. But I was also thinking back to Marshall McLuhan's *Understanding Media*. I was convinced that in a few years civilization as we knew it would collapse under its own sickened weight. The lights would go out permanently and we'd all be crouching over fires on the darkened hillsides, thumbing our thoughts over egg-shaped electronic machines that hadn't been invented yet.

Over this menagerie of clashing hormones and cultures, my mother and Johnny presided with singular forbearance and grace. There were runs to the Grand Union every day to fill the back of the station wagon with bags of groceries and gallons of milk. Cooking took place communally and at all hours. The vegetarians among us stirred summer squash, tomatoes, and zucchini in a pan until their plant fibers merged into an undifferentiated yellow paste, while the carnivores grilled steaks on the patio. In my role as house food scientist, I sometimes made a dish called seitan, also called "wheat meat," which tasted similar to the way it was pronounced. Seitan was made by forming a ball of bread dough, then washing away the starch in cold water until the dough reached the jellylike consistency of raw chicken. The resulting mass was then cut into slices and fried with soy sauce. To my amazement, my stepfather not only ate all that I served him, but asked for seconds. I could only conclude that he was either the most diplomatic man I'd ever met, or that he had no taste buds.

Although all around were the clapboard homes of Episcopalians, my mother and Johnny conducted their affairs like enlightened Epicureans. Neither he nor my mother could reconcile themselves to the idea of a Christian afterlife. Therefore they resolved that their progress to extinction should be along the path of dignity. Although they were both in their early forties they enthusiastically began preparing for old age. To this end, they refitted the dining room on the first floor to be their bedroom, to spare themselves the future humiliation as two infirm people of having to totter to their bedroom at night. "You don't want to have to watch us *crawling up the stairs*, do you?" asked my mother rhetorically. That refrain became a kind of maxim for those years. All one of us had to do was make the slightest paddling motion with our hands, for example, to send the others into suppressed paroxysms of laughter. "You don't want to see us *crawling* up the stairs!" In truth, my parents had a more sensible motivation for moving their bedroom downstairs: to close off the second floor for energy reasons during the winter. That their bedroom was now dead center in the middle of it all, a kind of Grand Central Station for teenage activities, didn't seem to bother them at all. A pair of sliding glass windows put their bed practically on the patio, from whose posts and platforms on summer months eight or ten of us at a time would hang like apes.

Each night at nine o'clock Johnny would retire to this sanctum in his nightshirt with a manuscript from work that was rarely less than four inches tall. Upon the bedcovers various children, stepchildren, girlfriends, and temporary adoptees would assemble, basking like seals during the gathering-in season, along with a bitch dachshund named Willy, who though spayed was to be the founder of an unending dynasty. I'd watch Johnny skim down the typed pages of his assigned manuscript, looking for dead-wood, of which there seemed to be a lot. Occasionally he would scribble the initials "RI" in the left-hand column. This stood for "reader identification," and was meant to point out that at that point in the manuscript the reader would need a few words to orient himself and send his canoe back into the leaping flow of the narrative. This practice fascinated me. Was it really that easy to discern when a reader was floundering? And was it also so easy with a precise sentence or two to set him straight and send him back on his way? This seemed to have applications in real life, too. One day the mists that tumbled around me would part and a deep, reassuring voice emerge. "I can see you've lost your way, my friend," the voice would say. "Turn left at the next tree! Follow the path until you come to a door. You will see a sign that reads, 'Army Recruitment Center.' Knock and go inside."

Meeting my new stepbrothers and sisters marked my first exposure to the concept of the urban wunderkind. In the cretaceous and slow-moving Protestant school in which I'd spent my childhood, as far as I'd known there'd been no such thing as a "gifted child." I don't think I met a genuine "prodigy" in the eleven years I languished there. The qualities that were prized were blond hair, bluff good cheer, and athleticism; anyone who showed a flair for anything besides football and lacrosse was likely to be considered a freak. I grew up hiding from the other kids on the bus that I

was somewhat good at math, read books on my own, and knew the an-
swers to questions in the biology textbook. We tolerated one or two girls
who played folk music on guitar and a couple of horseback riders but no
one who could genuinely be called a genius. There was one boy who
dragged his foot slightly, one of the last victims of polio, whom my classmates called a "brain," but I think we just felt sorry for him.

The Zinsser kids, on the other hand, led with their cerebral cortexes
the way a boxer learns to jab with his left. All four were tough, loquacious,
and uncannily bright; if you couldn't keep up with the conversation they'd
let you know you were stupid and then they'd let you know exactly *when*
and *why*. References to Florentine painters, noir writers of the 1930s and
1940s, baroque music, the Italian of Dante, and the locations of the best
London tailors dribbled from their lips at the breakfast table the way ma-
ple syrup dribbled from mine.

Still, we all burned the same high-test mixture of optimism and hormones. Not one of us was studying to be a doctor or lawyer, tax accountant,
management consultant, veterinarian, engineer, or anything that could
remotely prepare oneself for the task of making a living. We were all going
to be artists, and if not artists, then actors, and if not actors, then directors,
composers, playwrights, writers, poets, or opera singers. And if none of
those, then we were going to be people who publicly discussed, lampooned
or criticised artists, actors, directors, composers, playwrights, writers, poets,
or opera singers.

On a given evening, my stepbrother Steven might be playing a board
game of his own invention, a game that literally only he could play, in which
the goal was to cast an opera using the divas of all time. I would be in my
room trying to hot-glue together an egg-shaped geodesic dome whose seventeen different lengths of struts I had laboriously calculated. My cousin Anne
would be in the horse barn sleeping inside of a giant metal dog head that a
boarding school friend of hers had constructed. My stepbrother David would
be listening to music and disordering his senses, à la Arthur Rimbaud, in
preparation for writing his first roman à clef. Nina would be shaking the dice
cup for Boggle, a game she played with the spelling acuity of a T. S. Eliot, the
vocabulary of an Ezra Pound, and the raw aggression of a Leon Spinks. My
sister Lisa would be out, as usual, "discovering Black America." What the
rest were up to I've no clue, but perhaps skinny-dipping in the pool would be
a good bet.

Despite the constant thrum of adolescent effervescence, a certain watchfulness hung over us all. Round the back of our heads, and just out of the corner of our eyes, hung dark and menacing shapes. All of us had come from broken homes, and some from homes that had been broken more than once. Each of us had been let down by a parent in the deepest and most traumatic way possible. I don't speak for my siblings, but they would no doubt agree that there was *something* dark and scary out there. This thing, this hovering miasma, which operated in broad daylight, was like the tug of the tide in the waves when you were swimming, subtle and powerful; it could pull you hundreds of yards down the beach without your noticing or knock you off your feet. Succumbing to its power was a fallback position, perhaps, should the battle of life prove too overwhelming. And who was there to say such an eventuality would not in some cases be welcome? It seemed a powerful temptation, overall, to simply drop your arms and let it all go, the stress and strain, the heartbreak and anticipation, simply let it all suck down the drain, with a loud rasping sound.

Every once in a while one of us *would*, actually, let go and in the subsequent skid have to be put under professional care. One night I sat up late with one of my many siblings as she prepared herself to leave the next morning. It would not, of course, be to a madhouse in the traditional or Dickensian sense, with high redbrick walls stained with soot and tears, and black wrought-iron bars crisscrossing the windows in elaborate patterns. The place to which she was committing herself was a model of modern psychiatric science, set in a pretty and well-touristed part of the New England landscape, an institution once led by Erik Erikson, who was perhaps the most compassionate of the spawn thrown off by Sigmund Freud.

She and I had decided to prepare ourselves psychologically for her coming ordeal by staying up late to watch *Chiller Theatre* on a small black-and-white TV brought into the guest room at my mother's house, which was where my sibling was exiling herself that summer in order to allow her demons to incubate properly.

Chiller Theatre was the Saturday night presentation of WPIX, or Channel 11, the "local" television station, emanating from somewhere in New York City. Movies shown on *Chiller Theatre* depicted men and women being transformed, mentally raped, flesh ravaged or turned to goo, or made robotic and docile by aliens or radiation, or both. Usually it was teenagers who first discovered these alien landings, and therefore were the first to endure the crawling of disembodied hands or to be sucked dry by spiders while hanging upside down in cocoons. Women whose bodies were interfered with by insects or invaded by aliens, and whose minds were overwhelmed telepathically, came back wearing blank stares and speaking in horrific monotones, exactly like the women who were gang raped by motorcycle thugs or bands of renegade Indians in the teen thrillers.

The night before being committed, the movie we were watching was *The Snake Pit*, a late-forties melodrama about a woman who's been committed to an insane asylum but can't remember why. It was probably not the most appropriate film to watch that night. As we saw Olivia de Havilland's look of despair as she wobbled on a catwalk over a stewing pit of madwomen who called and tugged at her shoes and begged her to come down to join them, my thoughts were contradictory. We were both, I thought, suspended upon a catwalk ourselves, trapped in the never-never land of late adolescence, both (I felt) trying to escape the sulfurous clouds of childhood. The way to go was up, not down, though. On the other hand, I understood the desire to simply wrap your arms around your body and drop into the seething mass.

My sibling wore shapeless muumuus to cover up her Venus of Willendorf physique. She was a talented guitarist and had a wicked and pointed wit, compiled with good basic humor.

"Don't go," I said. "What's the point?"

She was finger picking the opening bars of Dylan's "Don't Think Twice, It's All Right," a refrain of almost unbearable sadness, beauty, and complexity. She waited until the right moment came around at the guitar to speak.

"No point," she said. "I have to do this."

"You *have* to?" I said, with skepticism showing fully in my voice.

She nodded, once again allowing the music to carry her over to the next thought.

"This all has to stop," she said. "Not forever. Just for now."

I knew that things had happened. I knew that she had settled into a trance of fear in her freshman year in college and had to be brought home. And yet what did all of that have to do with now? Just when the fruits of postwar adolescence were falling in our laps—the cornucopia of drugs, sex, and driving in cars that had the possibility of making living worthwhile— why did she have to give it all up?

"How long are you going to be there?" I asked.

"A year maybe. Maybe two," she said. She switched to the opening bars of "Fire and Rain" and smiled. "It may help my career."

"Ha, ha," I said.

I knew that James Taylor had sojourned in the very institution she was on her way to. There, it was said, he'd been forced to choose between remaining to gradually work toward sanity, or ignoring doctor's orders and embarking on a career in rock and roll (was it ever a choice?). In his room, on a dark night, he'd penned the opening words to a new song:

> *Just yesterday morning they let me know you were gone*
> *Suzanne the plans they made put an end to you.*

I assumed that Suzanne, whoever she was, had shuffled off to some harsher regime of cells, restraints, and electroshock therapy, while Sweet Baby James had caught the red-eye to London and thence to a freshman recording contract with Apple Records. Years later, my stepbrother, Little Peter, would walk away from the Austen Riggs Center (the place I am speaking of), the first of his many escapes from rigged normalcy. But Little Peter was only perhaps six years old then, still a feted young princeling on West End Avenue.

"What will you do there, in this place?" I persisted.

"I don't know," she said, pointing with her chin at the TV screen, where white-uniformed orderlies were strapping poor Olivia down to a table in preparation for either a gang lesbian rape or some novel kind of Soviet-developed galvanic therapy.

"Oh, come on," I said. "That doesn't look like fun."

"Oh, they will probably have all kinds of therapeutic crafts for me to do," she said, in an artificial singsong voice. "Clay building, basket weaving, gourmet cooking, water-painting. Perhaps they will even let me play guitar, if they decide it's not part of my illness."

"Great," I said. "Look, it all seems so simple to me. Why don't you just stay here with us?"

A half a minute of silence ensued while she played.

"And do what?" she asked helpfully.

"Live," I said lamely.

"Oh, *that!*" she said. *"Live!"*

"Ha, ha," I replied.

"Ho, ho!"

"Ha, ha!" I repeated.

And she began to scrabble at the strings of her guitar:
(she sang)

Remember when you ran away and I . . .
And begged you not to leave . . . ??
Well . . .
You left me anyhow . . .
And now you see
I've gone completely out of my mind.

(and I joined her for the chorus)

They're coming to take me away, ha-haaa!!
They're coming to take me away, ho-ho, hee-hee, ha-haaa!!!!!

"So, what *is* wrong with you?" I asked afterward, emboldened by the silly words we had just sung.

"That's for me to know and you to find out," she replied. And that was when for the first time I saw in her eyes that she was, truly, scared.

"No, really," I said. *What is it? I thought to myself. Is it something we've done? Is there something we could do now, differently?*

"It's nothing," she said, her liquid brown eyes looking down and away. "Just something I have to do."

And of course the next morning she was not in her room. And she stayed away for a long time. I can't say that she ever returned. She gathered up all of her trajectory into her own hands, and she took off over the hill and into the starry sky like a homemade rocket. Eventually there was a small *pop* and she came down floating, swinging on a small plastic parachute. But she was a long way away by that time and there were miles of forest between us.

My mother, who felt she'd been "saved" by psychoanalysis, was the first to say, "Get help!" I was so thin that she first engaged the views of our family doctor, Dr. Brown, a tall gray man with a fringe of feathery white hair. He prescribed a course of testosterone pills. "You will develop muscles in your arms and shoulders. You'll look better and feel better," he said. I threw the bottle in the trash on the way out.

Next, a middle-aged Westport psychiatrist with the shoulders of a line-backer was recommended, Dr. Rosenberg, a man who had done wonders with some of the other teenaged kids who no longer saw the point and were on the verge of dropping out of high school or committing some other atrocity.

I arrived at Dr. Rosenberg's office reeling, after spending all night writing an English paper on the neurological perceptions of the Impressionist painter Seurat. I wasn't sure whether the subject of sensory neurological break-throughs were what was expected of this paper by my honors English teacher, Miss Sanskrit, but the pair of amphetamine capsules entitled "Black Beauties" I purchased in the school parking lot that afternoon ensured that I would spend the night squeezed into an armchair in my bedroom, madly typing on a plank drawn over the chair arms, with the full moon reading over my shoulder.

When I explained to Dr. Rosenberg that the floorboards of his office were tilting, the psychiatrist bitterly accused me of intentionally taking the pills so as to bring an altered state to his session—some kind of "cry for help," I suppose. I denied that. He reinstituted and elaborated on the accusation. Our argument lasted for weeks. The weekly recriminations and ritual denials were only interrupted when my SAT scores were returned from the high school office. The assistant principal threw them at me with a look of accusation as if I'd been caught keying his car or pissing into its gas tank. The numbers on the page seemed wrong, surrealistically high. Somehow in the year since I'd left Exeter, during which time I'd applied myself to little but scarfing down eighteen-cent hamburgers, imbibing cigarettes, and trying to get into Carla Winkler's pants, my SAT scores had climbed by 150 points.

The scores seemed to enlist an unusually hostile reaction from Dr. Rosenberg as well. He heaved his bulk out of his chair toward me menacingly, his graying muttonchops bristling. "Go!" the middle-aged psychiatrist shouted at me. "Go! Get out of my office! What are you waiting for? Apply to Yale!"

The ensuing several weeks of bustle bore no fruit, of course. That venerable institution had no interest in acquiring an anorexic slacker who'd been kicked out of a respectable boarding school and was currently scraping out the bottom quarter of his public high school class, even if he could boast a half a dozen alum as his nearest relatives. In truth, I never put my heart into it.

Chapter Fourteen

My life began to tumble. Bone thin, in ripped jeans, with stringy hair down to my waist. I almost never washed or showered, so that Connecticut ticks grew fat as sweet peas on the blood of my scalp. I developed a terrible notion, probably from a too-early reading of Kerouac, that in the great romantic dark night of the American continent I might dissolve, literally rub myself out and disappear, and I grimly set out to do that.

For a year after high school, I attended art school in Kansas City, Missouri. Although I made a few steadfast friends, I left in a state of horror. Perhaps I'd been miscast as an art student. Then I drifted up to Chicago, where I began to do odd jobs for a Polish hardware store on Fullerton Street in the near north side. Eventually I became a full-time glazier. It was satisfying work to scrape out windows and fit them with clean new panes of glass, to fill dim and hopeless apartments with a little fresh light. There was an easy formula to calculate how much to charge my customers, who were mostly dirt-poor members of Chicago's sprawling, under-serviced Hispanic ghetto.

Chicago was a good place in which to lose oneself, I thought to myself. The young people I met were misshapen and terrified. Most of them had been members of blue-collar gangs when they were young and had developed falsely high opinions of the ethnic Lithuanian, Polish, Irish, and Italian bungalow neighborhoods in which they'd grown up. "Hey, you from Cicero?" one would crow, upon meeting another, and huge crooked smiles

would light up their faces. I didn't fit into their map-based sense of camaraderie, but that suited me fine. I could make the rent on the apartment I
shared with my girlfriend Margot in a couple of days' easy work. The rest
of the time I spent taking a class or two at the Art Institute of Chicago,
sketching, writing in my journal, and working on a film with a friend
who owned a 16mm camera. The project consisted of me walking the
grim, torn-open neighborhoods of Chicago's downtown, filming snippets
of whatever I saw. Sometimes I appeared in the film, a figure lurching in a
torn thrift-shop overcoat, a homeless drifter, an outsider. My goal was to
make a grand experimental film that would sum up my Chicago experience in the soaring style of Dziga Vertov's *Man with a Movie Camera*, or
Walter Ruttmann's *Berlin, Symphony of a Metropolis*. My ambitions did not
include the idea that I would ever finish the film, or that anyone would
ever see it, though.

Even as I walked down the broken reaches of Halsted Avenue, with the
wind tearing at my jacket, I sometimes wondered how my other siblings
were doing. Had they managed to escape, as I thought I had, from the stifling glass bubble of Peacock Point? My cousin "Little" Ward Appleby, for
example—how was he doing? As the only two boys in what seemed like an
overwhelming sea of sisters—five in all—Little Ward and I had shared a
common perspective. He'd eventually come to live with us in Connecticut
after his mother died, though he was often at boarding school. He grew
into a tall, cheerful teenager with a curly mop of brown hair, who liked to
fish. For a couple of years he'd gone to boarding school at Phillips Acad-
emy Andover, in northern Massachusetts. Then he dropped out, giving
no special reason, and worked as an apprentice carpenter in Vermont for
The Putney School, with whom my mother had connections. His trajectory had seemed fairly normal, at least for a member of our family, and, as
he was a few years younger than I was, I had ceased to take much notice
of him.

In fact, I thought about my family as little as possible, in fact, but every few
months the urge to reconnect would become overwhelming. I'd buy a ticket
and fly home to stay with my mother and stepfather Johnny in the house in
Connecticut. On this occasion, our extended family was gathering for
Thanksgiving weekend. As I drove down our driveway in the blue Datsun
truck, I saw Little Ward climbing one of my favorite trees, a giant copper

birch that, since it needed no tending, had survived my parents' devastating attempts to garden. Naturally, when I saw Ward halfway up the tree, I got out of the truck, leaving my bag in the back, and joined him.

Ward was dressed in a typical Vermont outfit: hiking boots, plaid shirt, and jeans. As it happened, I was wearing almost the identical garb, my Chicago working clothes. We were both skinny and wiry and our progress up the tree trunk was fast, perhaps even competitive. Soon we'd each straddled a limb thirty or forty feet off the ground, looking out over the lawn, which we could easily see, as the birch had dropped most of its leaves weeks before.

"How's it going in Vermont?" I said stupidly.

"Oh, you know," said Ward, waving a hand. "How's Chicago?"

Chicago was an unmitigated disaster, thanks. Although I didn't know it at first, my art-school girlfriend had been a hidden anorexic. For a calendar year Margot had been a hearty 145-pound Valkyrie, then, under my very eyes, she had shrunk to a hollow-cheeked, apathetic, barely-walking bundle of sticks—thanks to a deluded diet she'd taken on. Strangely, for the space of two weeks in the middle of this frightening deflation, her body had reached a confluence of perfection. Her skin had grown luminescent, her eyes turned wide and moist, and her lips had assumed the cupid's-bow shape coveted by models. Photographers from all over Chicago, and some from as far away as Japan, flocked to photograph her luscious limbs. Her small breasts were like two pale, quivering bowls of flan. Her pubic hair was an island of crystalline black rising amid an undulating sea of her flawless, milk-white thighs. With her limbs rapidly becoming a civic resource, she remained naked for days, lounging on our thrift-shop sofa. Our door was open to everybody. Critics called her elemental, star-shaped pubic thatch incomparable, and then went on to liken it to the tangles of bare weeds photographed by Harry Callahan—a photographer in Chicago who was considered close to God. In the daily newspapers, Margot's charms were enumerated and weighed against those of Kiki, the saucy model whose derriere had been made famous by Man Ray in the 1920s, and the catlike legginess of Edward Weston's Charis, followed by the squint-eyed Appalachian innocence of Emmet Gowin's wife, Edith. Finally, though, just as word of her waxen beauty threatened to spread beyond the Loop and go global, the wand passed again. Margot began to shrink and grow listless. Her skin folded in upon itself, her eyes lost their luster, and her hair began to fall out. The photographers disappeared, and she lost all interest in me. I'd been sleeping on a friend's couch for months.

Little Ward waited patiently all the time it took for this reverie to rise and fall in my mind.

"Chicago's okay," I said.

For a few moments I smoothed the bark under my hands, listening to the crows caw overhead. What could this kid understand, anyway, about what I was going through in Chicago? The ground below my dangling feet was thick and muddy, running with water rivulets. In contrast, the grass beyond the skirts of our tree glowed almost luminously, an effect of the dying sun, I thought.

"I can't talk to anyone," said Little Ward suddenly. "I don't know what to say. When I try to think of something, it comes out stupid. I don't think I'm worthy."

"You don't have to be worthy. You don't have to be anything," I said, wondering what abject confession this young cousin of mine was about to burden me with.

"There are these girls," Little Ward went on.

Oh, Christ, girls! I thought.

Little Ward blathered on, but I'd already stopped listening. An odd, tinny sound I was trying to sort out turned out to be my mother calling from the window, holding up a telephone receiver.

"Sorry, got to go," I said, shinnying down the tree. "We'll talk later, okay?"

Little Ward nodded, unhappily.

The voice on the phone was that of an old friend. Her querulous Fairfield County accent was the best thing I'd heard in months. I wanted to run my hands through her reddish, slightly kinked hair. My mind filled with libidinous memories of the mossy outbuildings of the old Lapham estate, which had been turned into a town park just in time for the teenagers of my high school to use it as a bordello. The rest of the weekend I abandoned myself to driving from one house to another, in an idiotic reprise of my life at seventeen. I barely found time to schedule in the required Thanksgiving meal with my family.

This meal was the usual chaotic and multicultural laugh fest we'd become used to during the years of our combined families' unlikely coexistence. We reprised some of our greatest recipes, the yellow squash mush, the vegan turkey, the brown rice and tofu. There were new boyfriends, who had to be introduced to our ways. No one noticed anything different about Little Ward. He was neither quieter, nor less quiet than he'd always been.

The next day I drove into Manhattan to have dinner with my father in his apartment. Before I left home, I promised Little Ward that I'd come see him in Vermont. Why not? I might find myself up there.

"Sure," said Ward, looking away. I knew I'd disappointed him, but what the hell. I had my own tragic life to unfold, corner by corner.

My father's still-new wife wasn't particularly glad to see me, but I ended up staying over on a folding couch in the library. When the telephone sounded in the middle of the night, its harsh, frightening ring caused me to sit up, sweating and gasping. A minute or so later, my father came in without a word and handed me the receiver. It was my mother in Connecticut, telling me that Little Ward was dead. He'd driven up to Vermont that afternoon. In the evening he'd called the police to tell them he saw an intruder. Then he had picked up a small-caliber rifle and shot himself in the temple. The rifle he'd used had been brand-new. He'd bought it at a sports store in New Canaan the day we had climbed up into the tree, and had kept it in the trunk of his car all weekend without telling a soul.

Ward's death tore a bloody hole in my world. As I wailed in my father's arms, he, conducting himself with the utmost practicality, as he always did, carefully positioned his body between myself and the open window. I blamed Peacock Point, I blamed Ward's father, I blamed myself, I blamed my high school friends. Why hadn't I bothered to stay and finish our conversation in the big copper birch tree? With some inspired combination of words I might have reached into my cousin's head and stopped him from the course upon which he was so determinedly settled. But what sentence, what paragraph, can make up for years of feeling useless, marred—a defective part better taken off the conveyor belt?

With Little Ward's death, I felt a terrible truth about my family had risen out of the black waters like a huge whale, to show a fatal gash that sharks had torn in its belly. I didn't stay to attend his funeral. Instead I returned to Chicago, quit my job, broke contact with what few friends I had, and moved into the basement of a vacant building in the downtown Loop.

There the owner, a young, hip Chicagoan named Lewis, took me on as a kind of watchman while he thought about what he was going to do with the building. "Just don't answer the *dowah* after *dahk*!" he warned. I soon found out why. The winter was bitter, and at night homeless people often tried to break in through the front door. Only the barking of the landlord's dog, Smoky, with whom I slept for warmth, kept them out.

My hair grew as long and stringy as it had been in high school, and I began to wear the same clothes day after day. Some mornings I could barely summon up the energy to get out of bed. There was a small coffee shop catty-corner across a set of empty, brick-scattered lots, and sometimes I'd get up and walk there for coffee and an egg sandwich. Back in the small basement apartment was an old-fashioned refrigerator with a science fiction coil at the top that ran on gas rather than electricity. The hissing of this strange object marked my nights and dreams. Most days I leaned back in bed, listening to the chatter of Chicago's AM station, WLS, steadily reading through a box of paperback mysteries and science fiction novels I'd found on a street corner.

Curiously, during a long stretch where I hadn't seen or talked to anyone in days, there came a loud knock on the door one afternoon. To my amazement, it was my father. There he was, standing in his Armani overcoat in the pale winter sunlight with the tracks of the elevated howling over his head.

"Callooh! Callay!" he shouted over the railroad din. "My friend and I have braved the wilderness of Chicago to rescue you from yourself!" Next to him stood a fat man with flashing glasses and a fat cigar clamped under one index finger, whom I recognized as Vic Simonte, one of the other vice presidents at Bowne, a man who'd started as a typesetter, and to whom my father had loaned money and helped to become an executive, a man with a reputation as an up-and-comer.

Gulping with astonishment, I invited them to come into my humble abode, but they declined. They were about to have a night on the town, and wanted me to come along. I had to laugh out loud. My girlfriend Margot had worked for a couple of weeks as a topless dancer in New Town, and I could see that these were just the types of silly clowns who'd hooked dollar bills through her G-string and tried to lure her into their laps. Dad and Vic were so eager to get away to explore the back alleys of Sodom that Dad actually did a soft-shoe on the sidewalk outside my seedy condemned town house, with its broken stoop looming like a big claw.

The next day my father took me to lunch at a restaurant downtown. "Vic is a family man," he told me, slopping his coffee with a spoon and then dropping the spoon to the white tablecloth. "Boys, one after the other, all sturdy, smart, handsome critters, according to Vic," he said, "although to me, they all look like him. Anyway, Vic is very concerned about what he saw yesterday. He says he'd never let a son of his live in a hole like that, and if he was me, he'd take you out right away."

"What do *you* say, Dad," I asked.

Dad shrugged the way a clown does, sinking his head deep in his shoulders and lifting his open palms up to the sky. "I say, who am I to pass judgment upon any of my kids? It's not my philosophy to intervene in your lives."

"I wouldn't listen to anything Vic says, Dad. He wants your job, and he'll do whatever he can to undermine you," I said.

Dad was astonished. "How do you know this? Vic is my best friend!"

My knowledge was a little hard to explain. People had been looking transparent to me lately, maybe because I hadn't been eating enough. Sometimes, while I watched, unpleasant things stirred up from a murky bottom. In Vic, I'd caught a glimpse of something dark with fins moving.

"It doesn't matter, Dad," I said, knowing I was letting him off the hook, as I always did. "You can leave me alone here. I'm fine."

So my father flew back to New York and I went back to my carton of paperback novels.

In February, a hole opened up in the building's roof and freezing rain poured in, dripping all the way down to my basement apartment. I realized it was absolutely time for me to leave. I boarded a Greyhound bus, intending to return home to the East Coast, but for some reason my route lay to the north. I dozed while the city gave way to the suburbs and the suburbs to farm country. For hours the bony fingers of trees flashed over long rows of snow and dirt. I hadn't brought a book, or anything to eat, so the ride seemed to take a long time. I'd decided that I was going to quit reading again, anyway. I'd been reading for months and it hadn't done me any good.

The bus stopped in Madison, Wisconsin, and I got out at a college campus where the buildings were made of concrete and cut to sharp angles. I'd heard from someone in Chicago that Madison was a friendly place, and I began to think of looking for a job there. An hour of staring at the notices in the student union convinced me that there was nothing for me, though, unless I wanted to participate in a fertility experiment or become a research assistant.

Night was falling. The student union was on the edge of an enormous lake. Fishermen had drilled holes here and there and stood silently by their lines—tiny figures out on the gray snow. A thick blanket of cloud had moved in to cover the sky, and the horizon had all but disappeared. The lake was only partly frozen over, however, and black water seeped through the ice in large shapeless patches.

Signs along the lake edge every fifty feet or so warned people not to go out on its surface. The lake looked beautiful to me, though, all of that open space soothing and inviting. I dropped my pack on a bench and stepped out onto the ice. Soon I was a mile out. The last fisherman called out to me, motioning frantically for me to go back to the shore, but I just waved and kept walking. At first I avoided the black pools where water had begun to soak through the ice, but as the sky grew darker, I could no longer see them. Every once in a while my sneakers broke through the thin crust under the snow, so that soon my feet were soaked and freezing. Still, the whole scene took my breath away. It was like a landscape painting from which everything, all details, had been rubbed out. This was it, I realized suddenly. I'd finally achieved what I'd set out to do. Like my hero Jack Kerouac, I'd dissolved into the cold dark heart of the American continent; I was about to be blown out like a candle. For a long time there was just the irregular crunch of my wet Keds in the soggy snow, and the strings of lights on the campus swinging far away. And then there was only blackness and numbing cold.

Part Five

Of what we cannot speak we must pass over in silence.

—Ludwig Wittgenstein

Chapter Fifteen

My stepbrother's cross-country adventure ended up stretching out over the next two and a half years. Having now, it seemed, "permanently" left New York City, his life solidified into a great migratory pattern typical of the itinerant homeless: Denver, Albuquerque, Ketchum, San Francisco, Miami Beach. He was one of the few on the road, I thought, who could define Latin nouns, or knew how many variations Mozart had written on "Twinkle, Twinkle Little Star." A social security office in Idaho wired a disability payment of $540 per month (gradually rising) into his bank account, allowing him a three-day, government-subsidized lapse into debauchery. Otherwise, he lived without money or friends, doing what he called his "alone thing," digging through garbage cans and making nests here and there, expending the bare minimum amount of energy needed to stay alive.

He'd call me in the middle of the afternoon, standing at a gas station somewhere, in Fort Worth, or Ketchum, the sunlight at his back. If I were out of the apartment, he'd leave a dozen messages in a row, ranging from irrational to chaotic. At that time, I believe, he had a phone card paid for by his mother.

"Hello, Big Peter, it's Little Peter!"

"Hello . . . hello . . . HELLO!"

"It's Peter . . . your long-lost stepbrother calling to say hello and how are you?"

"Big Peter, it's your brother. I just wanted to tell you one thing, but now I've forgotten what it is. So if you will just please pick up the phone, maybe I'll remember. Or maybe not."

"Hey Peter, it's, uh, Peter again. That cop who followed me, man. He freaking tried to . . . he approached me again. If he approaches me again it's big trouble. Big trouble, big trouble. Big trouble. That's all I can tell you right now. Talk to you later when I talk to you. Bye."

"It's Peter. Uh, the first part of that message sounded kind of vague when I listened to it. Uh, somebody heard me, though. I'm just wondering if you got the first part of the message that I already left."

"So I don't know, I guess a message is just as good as talking to you. Probably even better at this point. Yeah, I think it's even better by now, man. So, if I call you back from jail, or dead, man, I mean, don't be too surprised. Cause these fuckers are out to do me in, and it doesn't matter whether I did anything wrong or not. They're coming to get me. They're fucking coming to get me. So, I'll talk to you when I talk to you. That's all. Bye."

"Hmmm . . . HUMMMM . . . Hah . . . hah . . . HAH!"

Chapter Sixteen

Little Peter's return to my life coincided with the birth of my first child, Alden—hands down, the most intense and primal event of my life. Where in America, and at what point, do average people experience such shock and pain and effort, such bloodshed, and finally such a deep and almost mystical payoff? The answer is, except when watching television, nowhere. Birth is it. Death may have lost its sting, thanks to medical science, but birth still hurts a lot.

We were living then in a cooperatively owned building just off Eighth Avenue in the Village. Built in the nineteen-thirties, before the suburban exodus, it was designed with the laudable intention that every working-class family should have an affordable, if not exactly palatial, aerie in which to perch. The building had never been fancy or luxurious, but had a part-time doorman and elevators and had held on to its reputation of being a safe and respectable, if unpretentious, building to live in, while the West Village neighborhood went through several decades of gentle de-gentrification.

In the seventies and eighties, the small apartments with their sunken living rooms, old-fashioned kitchens, dark floors, arched plaster entrances, and overabundance of tiny closets gradually filled up with an aging population of schoolteachers, social workers, school superintendents, choreographers, retired actors, and salesmen. By the time Hali and I moved in, the building was far along in becoming a "NORC," or Naturally Occurring

Retirement Community. To the co-op members who interviewed us, we must have looked like a plate of bright red salmon roe glittering in the sun at an outdoor fish market.

We found ourselves sitting in a small studio apartment blazing with lights, facing a wall-length mirror. Eight unamused middle-aged residents sat before us on sofas and chairs. They passed around copies of our last three years' income tax returns, along with financial statements, recommendations, credit reports, and personal declarations. Shaking their heads, they pointed at lines, and whispered. From the start the interview seemed to go badly.

"This line item on your Equifax?" came a question.

"Uh, that was back in ninety-two," I said. "A dry-cleaning bill. I think there was some sort of dispute."

"Will you write a letter?"

"A letter explaining the dispute?"

"Of course."

"What did you want to move to New York for anyway? You seemed to be doing so well in Kansas City."

"Ummm," I replied.

This went on for ten more minutes. Then a heavyset man in a black leather jacket with buckles who had said nothing before interrupted.

"Are you planning to have kids?" he asked.

"What?"

"You look like a couple who are planning to have kids. We don't *like* kids in our building."

My face froze in place. Kids? I paged rapidly through the sheaf of papers in my lap. There had been nothing about kids in the co-op application. Even dogs were allowed, I thought.

"Mr. Desidario is kidding," said a kindly woman with red hair after a pause, smiling. "Aren't you, Mr. Desidario?"

"Yes, I'm kidding," the man in the leather jacket said, without cracking a smile.

"I believe that concludes the interview," said the kindly woman. "You can go now. The rest of us will stay behind and talk about you."

Eventually we were allowed into the building after filling out several more financial statements and writing a few more groveling letters.

Our apartment, built over a busy intersection, was noisy, but filled with sunlight. Brilliant squiggles roved the ceiling from the reflected chrome of the cars speeding below. Far from the cliché of New Yorkers riding up the elevator and never knowing their neighbors, we now found ourselves surrounded, as if in some preindustrial hamlet, by interlocking circles of curious, intrusive, helpful friends, radiating from our cooperative building, our playground and our preschool—so that when my mother came to visit, she wondered, "Is there anyone in the Village you *don't* know?"

The walls and floors of our place were soon covered with animalistic images: rubber boots in the shapes of frogs' heads; jackets and backpacks in the shapes of lions, zebras, and hippos; bovine wash rags, yellow rubber ducks; pink pig nail brushes; and swimming dolphin and frog bath toys. Within this menagerie were examples of almost every mammal and crawling creature available on earth, and in addition there were lifelike effigies of extinct species—megalodons, brachiosaurs, velociraptors, tyrannosaurs, and iguanodons—as well as those of imaginary species—such as Mothra, Godzilla, and Garuda—and provisional species—such as Elmo and Oscar. From the TV screen blared a new gospel according to Disney, called "The Great Circle of Life," whose central tenet was something like reincarnation. Mommy always died early in the show, but in moments of danger and stress She would rise up over the trees to speak in echoing tones of consolation and advice, like a giant see-through ghost. Animals talked in the voices of old comedians, sharks begged forgiveness as they ate you, and spiders wove messages into their webs. To me it felt like the end of Protestantism.

The hum of women's voices in the lobby warmed and calmed me, though, reminded me of my great-grandmother's parlor at Peacock Point, where my great-aunts played canasta with the Russians and sipped tea all afternoon long. The women sat in our lobby with their shopping bags by their thick ankles, white fencepost legs divided by blue veins. Now and then one would heave herself up with a sigh and apply herself to the next task, a visit to the doctor, a visit from a friend, a look-in from a social worker, a walk to the grocery store, a perambulation with the dog. Many were living in rent-controlled apartments, the property of the former building owner before the building had gone co-op. They smoked in the sad labyrinths of their tiny apartments, surrounded by dusty stacks of magazines, newspapers, and junk, and left pots of water to dry up and melt on the stove, causing concern about fire among the board—which I joined, eventually, as meetings were informal affairs, lubricated by bottles of wine and trays of grapes.

———

There'd been an element of slapstick in the birthing room, as perhaps there always is. My wife's labor lasted for over four hours. As pushing became more difficult, the midwife propped Hali up in a sitting position on the hospital bed. Unfortunately, the bed had a lever exactly at knee height, so that each time I leaned over to whisper in her ear, my knee hit the lever and she plummeted back down to a reclining position. As I had been trained by our birthing instructor to speak to my wife constantly, Hali began to flop up and down on her hospital bed like a rag doll.

Adding to our stress was the young, bearded obstetrical resident who sat in his office at the end of the hallway with his feet up on his desk, tracking our situation on a remote monitor. All of us knew that he was only waiting for a particular combination of blips on the screen to appear before he galloped into the birthing room to start some dire intervention that would justify the expense of his medical degree. This resident had already ordered a fetal monitor and oxygen, as well as intravenous hydration, so that my wife had tubes and wires running out of nearly every orifice in her body. At random intervals, he would leave his desk in order to pop into our quiet, well-ordered chamber, stand like a fraternity cheerleader over my wife's bed where she lay in the agony of labor, and shout, "Come on, Hali! You can do it! Push! Push!" Our midwife was starting to develop a fearful, beleaguered look, knowing her job might be taken away from her if things didn't hurry up very soon.

Hali's brother, Eli, who probably hadn't seen his sister naked since the first grade, at this point was practically crawling up her uterus, gamely clicking away snapshots of her blood-smeared thighs.

Even if our student doctor didn't carry through with his implied threat to start cutting in the next few minutes, the midwife knew that soon she would be forced to intervene herself. Her tray of tools gleamed in the dim of the operating lamp, like the gynecological instruments for mutant women invented by the obstetrical twins in David Cronenberg's creepy movie *Dead Ringers*.

Hali looked at me in despair. Her face was puffy and a bloody patch had appeared in the white of her left eye, as if she had been the loser in a bad street fight. Then she closed her eyes and tried to push one more time.

Suddenly like a mole emerging from the broken earth, our son began to spit himself out from between her bloody thighs. The process was like retching in reverse. First, his head emerged, dark and green, the chin and skull sharpened to long points, so that he looked like a pterodactyl cub crawling free from the blackness of some hideous slime-covered primordial egg. I startled back in horror. For a brief instant the creature turned his own dark eyes onto mine, then, recognizing his own flesh, turned back to his monumental task; with a few instinctive jerks, he shrugged himself free and lay twitching in the midwife's strong, pale hands, now copiously slimed with blood and mucus. Thick purple veins roped my son's flesh. His legs were long, and incredibly thin, and sprinkled with a white waxy powder similar to that which is put on apples to preserve them, his feet doubled up unnaturally, so that their toes lay against his ankles. More startling were his testicles, which were the size and color of a pair of California plums.

Strangely, it was only at that moment that I realized that it was a boy—and that he was my son! I mean, I'd always assumed we'd have a girl: I'd lived with girls all my life and had gotten used to girlish ways. My wife herself had predicted a girl, seriously doubting that any male hormone–producing organism could have resided inside her body for nine months without causing grave damage to her system. There'd been certain signs, though, which we'd missed. Weeks earlier I'd dreamed I was sitting in an open motorboat that was cutting through the blue waters of the Caribbean, while a small boy with dark wind-ruffled hair lay beside me asleep on the cockpit floor. My mother-in-law, Priscilla, had also dreamed of a boy, but we dismissed her dream as too-obvious wish fulfillment, since every Korean mother has no greater desire than that her first grandchild be a son. A doorman in our building had also predicted a boy, based on the pointed shape of my wife's belly, but we'd heavily discounted his prediction too, as Hispanic doormen wish for male heirs almost as much as Korean grandmothers do.

Giant boulders dislodged themselves under my feet and rolled ponderously away. Suddenly I was on my knees, crying. From somewhere, I don't know where, a storm of tears overtook me like a summer shower, wracking my chest with sobs. At the same time, going off like a strobe in my cerebral cortex was the revelation, exceedingly obvious to everyone but me, apparently: "So, that's what all that endless fucking was about!" For decades, everyone I knew had been copulating as often as possible, and in as many places as they could find: their grandparents' guest bedrooms, 2:00 A.M. bus station waiting rooms, brick-covered vacant lots, disinfectant-reeking motel rooms, the backs of rusty vans up on blocks, the tiny rooms that banks reserve for safety-deposit box customers, upon the sandy floors of vacant apartments sprinkled with voodoo pennies, in SoHo lofts surrounded by coughing pipes, or floating through cumulous water vapor thirty thousand feet up. One friend of mine, now a mom, told me that she once—finding no other place to have sex with a stranger she'd met at the airport—had taken him out to a grass median strip between two runways to fuck to the roar of 747s landing. No one was thinking about having babies then, for Christ's sake! It came as a shock to be confronted so viscerally, for the first time, and after so many years, with the results of all of that heedlessly expended energy. What a blithering idiot I had been, not to have seen the truth much earlier! Soon I was crying and laughing at the same time, which Hali had warned me would cause hair to grow on my butt, but at that point I didn't care.

Hali and I looked at each other in dismay, as the nurses took our son off to a far corner of the birthing room to suction out his lungs under a set of powerful lights, and the midwife busied herself putting in a couple of stitches into her torn flesh. No special-effects crew on the set of a science fiction film could have dreamed up a more frightening spectacle. From that far corner of the room emerged a cacophonous chamber piece, composed of our son's outraged howling, the nurses' sweet endearments in Tagalog, and the deep-throated growl of the suctioning machine, which made a grotto-sound like the last of the bathwater draining out of an old tub.

A few minutes later, the attendants returned holding our piebald cupid, who had lost his saurian aspect and now presented the angry red grimace of a newborn baby. Hali bared her breast with unseemly haste. The boy opened his mouth, engulfed an entire brown nipple, and began to suck. As the bond between mother and son began to tighten, a thin ribbon that had connected myself and my wife through the years of our intimacy snapped, and the two parts fell to the floor and were swept up by a passing orderly.

Beautiful as he was, our baby seemed to be related to neither of us, to be a far-traveling sentinel from another planet, reaching Earth for the first time, both innocent and wise. Hali's parents thought him completely Caucasian. Mine thought him purely Korean. Hali's grandmother, or Big Halmonie, who occupied a small, subsidized town house outside of Boulder, Colorado, that always smelled of kimchi and boiled soy milk, expressed her own strong conviction as to what the mixture of our two kinds might bring.

The conversation between Hali's mother, freshly returned from the birthing room in New York, and Big Halmonie went something like this:

"How are his hands, are they big?"

"Yes, Mother, they are big," said Hali's mother.

"And his feet, are they big, too?"

"Yes, of course."

"And his *jaji?*"

"Big also, Big Halmonie."

With great satisfaction, Big Halmonie sighed.

"I *thought* so!"

That Alden's *jaji* was on the large side was not necessarily a legacy passed on to him from my side of the family, though. He had, in fact, a hydrocele, a condition of water-filled sacs in the scrotum, that gradually deflated before the end of his first year. In any case, convinced that Alden had inherited more than just sun-sensitive skin from his father's Visigoth ancestors, Big Halmonie insisted on passing on to Hali and me, through Priscilla, a great number of unnecessarily detailed instructions on how to tie the diaper so as to give the poor boy plenty of room where he needed it.

At first I carried my son everywhere, to art galleries and openings and museums, strapped to the front of my jacket like a figurehead, as a proud emblem of contrarian philosophy. In the arid world of art galleries and museums, I . . . I . . . had gone the opposite way of everyone else. Instead of producing the exquisitely crafted essay, and shaping a career, I had made this . . . *other thing*, this amazing replica of myself in flesh and blood. A baby is the ultimate trompe l'oeil. His little penis sometimes actually fountained up in the air like a whale's spout when I was scraping the mustard-colored shit off of his butt! What art review, what work of art, could be more complex in form and conception, more fraught with meaning, taut with metaphor, more laced through with irony than the tiny, lumpen, but full-throated object I carried on my chest?

I had trained myself to think of everything I did as a gesture, a wry statement, a summing up, a thrust, a bit of repartee. Even the clothing I wore was a part of an ancient and laden dialogue. Doc Martens had been the perfect antidote to hiking boots, which had been the perfect answer to narrow ties. Later there had been a lot of black clothing and then retro shirts from the fifties and finally pinstriped suits, à la Jeff Koons. *Which* amounted to the more flamboyant and magnanimous statement, the summing up of everything important? If art was all about the grand gesture, then my son was a slap in the face of the avant-garde. He was a big fuck-you to the art establishment. Deal with it! Next I was going to buy a minivan and move to Nyack. That would show them.

These were the thoughts that consoled me as I stumped around the slushy streets of SoHo and Chelsea trying to keep up with the art world, as I contemplated my already tenuous position as an art writer.

Yeah, here was this baby, number one son, drooling and carrying on in front of me wherever I went, gumming and slobbering on its Baby Björn carrier. My son was a volcano of piss, shit, mucus, and saliva. A lot of artists were working with body fluids that year. Nothing new, of course. Marcel Duchamp had used semen in a work as early as 1946 and the artist Piero Manzoni had grossed everyone out in the early sixties by canning his own shit and calling it *Merda d'artista*. Serrano caused a minor shit storm by taking a picture of a crucifix floating in urine. This was human representation stripped down to its most basic level. He was, actually, a real human, but small enough so you could throw him in a shopping bag. He was a maquette, a miniature, a scaled-down model. He had a butt and little shoe-button eyes and a set of tiny miraculously detailed fingers curling in his hands.

Here was a set of instructions turned into a fully realized art object, like a Sol LeWitt installation. At the same time, a baby evoked everything that was cute and commodifiable in our culture. Warhol had stumbled upon the emblematic value of babies years ago. Keith Haring had honed the image of the baby to a fine and culturally radioactive art object. Furthermore our baby was the product of chance operations, of the alchemical swirling together of male and female genotypes, with no possibility of predicting the outcome, à la John Cage.

And moreover, the two of us, working collaboratively, had made him at home. To hell with presentation! A baby is about process, odors, palpability, and living in the moment—and nothing about the art school culture of presentation, polish and craftsmanship. He's all passion and instinct and groping blindly in the dark. Fuck you! We're not talking about mock naïve, with all of its sly levels of mono and double entendres, and this year's crop of *art brut*. We were the true naïves, visionaries: a man and a woman, bravely slashing out a new aesthetic terrain all by ourselves.

Carrying twenty or thirty pounds of flesh and equipment around with me at all times made it difficult to cover the six or eight or ten shows I tried to get to in an evening. It's true that hauling an infant around freed me of the necessity of always having to check my altimeter to see what level of irony we were operating under. But I found talking over the top of a baby's head at art openings could get to be wearing, especially when I had to stick my finger in his mouth to keep him happy. And it was sometimes hard to get a chic forty-five-year-old gallery proprietress in a black sweater dress to take me seriously when I kept having to interrupt the conversation because my brat was screaming at the top of his lungs and I had to borrow a bathroom in order to change his diapers. No matter how nicely she acted, her face told me, "Come back when you are ready."

And forget about slipping off for a glass of wine, a smoke, a chitchat of gossip about what Gagosian or Gavin Brown or Jeffrey Deitch was up to. I suddenly noticed that the kind of information I used to absorb through my skin wasn't coming in anymore.

Before Alden had come along, we were starting to look, well, kind of *interesting*, a biracial couple, fresh out of Kansas City, which was to most New Yorkers an unknown landscape of hog farms, long fences, and snowy rail sidings—the wife as knowledgeable, or perhaps more knowledgeable than the husband (having actually attended a college where they taught something), the husband dutifully flacking articles and reviews for *Art in America* and *The New York Times*, supplemented with a few catalogue essays, online reviews, and squibs in publicly funded, alternative rags. As much as Hali would permit it—and there was a kind of grr factor there, because she'd also scooted her butt through the art scene a few years before while in college, had worked as a summer intern for Paula Cooper and been an art slave for Petah Coyne, and while these had been positive experiences, as a result she had developed a low tolerance for gallery pomposity and unfortunate fashion choices—we were starting to be a couple whom people invited over to dinner. Just starting. There had been flirtatious friendships, cementing relationships that began in the gallery.

So we were being delicately and provisionally courted, but having a baby quickly exploded that empty coquetry. We tried to go to a childless art couple's weekend place and ended up having a hideous time, the waves of puke streaming over an antique Chinese table, the lack of sufficient quantities of paper towels and wipes, the soiled blankets, the public elimination of violently colored waste products. I actually thought it quite fun in a regressive way, but there was horror in our hosts' eyes. We retreated in haste, and relief, blowing regrets and apologies behind us like air kisses. It was time to let go and accept that this . . . this *baby-tending* was all I could do right now.

At first, it seemed laughable that the welfare of this tiny delicate human had devolved to us. After all, plants withered in our presence, cats went feral, and desert creatures in terrariums soon dried out and expired. To ward off crib death we kept him flat on his back for so long that he developed a bald spot on the back of his head like a novice monk. Gradually we realized that a baby is a tough thing, its willpower far stronger than our own. Rather than a passive fragile creature, about to die at a moment's inattention, our baby had an unquenchable desire to live and be heard. The sound of his cackling cry in the middle of my exhausted night wasn't a negotiable subject (like almost everything else in my life), it was a command, an order from the top of the evolutionary pyramid, the Big Boss. I was no match for the power of his will; in my imagination he towered over me. Still, I couldn't help but feel resentful of those of my friends who'd had babies before me for not complaining enough, or at least not complaining to the extent that I could actually *hear* them. Perhaps you can't really *know* what parenthood is like until you are there.

We seemed hopeless at navigating the communal system of child rearing that seemed to be going on all around us. Important information was swirling like leaves in the wind, but always seemed to slip through our fingers.

I got used to the sound of the breast pump wheezing in the dark like a lost oil derrick. I spent hours trying to read the grimace of our baby's face, his fists pushed up against his neck, the red capillaries breaking up in a maze on his cheeks, reminding me of the face of my grandfather Hattie-Hattie, before he died. I traced my fingers along the hot stretch of his scalp. His blind thoughts were as different from mine as the porpoise's or the whale's. They were thoughts without words, armless thoughts, legless thoughts. This is truly how we will all end up, I thought, as wizened old men hunched in bed, dreaming the ancient dreams of our race.

I learned to negotiate the intricacies of the Maclaren stroller, with its levers that either cause it to spring up, or collapse violently, sending your baby through the air as if thrown by a medieval catapult; the implausible

Baby Björn carrier; the fiendish adjustments of the Peg Perego high chair, conceived, no doubt, by the cappuccino-churned brain of a frothy, childless, twenty-four-year-old Italian industrial designer in Jean-Luc Godard glasses.

I'd heard that with each stage of the baby's growth I'd have to mentally relive that stage in my own life, but I never expected the alternating surges of raw pain and happiness, that I would sometimes feel split open like a gourd on the ground, with my viscera spilling out, or that I would also have quiet hours holding my son in my lap, thinking nothing, just holding him, while the sun went down yellow and black outside my window and the cars honked and settled into their afternoon rush.

As I stared into my son's eyes, trying to pry into their dark mystery, I pondered how his arrival had filled me with such wonder and gratitude—mainly that my life hadn't turned out so twisted and skewed that something as beautiful and perfect as he was had come out of it. In moments of tawdry emotion, I vowed to raise him well and protect him from harm, as well as from the darkness residing within me.

It would be foolish to assert that every man who has stood where I stood hasn't made the same promise. No doubt every son vows to correct the mistakes made by his father, and then goes on to make worse mistakes himself. It's in the nature of men to make such promises, then walk away from them. They disappear into the calm of their workplaces to find surcease from the strain of living at home—but the workday is long, it addles their brains, they grow restless with sexual malnourishment and self-pity. At home they drink, lash out, and mock, and in their blindness and rage, they systematically destroy what was once best and most pure in their children, just as what was best and most pure in them was once destroyed. That was the history of mankind as I had known it. The pattern went back through the sulfurous swamps to the low, stinking rise where our pagan ancestors first built their earthenwork castles so that they could beat their wives and children and perform their unspeakable ceremonies in peace. There was no end to this history. The process was unstoppable and had incorporated itself lately into our genetic heritage. I was crazy to think that I could do any better.

My father would sometimes come by the apartment to watch—his eyes grown piggish with age—while I spooned food into my son's mouth. The easy way my son leaned over my knee to receive a mouthful of ground carrots seemed to fascinate him. "I was never that kind of father to you," he said. He wasn't apologizing, I knew—merely voicing an observation.

Chapter Seventeen

When Little Peter finally returned to New York in January of 1998 he was displaying a new kind of equanimity—distilled, I thought, from his thousand and one mad adventures on the road and a few brief stints in jail over the past couple of years.

He called about nine thirty in the morning, his voice rasping and happy—happy to be in New York, happy to be alive. I was still asleep, roughed up by a night of kid changing, kid feeding, and kid napping. He'd arrived on the midnight Greyhound, he said, and was sleeping on a slab of cardboard on a grate in Riverside Park, within fifty yards of the apartment building at West End Avenue and Seventy-fourth Street in which he'd grown up. When he woke up he could actually look up into the window of his old bedroom—or was it the library?

By this time, my daughter, Maya, had popped into the world—with the celerity, if not the precise sound, of a champagne cork sliding from a bottle. Life was one long celebration for Maya. She gurgled and pouted and rolled her eyes and pursed her lips and smiled in continuous succession, following with her bright eyes everything that was going on around her.

She had begun walking at eight months and carrying on full conversations with me even before that. When Hali went back to work, I got used to carrying Maya around on my hip wherever I went, listening to her comment on every blessed *t'ing* we passed (a word she'd picked up from the West Indian babysitters in our playground). Maya rode me like a cowgirl in her red button sweater, steering by tugging at my ears, wrist, and elbow, or pulling at the edges of my shirt, or by means of a steady stream of orders, pointed fingers, and invectives. If I ever left the apartment without her warm weight heavy on my hip, I suffered a continuous nagging feeling, as though I'd left something important behind, like my wallet or my watch.

My stepbrother and I made a date to meet on the steps of the Museum of Natural History at noon, Little Peter hesitating: "You mean EXACTLY at twelve?" I didn't want to ruffle his sense of continuous, unfettered time flow . . . I said yes.

I arrived at the museum early, and was sitting on the steps reading *The Wall Street Journal* when I heard a gravelly voice behind me—don't know how he'd snuck up on me like that. Little Peter was wearing a filthy red nylon windbreaker, jeans, and a wool hat. He had a half inch of beard and his hair was shoulder length and greasy. He was carrying two see-through plastic bags and a daypack—one of them held a sleeping bag. I was surprised at how glad I was to see him.

At his suggestion we went around the corner to a Cuban-Chinese restaurant—where to my surprise the waiters let us in without raising an eyebrow. I think they took my stepbrother for a European backpacker.

At first, Little Peter didn't want to talk over Maya's head: she was strapped to my chest. He asked several times if I would put her down. But in the restaurant, it was impossible. "If she keeps staring at me, she'll burn her eyes out," he said. Finally, she fell asleep and he grew more comfortable. We began to talk of the usual things—his indecisions, his future. I said he should look at the menu and decide what he was going to eat first before he decided what he was going to do with the rest of his life. I'd forgotten about the scar on Little Peter's face between and just over his eyes, a nasty, curved cicatrix that raises a portion of flesh on his forehead and accentuates his already heavy facial features.

Lunch arrived and he ate greedily, strings of melted cheese occasionally hanging from his lip. His left arm at times needed to be propped up by his right arm, but he told me that his hands were in pretty much the same condition as before. The meal was superb, a plate of fresh sliced avocado, tomatoes, and onions with lemon squeezed onto it, a kind of melted cheese sandwich, rice and beans. I never eat so well as when I'm with my stepbrother, or so cheaply . . .

In the middle of the conversation, he asked me very concernedly if he was taking up too much of my time. I said no, I would tell him if that was true. But was this a sign of the "new" Little Peter that he was even asking me that question? He claimed he was a lot better at "those" kinds of things than his family thought he was. They (Olivia and Franz) still thought of him as being totally self-centered and oblivious, but now that he was an adult, he'd learned to be more sensitive to others.

I told him that he'd suffered a lot of bad years and it'd be worth it to me to see his luck turn around.

Now that he was in New York he was full of plans. He'd been reading a John D. MacDonald book and wanted to move to Florida and buy a boat to live on, and become a full-time boat bum, like Travis McGee, the private eye hero of the novel. The plan almost seemed plausible, and I said so. He also wanted to take piano lessons, and I promised to call his old piano teacher (who never returned my call).

When Maya woke up and started making nonstop goo-goo noises, Little Peter wanted to know if she was all right. I replied that Maya could go on like this all day long . . .

Lunch over, we went out to find a hotel. While we were walking, Little Peter suddenly lagged behind as a policeman strolled by on foot, then made a big obvious circle in front of the cop. With that shit-eating grin on his face he looked particularly disheveled. The result was that the cop took much more notice of us than he normally would have.

The woman at the hotel desk, a pretty, young Asian with a round silver stud protruding just below her lip, kept staring at Maya, strapped to my chest. I think she could tell that my daughter was a *hapa* child—rude Hawaiian slang for half Asian, half white. She gave me a card and wrote the number of my stepbrother's hotel room upside down on it—that is, correct for me. When I complimented the woman on her unusual skill, she gave me a cute little smirk and said, "I've been practicing."

Chapter Eighteen

The next time I met my stepbrother—at the deli on Fourteenth Street—I discovered to my amazement that, following his new program of responsibility and self-improvement, he had already been in touch with his childhood psychiatrist, Dr. Desmond Heath, once or twice—and had even been up to see him!

Little Peter had started visiting Dr. Heath three times a week from the age of eleven—with a fourth session reserved for Olivia by herself, because, as she said, "Peter will never tell you anything important!" After my stepbrother dropped out of college, the doctor facilitated his nine-week stay in the psychiatric wing at Mount Sinai Hospital. There, he had been administered powerful antipsychotic drugs until he began to walk with his arms straight in front of him like a movie Frankenstein. When he finally returned home he cut the cord to his electric keyboard out of sheer frustration, because he couldn't make his fingers walk the keyboard the way he had before his hospitalization. Ancient history.

At Little Peter's invitation I met him at Dr. Heath's office for his next appointment. The building was on Park Avenue just before the trains come out of the ground at Ninety-sixth Street and had an ornate Spanish lobby with a doorman standing at a lectern.

Amazing how seedy the doctor's waiting room was, though, for someone who pulled in $150 an hour for his consulting time. A vase of artificial flowers; an Impressionist print in a yellowing mat; a kitsch drawing of a ballerina; some low-slung Danish modern furniture, circa 1960, re-covered in brown material; an air conditioner; wall outlets and a small, conical air-purifier (whose main function was probably to drown out the confessions of patients), all in yellowing ivory plastic, like bad teeth. The effect was like the lobby of a motel on Route 66—pretty dingy!

Eventually Dr. Heath came to the door, in a gray suit with a hospital badge. The doctor was short and thick without being fat. With iron gray hair curling around his ears, he resembled a younger and handsomer Norman Mailer, but not as tough. He was perhaps sixty, and spoke with a gentle, cultivated English accent.

I shook hands with the doctor, while Little Peter regressed. He enthusiastically bounded to a chair, telling me that I could sit anywhere but there, because that had always been *his* chair, and then slouched down like a teenager. The office was worn and comfortable, cluttered with a dated slab couch and many mismatched chairs and pieces of equipment of various kinds and vintages, such as fax and answering machines. Piles of files and books lay everywhere, on chairs, the floor, and any flat surface. The bookshelves contained the complete works of Freud and many others of mossy age. Still, a comfortable and cheerful place in which to confess your sins.

Dr. Heath himself seemed to think of my stepbrother as a kid. They quickly set up a bantering conversation, from which I was almost excluded. At times Dr. Heath seemed to bait Little Peter about his hallucinations and paranoia. I was not sure how therapeutic it all was, but the doctor did, I noticed, eventually discover the particulars of Little Peter's present situation.

"Now, Peter," Dr. Heath said, moving on. "You appear to be rather happy to see me. Is that true?"

"Always," said my stepbrother. "I'm always happy to see you, Dr. Heath."

"And yet a moment ago I saw a giant scowl on your face and your lips moving as if you were talking to someone. Did you mean to be addressing me?"

"No."

"Someone else in the room, perhaps?"

"Not really."

"Your stepbrother? Perhaps a voice in your head?"

Little Peter pinched his brow and mumbled. "Not really."

"Could you speak up, Peter, please. It's very hard to hear you."

"I was just . . . thinking."

"Thinking?"

"Yes."

"What exactly were you thinking, then, Peter?"

"I was thinking that we should be careful what we say here, because someone might be listening."

"Someone from the police, perhaps. You have never enjoyed good relations with the police, have you, Peter, even when you were a boy?"

"No, I haven't."

"What if I told you that the walls of my office were thick and perhaps even made of Kryptonite, so that no one could listen in, even with the most powerful microphones?"

"That would make me feel better."

"You trust me, do you, Peter?"

"I trust you completely, Dr. Heath."

"We've known each other such a long time, haven't we, Peter? When did your mother first bring you in to see me? Were you nine then? Nine? Something like that. Perhaps a bit older. You'd gotten into a little trouble at the school, hadn't you? Punched somebody?"

"Yes, I think so."

"Such a handsome boy. I don't think I'd ever seen as good-looking a boy as you were then. Or even imagined one. Like an angel, with blond, tousled hair and blue eyes.

"You know," Dr. Heath said, turning to me, "I told his mother after our very first session, 'No wonder Peter doesn't like to read books. What's going on in his head is so much more interesting.'"

I'd previously resolved to slow Little Peter's nomadic lifestyle if I could. My chief goal was to get him into Fountain House, an early and successful prototype of a halfway house for schizophrenics that is located in the West 40s in Manhattan. The place seemed to be nonrestrictive and fairly cool about their residents' coming and going. If I could just gain admission for Little Peter there, I thought, I could keep an eye on him without being responsible for his welfare and safety every minute. In a pinch, though, I'd settle for Spring Lake Ranch, the Vermont work farm where my stepbrother had already had a couple of (I thought) fairly successful stints.

Dr. Heath studied the Fountain House brochure. Then he looked up. "Peter, you will be better off living here, in this place," he said, in his gentle English accent, "rather than on the street, you know. With our new Mayor Giuliani cracking down on the homeless. Harassing windshield cleaners and so on. Putting people in jail."

But my stepbrother was adamant that, in his present state of equilibrium, he had the situation well in hand.

In any case, Dr. Heath took the pink and yellow quadruplicate Fountain House form that had been mailed to me and promised to fill it out with Little Peter next time he came up for an appointment. I wouldn't even have to be there! I breathed a vast sigh of relief that something was finally being done.

Afterward, as Little Peter and I stood in the rain at the corner of Park Avenue and Ninety-sixth Street, in full view of Dr. Heath's doorman, a pizza box sitting on top of a trash can caught my stepbrother's eye, and he immediately began rummaging through it. The box contained, for some reason, raw potatoes. He recalled that once in Times Square he'd picked up an open can of beer and taken a sip: it was piss.

As we waited for the Number 6 subway train, Little Peter said he thought it'd rain for forty days and forty nights and the world would drown.

"Do you often think about the world ending?" I asked.

"The world has already ended," he told me. "The ones who are walking around now are the lucky ones, the survivors."

A few days later, taking no chances about filling out the the Fountain House application, I walked over to pick up my stepbrother for a second appointment with Dr. Heath. Little Peter's hotel room was four flights up—no elevator, of course. I found him standing sleepy and half naked in the doorway. His chest was covered with pinpoint, black blemishes—the result of his long-term Dumpster diet, I wondered? He had no idea why I was there, since the hotel clerk hadn't delivered my message as he'd promised.

When we arrived at his office, Dr. Heath was his gentle, relaxed, witty English self. At my request, the doctor placed a call to Fountain House and managed to get a woman, Margie, on the line, who was British. Funny to hear him flirt with her: "Where do you come from, love? Oh, London? I'm from Devonshire. Did part of my college work at St. Mary's in Paddington." And so on . . . Not sure if I remembered the English places right, but you have the idea.

While this potentially life-changing conversation was taking place, Little Peter's look turned alternately wary and muddled; he frowned and then opened his mouth as if he were going to say something, then closed it. His eyelids fluttered almost shut, then he opened them . . . a flash of brilliant blue, his irises now somewhat bleached and pale. He lifted his heavy hands and made vague gestures as if rehearsing an orchestral piece, tilting his weighty forehead to one side. Most of the time, when Little Peter talked to me, he spoke in childishly sincere tones that mirrored his deep enthusiasms and beliefs. At times like this, though, he was fully capable of pondering himself into a corner, causing the machinery of his thoughts to lock together painfully into knots of frozen and rusted gears. Then he'd halt and cover his eyes with one gnarled and rubbery hand. Dr. Heath called it his "Rodin's *Thinker*" pose, when he was completely perplexed and concerned with his own mentations.

"I'm not like that anymore!" Little Peter blurted out loud, suddenly.

Dr. Heath put his hand over the phone and we both turned to look at my stepbrother. What could he mean?

Eventually Dr. Heath reached into a drawer and came out with a bottle of prescription pills. He handed them to Little Peter. My stepbrother scratched the top of his head at length, then squinted and looked around, uncomfortable.

"What are they made of?" he asked.

"This is a result of molecular biology," said Dr. Heath. "The Haldol pills you used to take, you remember? Those dealt with the dopamine receptors in your entire brain. This is designed to plug up the receptors only in your frontal lobes. These will clear your thoughts, allow you to take them in order. After a few days you will feel much more reasonable, happier. I've had great results at Covenant House, with my kids telling me, 'Dr. Heath, we like those pills!'"

He went on: "Usually in a case like yours there are two types of symptoms. First the dreamlike ones, the hallucinations and breakthrough thoughts. The pills will deal with those effectively. And then there are the relational symptoms, how people relate to each other. These also work remarkably well with the relational symptoms. You'll get along better with people. Understand what they are saying. Won't feel as alienated."

When Little Peter left the room to get water to swallow his pill, I took the opportunity to complain to Dr. Heath:

"This is a lot of work."

"You're a saint," was his response. Which, of course, made me feel like a complete fool.

The next day I found Little Peter hanging off his hotel room door, half-crazed with anxiety brought on by his new antipsychotic medicine, Zyprexa, even though it'd been a full twenty-four hours since he'd taken it.

As I followed him into the room, he began to pace back and forth, helplessly dangling a plastic bag from his fingers, and spouting anguished questions. "Where did I go wrong with my life?" he asked. "How do I get all my things into this bag? This place is a mess! I feel that at a certain point in time I should have participated, but I didn't. Something's wrong with my head. I have too many things to think about! Do you have a comb? Is my hair all right?" The change was quite pronounced. Overnight, he'd been transformed from an uncaring, low-affect, sidewalk psycho into a stricken New York neurotic of Woody Allen proportions.

Just when I was getting used to the new, self-assured Little Peter—who'd arrived in town so proud of his homeless skills, so sure of himself, so willing to endure any kind of hardship to save his freedom ("Don't get me a hotel room," he had told me. "I don't want to get soft. I'll just sleep out on the street a few nights . . . until I get my bearings.")—this new hyper-neurotic stepbrother comes along.

In his agitated state, Little Peter decided that what he actually longed for was a long restful stay at Spring Lake Ranch in Vermont. "Great!" I told him, and dragged him to a Greek coffee shop nearby for a heavy dose of omelet and hash browns so he could think it over. I figured that a full stomach would tone down his frenetic soul-searching, and I was right. But his resolve to rechart the blighted course of his life stayed firm. He jumped to the pay phone and with surprising efficiency placed calls to the admissions officer at Spring Lake, his mother, and Dr. Heath, one after the other—not bad for a man who'd been officially classified as a mental misfit!

Finally I'd had enough of his jitters. I gave Little Peter a twenty and left him at the Formica table, polishing off the last of his omelet.

He asked, "Where are you going?"

"I have to meet someone. I'm already late."

"An art project?"

"A writing project."

Actually I desperately wanted to go home and be alone. Thus I prevaricated from day to day to preserve myself from my stepbrother's endless needs.

Later, in a telephone conversation with Pam Grace, the admissions director at Spring Lake Ranch, I discovered that Little Peter's prospects there weren't as secure as he'd hoped. The last time he'd stayed at the ranch, she told me, he'd stalked the cook's daughter and stolen a car to escape in. "Of course your stepbrother can stay at the ranch if he intends to participate in the community," she told me icily. "But if he just wants to do what he wants to do and nothing else, then we don't want him."

By the next morning, when I tried to roust him from his hotel room, the pill's effects had worn off, and Little Peter was back to his insouciant, self-possessed self.

"Just let me get my pants on!" he bellowed through the door. "Isn't this something that can wait?" (I had actually arrived two hours early, but so what? I was on a different clock. I had to deal with two kids in diapers: he didn't.) He opened the door at last, then unhurriedly lit a stick of incense and began to stuff his belongings into a duffel bag. Gone was the paralyzing anxiety, his bothered fidgeting about the place. "Good coffee!" he complimented me, on the cup of Starbucks I'd brought for him. "How cold is it?" he asked, then lifted the window a few inches and waggled his fingers underhanded in the fresh air to get a reading.

That afternoon, after paying his hotel bill for another week, I totaled up my Little Peter–related expenses since he'd arrived in town on January 7. It came to the astounding and somewhat sickening sum of $893. I was reminded of the line from the movie *Gandhi*, when the rich patroness says to Ben Kingsley, "My dear friend, you have *no* idea how much it costs me to keep you in poverty!"

I had to somehow make all this expenditure of time and money worthwhile, as though Little Peter and I were eventually going to arrive together to some grand conclusion. Could it be done? Was this just some idiotic, pointless adventure? A fool's mission? Self-promotion disguised as do-gooderism? There was no doubt that the whole operation was losing its spice for me with each repetition. Since I was really not a saint, what was I trying to do here?

Actually I'd been saving up my psychic reserves to talk to Dad about footing some of Little Peter's expenses. The cumbersome business of e-mailing Olivia and then waiting for a check to arrive was starting to break down. Fortunately when I called, I caught my father in a ruminative mood. Dad, typically, wanted to know if Little Peter knew anything about sex. He thought not and I honestly couldn't tell him much.

Most young male drug addicts in New York find a way to trade sex for cash but I didn't know about Little Peter. (There was always the question of what homeless men do with each other, since women are far between in the subway-grates set, but I don't know about that either.) My stepbrother's addictions weren't strong, I told my father. He'd learned to wait patiently until the first of the month for his disability check and then binge.

"Like the cowboys," my father put in.

"The cowboys?"

"Yeah, there were a bunch of stable boys from Germany and Czechoslovakia in Darien at the riding stables when you were growing up," my father said. "Every time they'd get their checks they'd disappear for three or four days. When they came back to work they were always drunk and bruised and cut up."

"At the Ox Ridge Hunt Club?" I asked, remembering the pretty dark-haired girls of my Fairfield County youth riding on the bus in their long leather boots and hard black hats and jodhpurs with tantalizing leather patches sewn into their inner thighs. It was hard to imagine a bunch of wild Czech cowboys being allowed to decamp anywhere near those precious beauties.

I heard the ice rattle in his drink. "Yes, at the Ox Ridge Hunt Club," my father repeated. "Can you believe it? Amazing."

Amazing, too, the insight my father could summon up at times. No doubt a high percentage of the old-time cowboys out West were like my stepbrother, I thought . . . socially allergic, preternaturally strong, impervious to cold or heat, full of strange haphazard theories and premonitions . . . accustomed to stumble into the nearest prairie town with their hard-earned paychecks once a season, to be wheeled out three days later in a creaking ox cart, a tangled pile of drunks with their mouths open, their eyes blackened, and flies feasting on their dried and cracked lips . . .

To my surprise my father agreed to fund Little Peter's stay for the next two weeks.

"You just tell Peter this isn't a free ride," he said. "I want him to give me something back for what I give."

"Like what?"

"It could be a letter. It could be a dollar. I don't care, just so long as he pays me back with something."

Chapter Nineteen

Shamefully, I'm not sure whether I ever had Little Peter fulfill my small promise to my father. Other things popped up, in the sky clouds formed and evaporated, on earth pants tore, the phone jangled, loose buttons fell off shirts, orange goo built up on a kid's lips, and my stepbrother remained stubbornly, childishly himself. Before I knew it, we were on to something else.

Quite soon after my stepbrother's unexpected reappearance on Fourteenth Street, I started to keep a record of sorts, a noir journal to mark the dark passages of his mind. The more I chronicled our strange and sometimes sad conversations, the more I was convinced that his story, that of the perambulant American schizophrenic, had not been truly told, or at least not been told forcefully enough, to sink into the scarred hide of our national conscience.

At first I'd scribbled on whatever was handy: pages ripped from spiral notebooks, the backs of junk mail envelopes, recycled bits of office stationery. Eventually, if I didn't lose my notes, or toss them in the trash, I stapled the sheets together and threw them into a box under my desk. Then one day, responding to I know not what organizational impulse, I took out a hole punch and began assembling the fragments into a large three-ring binder, printing out e-mails, and sliding receipts and snapshots into clear pocket sheets meant for collecting baseball cards.

Once I assembled these oddments into calendar order, held the binder in my hands, and hefted its weight, I felt as though I'd come upon some chance by-product of history, a vaudeville magician's suitcase, or a yellowed album of clippings, or the flotsam and jetsam of a criminal dossier.

Little Peter's life was a crime I was attempting to solve, I realized. At least if there was no culprit, I might find out enough so that other exigencies might prevail. Such as in the circuitous Paul Auster novel I'd just finished reading, in which a detective entered an alley to stake out his prey, but remained for so long he wound up homeless and sleeping behind a Dumpster. And so I scribbled on, noting down dates and times, bits of conversations, places and thoughts, evidence, anything I thought in one way or another might be useful. At a minimum, I thought, I'd have a record that Little Peter and I had once, in a certain place and certain date, existed. And in these ephemeral times, that in itself was something to strive for.

At a certain point, I asked my old friend Jim Syme, a photographer, to drive up from his row house in Philadelphia to take pictures of Little Peter (and on occasion both of us) perusing the homeless byways. I had some vague idea that I wanted to add a visual element to my crimped and crabbed-together "Peter Diaries."

Jim was from way back in my life, a tall, thin, pockmarked, and self-deprecating photographer I'd befriended my first year in art school in Kansas City. He was a true sensitive, an original American reclusive poetical soul. I hoped that his offbeat outlook and troubled past—he came from a military/Catholic background and had lived all over America—would help me gain insight during my meetings with Little Peter, just as I hoped his photography would add a new dimension to my scribbled pages.

Jim talked about his dreams as if they were real life, and drew sketches that reminded me of early Dylan songs, of black crows and flying saucers hovering over prairies. When we were both in art school, Jim and I had hitchhiked across the desert states together, and over the years he'd taught me everything I knew about the *yee naaldlooshii*, or Navajo Skinwalkers—strange malicious spirits that ran alongside your speeding car at night in the desert and tried to suck out your soul—as well as the secret government laser installations that are buried inside New Mexican mountains.

Our car adventures together were often fraught with poltergeists and supernatural occurrences, as well as more normal roadside strangeness. Once when we were camping in an Anasazi ruin outside of Gallup, New Mexico, our entire picnic tabletop suddenly flared up in blue and yellow licking flames—the ancient gods' retribution, we thought, for the pottery shards we'd picked up illegally along the trail. That night, as we slept, our tent was beaten by gusting winds, and Jim and I both suffered terrible dreams in which we staggered through the rocky valley strangling each other. Another time, years later, as we were sitting across a table in my East Village apartment, the corner of a small Persian carpet near us silently lifted and turned over as if gripped by an invisible hand. When our coffee cups then began to slide by themselves across the tabletop, there was nothing to do but look at each other and laugh.

Hali had been fairly tolerant of Jim over the years, I considered. She'd grown up with a wide definition of extended family and right away accepted him as my adoptive brother. Curiously she'd had no problem believing in Jim's occasional clairvoyant spells, animist beliefs, and telekinetic intrusions—these fitted roughly into the belief system soaked into her as a girl by her ancient Korean grandmother. But she viewed such ESP indulgences as signs of weak and porous characters on both of our parts, rather than strengths.

At any rate, on Sunday Jim arrived with a heavy bag of equipment, as planned, and we took the subway uptown, to meet Little Peter by the equestrian statue of Theodore Roosevelt on the steps of the Museum of Natural History. After a while I spotted my stepbrother, his back to us, loaded down with all his belongings, gliding alone through the crowds of tourists and museumgoers, oblivious in his slow, bobbing, dolphinlike gait. When I called out, he barely acknowledged me, but stood waiting with his eyes blinking, half turned away.

I watched carefully to see if the chemistry between Jim and Little Peter was right, especially if we were, as I suspected, going to start a long-term project together. When Jim first took out his camera, Little Peter's face froze, but after a while, despite his fear of cameras, police, and surveillance, he loosened up and let out a wary grin.

As we walked, Little Peter said, finally, that he remembered Jim from somewhere. That could have been true. Fifteen years ago, when Jim and I had both lived in the East Village, we'd picked my stepbrother up at my father's apartment and driven him to New Haven to deliver him to boarding school at Choate. Little Peter had hung over the backseat in the headlight-flared darkness and told us proud, eager stories about cutting classes, picking locks, winning at soccer, and the illicit antics of upperclassmen. Of course, I remembered the trip only on the vaguest of terms, but it was interesting that, at one time, the three of us had shared a car for several hours, and told the kind of stories people tell when they are staring straight ahead into the headlights and the endless curl of nighttime tarmac.

Thinking of this made me recall my own disastrous boarding school experience. To say I was unhappy would have been an understatement. I was miserable. The dean had caught wind I was a bad apple and had spent a semester trying to drive me out of the school. Something of what I was going through seemed to touch my father, though. Perhaps he thought back to the times when he had been cold, hungry, mocked, and puny in German boarding schools run by actual and soon-to-be Nazis. It's also true that by then he'd started his affair with Little Peter's mother and his own life was beginning to turn upside down. At any rate, at night, often at around nine o'clock, I'd get a knock on my dorm room door: some kid telling me I had a phone call.

In Soule Hall, the pay phone was at the bottom of a spiral staircase composed of worn white marble slabs, as in a medieval castle. All the rooms opened directly off this staircase, so that anything said at the bottom was amplified and carried upstairs.

As soon as I took over the phone, Dad's deep voice vibrated in my ear.

"*Ach!*" he started, clearing his throat. "*Ach, achh, ach!*"

"Hi, Dad," I replied.

"I'm just trying to decide whom to vote for in the election," my father said, coming out of his phlegmatic fit. "I'm thinking about Eldridge Cleaver. But don't tell your mother yet."

Eldridge Cleaver was the presidential candidate of the Peace and Freedom

Party. I'd read Cleaver's book, *Soul on Ice*, of course, but I couldn't imagine him as president. Hadn't he coldheartedly set out to rape a series of women in the ghetto of Los Angeles as a kind of amateur political science project? I myself had been spending Sunday afternoons knocking on doors and passing out leaflets for Hubert Humphrey, not that I could work up much enthusiasm for the Democratic candidate. The hands that reached out for my pamphlets were white, puffy, and free of calluses. In New Hampshire, a deeply Republican state, my leaflets were about as happily received as free condoms would have been.

"Dad, there are so many voters, I'm sure it doesn't matter who you vote for."

"Huh? What do you mean?"

"That's what's good about living in a democracy, Dad. You kind of get lost in the shuffle. If you're lucky no one will notice you at all."

"I just want to do what's right and make a difference for once."

"Just don't vote for Richard Nixon," I said. "That's all I ask."

Another night as I stood on the frigid marble landing in my pajamas, he told me, "I'm thinking about quitting my job."

This seemed reasonable to me, considering we were all going to be camping out on hillsides soon warming ourselves on bonfires of burning books. "What are you going to do?" I asked.

He told me that he'd just gone through a month-long battery of aptitude tests to determine what job he was actually best suited for in life. I think he was hoping to return to the coldwater flat in Greenwich Village he'd had after the war, where he wrote terse, Hemingway-inspired short stories, took pottery lessons, and screwed the young women in black leotards who crept down the fire escape to his window—sometimes two at a time, he claimed. Instead, the tests had told him what he hadn't wanted to hear, that he was best at what he was already doing, holding down a high-level executive position in a mid-level firm near the bottom of Manhattan. That was disappointing news.

"I'd really like to be the guy in the park who picks up trash with a nail on the end of a stick," he confided. "What do you think?"

I was thinking that I was standing in my bare feet on a block of marble the temperature of ice.

"Dad," I said, "that sounds a little like what Holden Caulfield told his sister Phoebe in *Catcher in the Rye*."

"What the hell are you talking about?"

"You know, the book about the kid who leaves boarding school and wanders around New York on his own? He wants to be the guy in the song 'Comin' Through the Rye,' standing on the edge of the field where a bunch of kids are playing, making sure they don't fall off a cliff, or something."

"So you're saying I'm not original?"

"Dad, no one's original. That's what they're teaching me here at school. I've got to go. My feet are getting numb."

"Okay. Your mother sends her love. And will you please stop writing all this crazy crap about how miserable you are? It just upsets her."

"Sure."

He paused to clear his throat. "The more I've thought about it, son, the more I've realized that it doesn't matter what happens to you or me *personally*, get it? Everything eventually comes round to where it was before. Life is a continuum."

"A continuum of what?"

"Never mind what. Jesus Christ. *A-a-a-y—AAHHH-yi!* Why are you always trying to draw me into an argument!"

"I just asked you."

"A continuum of itself, you snot-nose bastard. I did my homework when I was your age, and now you do your homework and no one wants to know your goddamn opinion about it. It all goes around in a circle."

"Okay, I guess so."

"Get it? Got it? Good! Now quit your ass-wiping and knuckle down to work!"

In retrospect, I should have spent more time conjugating German verbs and solving differential equations. Instead I was reading subversive books like Burroughs's *Naked Lunch*; Freud's *The Interpretation of Dreams*; Jung's *Memories, Dreams, Reflections*; Edward Albee's *Who's Afraid of Virginia Woolf*; and Alain Robbe-Grillet's *The Voyeur*; all likely to make a boy question the relevance of living in an isolated boarding school in the northern reaches of New England at the dawn of a cultural revolution.

What finally got me kicked out was getting caught hitchhiking away from school without permission a couple of times, the first to help my roommate find a dog, and the second to visit the nearby Groton School, where a kid was supposedly drinking shoe polish to get high and having an interesting nervous breakdown. Neither of the boys with whom I was bagged was kicked out. Just me, the bad apple.

"What's the matter with him?" Jim had asked, after we'd dropped Little Peter off in front of his dorm at Choate and watched him go slouching up the steps with his duffle slung over his shoulder.

"Nothing," I said. "He's just a teenager. That's the way teenagers act."

"No, they don't," Jim said. "Not where I come from."

Still, despite Jim's earlier negative first impression, by the day's end, I was congratulating myself more and more that Jim was a great choice to be Little Peter's "personal" photographer. There was a certain element of pure guilelessness in my friend that matched a similar trait in my stepbrother. In dealing with my stepbrother, Jim was modest, soft-spoken, and unobtrusive; he had the ability to talk authoritatively about places that Little Peter had lived, such as Albuquerque; he'd also had a certain amount of job experience in dealing with the mentally ill. My only criticism was that Jim was taking too few pictures.

Little Peter remembered a Mexican barber he'd once patronized on West Fourteenth Street. We subwayed down, and sure enough, found a below-street shop with three chairs. The barber used electric shears on my stepbrother, and I sat down to have mine trimmed too as soon as the next chair was empty. Jim seemed reluctant to break in or ruin the mood of the place: but finally at my urging, he started to use the camera.

Outside in the street I noticed a large overhead sign that read something like "Nuts, Nuts and More Nuts." I pleaded with Jim to take a picture of Little Peter and me standing in front of it. But Jim just laughed hysterically—too long, too high-pitched, and too loud for my taste. I imagine he thought I was kidding. He refused to take the shot.

A few days later, I subwayed uptown to have lunch with my mother. Jim had sent me a few of the photographs he had taken that weekend, and they were superb, banishing my worries that we were wasting his or my stepbrother's time. Excited, I took a packet with me to lunch and showed them to her.

My mother carefully leafed through the pile one by one. Finally she asked me, "Do you realize how handsome your stepbrother is?"

"Not really!" I said. My mother has not lost the power to amaze me, and in this case it was in her appreciation of men.

"Well, he is!" she insisted.

Chapter Twenty

After that Jim began to come up nearly every weekend to continue his photo series of Little Peter and me. Almost immediately he and Little Peter had developed a rapport that at times I found impenetrable. They shared interests in sailing, in traversing the vast unknown desert spaces of the Southwest, in flying saucers, government plots, and in grand technological conspiracies of all kinds. Of course it had been at my urging. But I did begin to feel uneasy that, almost every time I saw my stepbrother now, it was in the company of Jim.

In a quaint spirit of liberation I woke up one morning and thought to myself, *I'm sick of having all of this camera paraphernalia around whenever I visit my stepbrother. I should just get up and spend the day with him. A day without cameras, just Little Peter and me. To hell with cameras! To hell with photography! To hell with Theater of the Absurd! Or whatever it is we are capturing.* Because in truth all of this documenting Little Peter had started to make me feel guilty that I was in truth ignoring him.

If I'd been listening to myself more closely I might have recognized the call of the weekend warrior—the neglectful parent who, having left his kids alone all week, vows to make up for it by spending "quality" time with his offspring on the weekend. Every Saturday the playground was full of parents like this, dressed in Polo casual, with predictable results: frustrated fathers, squalling kids, overturned cups of takeout coffee, ears glued to cell phones, and screaming matches about where to order out from.

Little Peter was in unusually high dander when I met him later, and I could smell beer on his breath. He was carrying a couple of overstuffed Gap bags and the blue ink had rubbed off on his hands, making them look filthy. He also had a big horseshoe-shaped sore on his chin under his beard that he said was a pimple.

"Oh, boy, we are going to have a really, really good time today!" he sputtered, rubbing his hands together. He was still sleeping on a grate under his old building on West End Avenue and had gotten thoroughly wet the night before.

"Did I ever tell you about Tony, my black friend?" my stepbrother asked. "He's always at the door at H&H Bagels."

"Not really," I replied. I was thinking I had until four at the latest.

"You have to learn to listen to me, and pay attention!" he scolded as we rode uptown on the subway. "The main thing is not to get arrested, because cops are unpredictable, and I'm not sure what their plan is. But the other main thing is not to worry. Just relax and listen to me: *Listen!* Because I have the instinct that will always tell me what to do!"

So I told him I *was* listening, though I could feel myself retreating into my head, because no matter what happened, getting arrested was not even a possibility. As I'd pulled on my pants that morning a little piece of paper had fluttered out and fallen on the floor. It was a note from my wife: "Nothing bad is going to happen to you today." Yeah, but how did she know? When I thought he wasn't looking, I shifted most of my cash from my wallet to my shirt pocket. One of the moms I knew from the soccer field was a bulldog lawyer, the kind who'd come down at 3:00 A.M. to pull you out of Central Booking. I began to wish I'd written down her number on the back of my hand. I found myself imagining what it would be like inside the lockup wearing shoes without laces and pants without a belt.

Meanwhile, the Number 1 train rattled on. At Seventy-ninth Street, Little Peter jumped up suddenly, and said, "Okay, we're getting out!"

We rushed out of the subway to upper Broadway. But his friend Tony the crack dealer, who normally would have opened the door for us at H&H Bagels, wasn't at his usual station that day. Disappointed, Little Peter turned down one of the side streets and walked halfway down the block. I assumed he was still acting on his finely tuned street instincts, so I followed.

My stepbrother looked around, sniffed the air, and at once started taking a piss against the door of a parked car. I walked away disgusted and sat on a stone bench.

If the cops are really watching, they'll pull him in now, I thought to myself. *And if they do, they're welcome to him.*

Nevertheless, I had committed myself to dogging his tail for the next few hours. Little Peter let his hunches pull him here and there. He explained that he'd befriended a bunch of homeless Mexican men who'd encamped in the old Rotunda under the West Side Drive. "You have *got* to meet Nacho," he said, as we retraced our steps, walked up Broadway a block and down Eightieth Street. There we entered Riverside Park, even though he commented that chances were his friends wouldn't be home.

"This is just an exercise in futility," he said.

"Well, it's exercise," I replied.

The air on the park pathways was cool and luminous, cut with veins of tree shadows. We cut under the West Side Highway through a darkened tunnel and passed a pair of windows screened with heavy wire. The windows exuded a crude damp smell, and I heard men knocking around and talking inside. I grew nervous, since the tunnel did not have obvious exits.

"We're going to have to go slowly," he explained, since, unfortunately, he and another of the Mexicans, Lupo, had gotten in a fight that morning. It seemed my stepbrother had drunk a six-pack of beer in lieu of breakfast. Then he'd headed for the Rotunda to find his friends, but the moment he'd shown up, Lupo had told him to get out of the way, because he was feeding the pigeons. Little Peter'd protested, "You can't just tell me to move like that!" but Lupo had just repeated, "Move it!" So they'd gotten into a yelling match, you know: "Fuck you!" "Fuck YOU!" and all of that kind of witty repartee.

We came out suddenly into the deep well of the Rotunda. As I gazed around in wonder at this seeming Taj Mahal of moral degradation, I could see why Little Peter called it the "Homeless Hilton." Around a series of Roman-style brick archways were an impressive number of bodies huddled under dirty blankets and quilts. Near me, a black man in layers of clothing picked through a shapeless pile of damp belongings.

This neglected structure was formed by the traffic turnaround on the raised highway above us. When I looked up, the sky made a perfect circle and I could hear the car tires whizzing and slapping. Ahead, a cake box of peeling plywood covered an enormous forgotten fountain. A repository of wire shopping carts and cardboard boxes were set out against a curved brick wall on the side of the Rotunda where the sun hit warmly. On the far side, a rectangular break in the wall opened like a picture window, providing a wide view of the boat basin and the Hudson River. I could see sun glittering hotly on the windows of a cut-rate housing development someone had built far away under the cliffs of New Jersey.

"There they are!" Little Peter called excitedly. "They're here!" He broke into a trot.

In the damp, uninviting shadows of the brick arcade, I saw the comatose figure of a young Mexican man in a red jacket lying halfway under a yellow blanket against the wall.

"Hey, Lupo, it's all right!" Little Peter called out to the man. "We had a fight this morning, but it's all gone now."

"What fight?" the man asked, looking over at us, his eyes confused and bleary. "What's the matter?"

The Mexican was only half awake. He levered himself up a little off the ground and tried to reach for my hand to help himself up, but missed.

"The fight! We had words this morning," Little Peter explained. He showed with his hands that the anger had all been thrown away, tossed aside. "It's over. *Pfft!* Gone!"

"What's the matter?" asked Lupo again, unsteadily taking his feet. "What's wrong?"

"You are my friends!" said Little Peter.

Lupo looked at me with bloodshot eyes. He caught my hand this time and held on to it, partly to keep from falling back down.

"This guy, is he your friend?" he asked me.

"He's my brother," I said.

"Your brother? *Sí?*"

"Yes."

"He speak Spanish and English," Lupo told me haltingly, in the language of the thoroughly smashed. He waved his hand, indicating Little Peter. "He's a pretty good guy, but I can't understand him." He peered into my eyes using them as a point of navigational reference. "You look like a pretty good guy, too. Wanna have a beer?"

He started groping into the folds of his sleeping bag, presumably looking for a can of the stuff.

"Gotta keep going," I said. "Thanks anyway."

"Whatsamatter?" he asked. "You don't wanna drink with me 'cause I'm a Mexican?"

"Yow," I said. "Whoa!"

"He my friend . . . you my friend. We drink a beer."

One of the things that I hate about the so-called street is the number of stupid conversations you are continually being forced to have with people who are either high or brain-damaged or both. Stickiness can be a successful evolutionary survival strategy: burrs that hitch on to your sweater or sock as you pass, strings of a spider's web that glue and wrap you up, the ancient and redolent resins of opium and hemp that adhere to your neuronal tendrils. Also, homeless headaches like Lupo, who motion you over, try to shake your hand, breathe their wine-smelling breath in your face, and effusively inform you that you are a stand-up comrade, implying that all the world are equals, then try to suck a quarter from you on the basis of your thirty-second friendship. This has been going on since time immemorial and certainly since I was a teenager taking the train in to hang out with the hipsters in Washington Square Park on weekends.

I glanced down at Lupo's belt and saw he had a knife strapped there. I was aware of the possibility that our conversation could turn sour in a second. Violence is a part of living on the street. You have a little misunderstanding, you work it out by punching each other in the face until one of you drops. Little Peter had discounted the possibility of violence here, but he'd been in plenty of inane, pointless fights himself in his time, including the one this morning.

"Where's Nacho?" Little Peter asked, interrupting.

"There!" Lupo waved his hand, still rummaging through his belongings.

"Is that him?" Little Peter asked, pointing to where a tiny shape lay under a blanket. No part of the man's body was showing.

"No," shouted Lupo. "Don't touch him!"

"Where's Nacho?" Little Peter asked again.

"Over here," Lupo pointed. He abruptly stood up and started walking on cat feet through a brick archway down a pathway into some deep brush.

"Here, my friends!" he called back to us.

"Nacho! Nacho!" Little Peter called, running ahead. I started to hang back, but Lupo turned his head and beckoned me to follow too.

I followed their path as it led up the hill through a copse of trees. About twenty yards ahead I saw the legs of three or four men who were sitting on logs, and above them, the deadpan Indian face of another man standing.

"Come on!" called Little Peter to me again, thrilled. "Nacho, my friend!"

I could see now that there were six guys in the clearing of the trees, four standing and two sitting. With Lupo, that made seven. There were too many men. I was not much of a fighter. My instincts usually warned me when to back out of a situation. They were warning me now, loud and clear.

"*Come on!*" shouted my stepbrother, almost out of sight now.

I called loudly through the trees. "Hey, Peter, come over here."

"What? What is it?" He ran back on the path, panting, his eyes wide and bright.

"I want to talk to you about something."

I was surprised when Little Peter followed me back into the Rotunda. I walked him across to the other side, as far as possible from the sleeping bags of the homeless Mexicans. We stood against a wall.

"This just isn't my scene," I said.

"But I want you to meet Nacho. He's the *man*! Now everything will be all right, you'll see."

I gave him a couple of bills. He stared at them dumbly.

"Go ahead," I said. "You have a good time."

"What's the matter?"

"I have to follow *my* instincts, Peter," I said. "I don't know these guys as well as you do. I don't trust them."

"Are you sure?" he asked me. His disappointment showed nakedly in his face. He'd badly wanted to share his friends Nacho and Lupo with me.

"Sure," I said.

"Okay," he said.

"Call me later," I said, as my stepbrother ran away.

I looked at my watch. Shoot! I was already on the verge of being late to pick up the kids. Amazing how time flies when you are involved in something tedious and seedy. As I hurried off toward the subway, I thought about how nice it would be to be sitting at my desk back in our apartment right then. I stumbled by well-dressed Upper West Side businessmen with jobs and money in their pockets. I stopped at a newsstand to buy a copy of *The Wall Street Journal* to read on the subway and a coconut Mounds bar to calm my nerves.

When the subway car arrived with a blast of hot urine-smelling air and a shriek of metal I stepped in and allowed it to carry me back to my life. Well, I was nibbling my way timidly into Little Peter's world. Perhaps I'd learn as much doing it a little at a time. I wondered if Hemingway or Kerouac would have acted differently. Both writers spent time hanging out with hoboes and bums. I wondered who of the people that I knew would have followed Little Peter into that thicket to meet those Mexicans. Few but me, of course, would have dared themselves into such a stupid situation in the first place.

Chapter Twenty-one

The next morning there was a front-page story in *The New York Times* about how video cameras on every light pole watch everyone all the time. More truth to Little Peter's paranoia?

By arrangement I rode the subway up to meet Little Peter at Dr. Heath's office—the E train was clogged with rush-hour commuters, frantic to push through the doors before they slid closed. A baby was crying. Rain and wind outside . . . I arrived late.

Dr. Heath asked me in his gentleman's English accent, "Did you smell anything when you came in? Peter, have you had a chance to do your laundry? How about your jacket? Because I thought I smelled your jacket in the waiting room when I went to get you."

Little Peter mumbled, "I did my laundry. Well, maybe I haven't had a chance to take a shower in the last few days."

We talked some more about Fountain House. I discovered Little Peter had ruined his chances there by showing up at the front door without an appointment and trying to bully his way inside. An ugly leviathan of a guard had turned him away—an unbelievable ogre, a one-of-a-kind, he said. Little Peter wasn't sure he wanted to join a club that would keep a guy like that as a guard.

The whole thing is hopeless, I thought. The idea of my changing Little Peter. It seemed much more likely that he would change me.

Hali and I invited my stepbrother to join us, en famille, at a Malaysian restaurant on Bleecker Street called Sarong, Sarong. The place was run by a crew of willowy young Chinese transvestites—a strange choice, one might say, but Little Peter and I had eaten there a few times and he liked the vibes. The waiters all knew us by now and were very friendly.

Little Peter must have been nervous, because he arrived at the restaurant early and called from the pay phone several times to make sure we were actually coming. When we arrived—Hali, myself, Alden, and Maya, the whole menagerie—we found him sitting at the bar staring into the glass of water in front of him, seemingly perplexed, as if someone had told him that if you looked hard enough you could see microbes swimming in the water.

I'd rehearsed Alden on the art of looking "Uncle Pete" in the eye and shaking his hand. But my son forgot to say hello; instead he ran to study the artificial gas fireplace at the bar, fascinated by its blue and yellow flames.

Little Peter wolfed down a plate of beef curry and, as usual, ate everyone's leftovers. He was amused by Alden's request for mandu—the Korean word for dumplings—especially when I told him that Alden often consumed so many so fast that he threw up. I suppose it added a certain zest to the meal to know that, at any moment, we all might have to scramble for cover.

Afterward, he belched and described how he could reduce all human drama and every situation to a mathematical formula. I replied that if he really could do that he'd be the untold genius that liberated mankind from the uncertainty of its fate, a Nobel Prize winner.

"I can't guarantee that I was the first to think of it," he said modestly.

I could see how some people might call my stepbrother handsome. His jaw was square and his hair blond and just unkempt enough to seem cool in an urban hipster way. Still, I noticed, not for the first time, how much he resembled my heroin-addicted (and now also alcoholic) friend, Lester Bergamot. Same gray face, drained of all color (from avoiding the sun and too many vampirish New York nights spent out or underground); same anxious look, resulting from constant fretting about cops; same tightened neck cords, stemming (I think) from washing his bloodstream with harsh, badly purified drugs.

Alden solemnly handed Uncle Peter a marker pen and asked him to draw a picture. Little Peter took the task very seriously, and after ten minutes of intense, eyebrow-clenching scribbling, came up with a schematic that resembled a crystal spacecraft.

Despite what was for him a relatively complex situation, Little Peter remained polite, deferential during the meal. Hali asked afterward if he'd been on his best behavior, and I replied that he was usually like this now—quiet and philosophical, if occasionally somewhat dark in his thoughts. As it was, Little Peter led the conversation, asking us about Mexico, where we'd been on vacation, asking questions about Alden and Maya, and telling us stories about himself growing up.

His first memory of Franz, he recalled, was of a big, overbearing man with a booming voice. He remembered, too, an early vacation in Jamaica, or someplace tropical (I believe, upon further inquiry, that this was actually Florida), where Franz sat in a chair and got very drunk each night, ordering everyone around in a loud voice.

"It was like a hammer fell on my life," he said. "There was an immediate personality clash."

Toward the end of dinner something started to eat away at him. My stepbrother's personality appeared set far back from his eyes, his brow wrung up in a caricature of worry, like a gargoyle. When he got up to go to the bathroom, his tentative motions, even in my peripheral vision, set off primitive danger signals in my brain stem. I was almost surprised that no one dialed the police.

Little Peter would be leaving New York tomorrow, he told us when he returned to his seat. He planned to take the Greyhound to Florida the next day, as soon as he received his disability check. With a layover in Atlantic City, of course, to play the slots. Actually, he had a budget scribbled out in ballpoint pen on a paper plate that was folded into quarters—so much for a Sony Walkman, so much for the bus ticket to Atlantic City, so much for the slots.

He was far from deciding, he admitted. He wasn't sure of anything until he held the money in his hands. He might just as well ride down to Mexico City, he said—or perhaps go up to Bangor, Maine, to visit Stephen King (whom I assumed he didn't know). He was also considering a return to Spring Lake Ranch, or just a longer sojourn here in New York—though it was apparent to me that he was getting restless. Ultimately he'd like to go to the Caribbean.

He asked, "Have you ever had trouble making up your mind, and it just won't come, no matter how hard you try?"

"The idea of you going to Miami Beach appeals to me most," I told him, finally. "You'll be warm there and might even be able to latch into some interesting boat life. If you call me from down there, I'll help you figure things out and maybe even come down to visit you at some point."

When we shook hands outside the restaurant, I realized this really *was* the end. The orange "Bud" hat that someone had given him made his eyes an intense pale violet. The kids took his hand, one by one. "Good-bye, Uncle Peter!" they said. "Good-bye!" (My stepbrother called me later to tell me that this dinner with my family had been a momentous event for him, something that had happened perhaps only one or two times in his life—or perhaps never before. That was an exaggeration, but I appreciated that his feelings were genuine.)

I told him I was sorry the plans we tried to make—piano sessions, Fountain House, an apartment for him—had all fallen through. For two months he'd been hanging around, "staying alive and enjoying what the city has to offer . . ." in his words.

"Life is about cycles," Little Peter said.

I was still rather pissed at Dr. Heath, who didn't seem to have come up with anything of practical value for his gargantuan fees. But Hali counseled me that it was Little Peter himself who was ambivalent and couldn't make up his mind.

I should give the doctor a call, though, and tell him that Little Peter has flown the coop and to suspend all present operations (if any). And I needed to call Jim, too, to tell him not to come up the next weekend. Another chapter closed. Not to say I wasn't somewhat relieved . . .

Part Six

And we thus drift toward unparalleled catastrophes.

—Albert Einstein

Chapter Twenty-two

When—as happens sometimes—the complicated façade of my life starts to crumble, and everything I try seems fake and forced—when even my wife looks at me with exhausted eyes and tells me to go find someone else to brood on, a deadly stillness starts to collect outside my window . . . When I'm really tired of my world, in other words, I retreat to my closet office. My wife's father sometimes calls me the disappearing son-in-law.

There, on a high shelf above my desk, I reach for—not the *Music from Big Pink* CD case with its deadly green rectangles of Afghan-grown scouring powder. Leave that for another time. Instead I pull down a small, heavy, cardboard box. It contains a stereoscopic viewer, made of dense black plastic with two contrastingly bright red knobs. Jammed around it are twenty-two slides encased in rectangular strips of glass as if prepared for a microscope. The slide viewer, a "Realist," made in the late forties, is solid and compact, like a pair of binoculars. It feels heavier than it should in my palm, as though it contains unknown and forgotten mechanisms. I treat it with respect and awe as accords a time portal into the past.

When I slip the first slide into the viewer and press my eyes to the glass elements, at first all I see is a few lazy amoebas floating in blackness, accompanied at intervals by the silent digging of a large tined pitchfork, which I recognize eventually as my eyelashes. The red disc on top of the

Realist depresses with a squeak under my finger, and *presto!* a magic world appears. I am suddenly in my great-grandmother's library in the Big House—a room into which we used to jokingly bring guests to see the hindquarters of the lion and the rhino whose snarling front halves graced the panels of the Trophy Room next door. This doesn't appear to be an illusion. I do not *almost* feel that I am in the room, I am actually in the room.

My mother and her sister, Alessandra, stand facing me, smiles lighting their faces. Although they are frozen in place, they appear quite alive to me. After all, they are posing. The picture is crystal sharp and the 3-D effect is incredible. By shifting my eyes I can look past my mother and aunt, down into a hallway, through a door, and into a window. In the mirror behind them, the camera flash has silvered the edges of my aunt Allie's veil and her Grable tresses. The pineapple knobs of the Louis XIV armchair almost grate against my jawbone. My mother looks at me with faintly questioning eyes, as if she wishes I would hurry up and take the picture—although I protest, I am not born yet.

My aunt Allie displays one of those uncomplimentary expressions only the most uncharitable flash camera will catch; her drooping jaw shows long equine teeth and lips downturned in permanent discontent. Her cantaloupe lipstick and matching nails pay tribute to an exquisite bouquet of orange carnations sprinkled with tiny pink rosebuds she holds in her hands. She is attired in a superbly tailored gown of watery dun silk, which bells inward below her knees. In contrast, my mother wears only a simple and inexpensive white confirmation dress that was picked off the rack somewhere. Her nails are free of polish; the tips of her long fingers intertwine like an unfinished thought. Her spray of lilies of the valley echoes the unpretentious strand of pearls on her wrist. The dress swells from her beltline almost to her heels, leading me to wonder if, by some chance, she is already pregnant (of course she isn't). The lace tiara upon her head is the kind that a guileless Amish girl might choose. Her dark pageboy brings up her high cheekbones. Her lips, glossed the same orange as her sister's, whom she has always followed, upturn in quiet happiness. This is her wedding day.

Just who took these twenty-two pictures is a bit of a mystery. My parents kept the viewer and its precious box of slides for years, carelessly tossed on a closet bookshelf upon a stack of *National Geographics*. When they divorced, my mother inherited the slide set. Perhaps twice a decade she and my stepfather would take the slides out, more for my stepfather's pleasure than my mother's, for my mother was always trying to erase her past, while no one appreciated the beauty of silk drapes and ormolu more than Johnny. Gradually, not through mishandling, but simply through the passage of time, the glass slides sullied and cracked. Later when my father in his old age grew besotted with the past, he begged the viewer from my mother, promising to restore the slides to their original condition. This he did, and eventually the alchemical mechanism devolved to me.

As I drop in slide number two the scene shifts instantly to the grand staircase. Here my grandmother Froggie leans, in a careless flapper pose, looking down, a fashionable and still defiant woman gripping a brass stair rail. Her gray-blue silk dress, embroidered with white clouds, shimmers like a French ceramic; she is big-boned though thin, and her face at that moment looks worn and far from carefree. Indigo walls are emblazoned with fanciful birds. A door thoughtlessly thrown open upstairs reveals a guest room, a window blind, hot sun peeking through drapes . . .

Behind my grandmother is the enormous life-sized portrait of herself as a very young woman, perhaps still a teenager, plump and cosseted, her raven hair spilling about her shoulders. She's seated upon the back of an also life-sized white horse, who must have been a beloved animal. The whole scene is lit impressionistically and romantically in fresh rays of slanting morning sunlight.

That hot planet that glows directly in front of the camera flash—that's the back of my grandfather's head. He was not a vain man, and I never thought he'd be the kind to grow his hair long in order to comb strands over his bald spot, as he does here.

Allie leads the way alone down the grand staircase, her beautiful silk dress swishing richly, passing the ornate grandfather clock on the landing. The procession winds around the bottom of the staircase, passing Jean-Antoine Houdon's frozen gamin, carved in black marble, who shivers and clutches herself.

Leaving the portrait to ruminations and regrets, I hurry to catch up to my mother, poised in the doorway to the garden, with my grandfather, Big Ward. He appears resplendent in his dark blue jacket and white ducks, though the camera has chosen a moment to freeze him in which he looks watchful, troubled. This is not celebration, I think, but cerebration. Ward's shoes are white, as is correct for the season. He whispers something and my mother smiles. Nearby, a curtain of hauteur wraps Allie entirely, and I wonder if she is simply unhappy. Her shoes and belt, I notice, match the tomato bisque of her lipstick and nails.

My mother and grandfather proceed down the path through the garden, towards the Casino, where the wedding is to take place. The flagstones are wetted for effect, perhaps by the photographer, using a garden hose. The flowers along the pathway are so sharp they cut into my retinas. You can see that my mother and grandfather are taken from the same mold, both angular and thoughtful, as they gaze down at their feet.

Again it is Allie's job to lead the way, and this time she looks abject and helpless, as if she has learned from her own dark experience what a grave mistake a marriage can be. I see now clearly that Allie has a wandering right eye, and recall with sudden precision the venetian-blind glasses that her daughter Anne will be forced to wear much later in an attempt to pull her eyes to the front.

The wedding ceremony itself is a dark mystery the cameraman apparently did not wish to disturb by recording. There are no bridesmaids, no fatuous minister, no earthy excerpts from Song of Solomon, no winking references to twin roes or foxes at play in the ripening vineyards. When the next slide drops my father and mother have stepped out on the cut grass, already voluptuously and freshly married. My father is an arch twenty-seven, my mother is twenty-two. They are in motion, left and right foot raised oppositely, in a lithe pas de deux, gazing at each other in the full hilarity and knowingness of the moment.

In this moment, my mother finally displays her teeth and her inherited Cheney nose (in geometric terms, it might be described as an arc a quarter of a circle in length). A salty breeze, blowing off the Sound, sweeps my father's curly hair back from his high forehead. He looks very much the Yale man, jaunty in a navy jacket with a sprig of lily of the valley in his lapel, his white khakis. The jacket and pants will serve him well over the years, for he'll be married twice more in them. As my mother and father clasp hands and prepare to step into a limitless future of resplendent Connecticut evenings, pearlescent diapers, and frozen pot pies, I wonder if their seemingly artless pose has actually been set up by the wily photographer, though I suppose it wouldn't make much difference if it were. A wedding is choreographed to make lasting images rather than lasting relationships.

Behind, at the granite breakwater, waves arrive in pairs, cocky and full of gloss at first, only to tumble and deform, roiled and unsure, against the implacable rocks of the shoreline. And from the direction of the whitewashed portico of the Casino, a neoclassic blur visible over my mother's shoulder, comes a celebratory volley of popping champagne corks, which I recognize as an auditory hallucination.

I blink and rub my eyes as the next slide drops. Without further ceremony, it seems, my mother and father have lined up with their best man and maid of honor on the steps of the Big House, facing the Long Island Sound. Smiling, the men flank the women. My father looks like a pleased schoolboy now, a pleasant-faced Choatie, the hip cat who ate the canary. Johnny Findlay, my father's roommate at Choate and Yale, looks positively rakish in his heavy afternoon shadow. In his place at the end of the foursome, Findlay stands tall and pale with his hands behind him—at the camera flash, his eyes narrow to such a rich look of devilment that I can't help wondering if he is thinking of giving my aunt Allie's rump a grope behind the group's back.

My father often talks with regret about Findlay. His death at a young age due to alcoholism and plain foolish behavior saddened my father, and made him cynical about happiness and friendship in general. Findlay, a year ahead of my father at Choate, had made my father a sidekick in his misadventures, a Pancho Villa to his striding Don Quixote. Findlay was a handsome, sophisticated, insincere lady-killer, a teenager privileged enough while at boarding school to own both a driver's license and a car.

"He was an apple-polisher first-class," my father remembered. "Why did I like Johnny so much? I guess it was because he paid attention to me and let me in on his phoniness. We broke the rules together. He taught me how to smoke . . . I often wonder what he'd be like today were he still alive. His untimely end probably saved me a lot of bother."

The action moves into the Big House, and under the spell of the viewing glasses I find myself drifting in with the guests, swept by their ebb and flow. I feel sharply, almost preternaturally alive to every sensation and to the forces of their personalities.

I am not supposed to be here. As a child, most of the doings of the Big House happened at night when I was required to be in bed. I viewed doings like this by creeping down the stairs, and crouching behind a screen. The scene is thus imbued with the aura of the forbidden. There was, in the Big House, at the end of every corridor, an inconspicuous, white-painted door that led to the servants' quarters. There was my true place, among the plain cupboards and closets and drawers and deal tables upon which the servants ate and prepared food. Here my sisters and I, with my cousins, would sit and chatter and listen to the servants talk. Here we would wait to be taken to the beach, or to lunch.

The photographer has gathered everyone for a group pose. Goggie seats herself grandly in the center, in a drawing room chair, ramrod straight in a stiff black Mary Poppins hat. She folds her fat hands in her lap and looks straight into the lens with unflinching pale blue eyes. In contrast, Grossmama Hasslacher, my father's grandmother, a woman I wouldn't meet in my lifetime, gazes to the side in distraction; her pallor is deathly and I wonder whether her circulation is poor.

Under a large dim Flemish landscape my grandfather, Hattie-Hattie, takes his place with aristocratic ease beside Mimia, who is robed in a green silk dress and an ingratiating smile. She has something odd pinned to her shoulder: a monkey or a succulent. My best taxonomic guess identifies it as a fanciful Schlumberger brooch, probably purchased at Tiffany's with much anxious titting and tatting. Mimia was terrified of the Davisons and would have wanted to impress them with both her daring and her sensible taste.

Next to his mother stands the groom, his cheeks flushed with champagne. My newly husbanded mother perches by him, birdlike, somewhat watchful. Then Allie, who looks positively vicious now, for she's being forced to stand next to her husband Edgar for the first time tonight. Among this gathering of robust Huns, Edgar appears genetically recessive, with a washed-out Yale forelock and pink rabbit eyes.

Next to him, my paternal aunt Olga looks exotic and South American, with her wide forehead, her tight black curls, and a white carnation rakishly pinned to one side of her hair. Uncle Ulrich, by several inches the tallest of the group, stands with arched eyebrows, a barrel chest, and the enormous protruding ears of a fresh army recruit, his red tie much too small for the yards of shirt it must cover.

By Ulrich, my grandmother Froggie, who in her youth was photographed many times for the society pages, poses in a bright, toothy smile, her right ankle crossed over her left, her hand stuck securely through my grandfather's elbow.

Among this placid semicircle, my grandfather, Big Ward, looks genuinely commanding. His body sweeps up from his white shoes to his chest in a pose of grace and self-sufficiency like a ship's prow; he radiates ease, muscularity, and intellectual power. He turns his head off to the right where, unfortunately for the picture, he grimaces with disgust, as though he has discovered something untoward about to happen.

My father always disliked my grandfather, Big Ward, whom he characterized as a cold fish. My father had learned to float on the plunging dinghy of his own intuition; in his way, he was an artist. But my grandfather was a straight arrow, kept upright by his belief in a set of institutions that were boxed one inside the other: marriage, the Republican Party, the Skull and Bones Society, and the American Civil Liberties Union (which he'd strongly supported despite a conservative bent). My mother adored her father almost without reservation, though. Big Ward, my mother whispered to me, could have become president. This was a not-too-obvious restating of the American dream. Big Ward had served as a spymaster in the Office of Secret Services during the Pacific War, directing an army of Tagalogs with hidden radios in dugout canoes. After the surrender, he was tapped to join the newly minted Central Intelligence Agency. If he'd agreed to join, he could have easily become the agency's head, and his career might have mirrored that of George H. W. Bush, the son of his closest friend at Yale, Senator Prescott Bush, who went from CIA chief to the presidency. But Froggie, who hated the thought of living in Washington, D.C., put a firm kibosh on the idea.

Nearby, my great-grandfather, Henry P. Davison, gazes benignly from his brown portrait, looking every inch the early-twentieth-century Captain of Finance, with his wide, serious face; squared shoulders; drooping ears; and narrow, discerning eyes. His lips were expressive and sensual.

As early as the teens, people in the press had begun making noises about Harry running for president on the Republican ticket, perhaps after Woodrow Wilson's term was over. In preparation for this possibility, Harry quit Morgan's bank and took over the command of the Red Cross—the kind of position that might be expected to wipe a little of the tar of Morgan's money off him. The plan probably would have worked, too, except for a skeleton that threatened to rattle itself out of Harry Dear's closet.

Harry had always been a capricious and carnal man. The same glad-hand personality that made bankers fall in love with him had made women swoon. While Goggie stayed home to mind the kids, Harry took as many women as he wanted—whomever and whenever he wanted. His mentor, J. P. Morgan, had so many mistresses that he was rumored to have been forced to set up a foundling hospital to take care of his illegitimate children. Harry always followed J. P. Morgan's example as closely as he was able.

One afternoon in 1915, a banker named Howard Boocock went into Tiffany's to have his wife's necklace repaired. When the clerk brought out an expensive clasp, Boocock said, "I don't need anything fancy. I bought this string of pearls for my wife myself and it's nothing special." "On the contrary," exclaimed the clerk, "that magnificent man Henry P. Davison bought these pearls from me and they're a fabulous string!" At that moment, Boocock realized the terrible truth, that his best friend and his wife Adele were having an affair. In a fit of madness, Boocock went to his East 70s brownstone, shot Adele while she played piano in the parlor, and then shot himself.

The true story behind the grisly murder-suicide must have been well known in society circles, even while it was hushed up in the press, because the well-informed writer Somerset Maugham based two short stories on the false pearl necklace gambit. The orphaned Boocock children were quietly folded into the batter of Peacock Point, where most important things were not spoken of, and their story twined itself with that of my great-grandfather's four children. Afterward, whenever the subject of his presidency was brought up, Goggie would grow pale and Harry Dear would murmur, "That could never be. That could never, never be."

Wandering among my parents' wedding party, an invisible presence, I am aware that sorrow follows each of the guests. In one corner of the living room, no less than four suicides pose side by side, their faces happy and expectant. How can I change the thoughts they are not yet thinking?

There is my mother, blissful and smiling in her simple white dress. What words of warning should I whisper to her about seductresses and secrets? There is my father preening in his navy blue blazer and khakis. How can I wipe the frat boy smirk off his lips? There is Johnny Findlay, my father's best man, who just a few years hence will be discovered floating facedown in the Gowanus Canal. Should I snatch the drink from his hand? There is my aunt Alessandra, striding haughtily down the staircase in her tailor-made gown. How can I pluck the tiny cancer buds that perhaps are even now forming in her breast?

My father's sister, Olga Consuela, her head thrown back, her lips carnation red, tosses a quip to someone invisible on the upper landing. She rocks and laughs, her toes slightly turned in, her silk dress flaring. Big Olga looks as though she is concluding a Latin dance number, her hands carelessly crossed over her stomach. Ulrich Ferdinand catches my eye momentarily. It will be decades before the broken box of their youths will be unlocked and its contents spilled out.

Something in this scene reminds me of an episode of the early 1960s television show *The Outer Limits*. In the episode I am thinking of, "A Controlled Experiment," a pair of disguised Martian scientists, named Diemos and Phobos One, descend to Earth in order to study a phenomenon that is unknown to their planet—namely *murder*. In a suitcase the two Martians carry a futuristic device called a "temporal condenser" that can speed up, slow down, reverse, and stop time in real life. Hiding behind a potted plant in a sordid hotel lobby the two aliens witness a pointless but typical homicide. Fascinated, they replay the scene over and over. A jilted blonde named Carla screams at her unfaithful boyfriend. "You're a two-faced no-good blackhearted two-timer!" Sometimes she hee-haws in slow motion, at other times she gabbles at super speed, or sucks her invectives in backward. She pulls out a wavering black gat from her purse. Points. A ring of smoke slowly seeps out. "Oh, no!" the boyfriend shrieks, holding up his hands— exactly as Oswald later did—as the bullet slowly enters his chest and bursts his aorta. At an exquisitely glacial pace he crumples to the dingy carpet and dies.

Diemos and Phobos One start out the episode as cold and superior beings. "Earthlings!" says One, speaking charitably. "They are a form of life, even if they are unspeakable!" But the longer they study our ways, the more they grow fond of our weaknesses—nicotine, caffeine, alcohol, and most strange and addictive of all, love. In the end, the newly humanized aliens find themselves rather impressed by the touching genuineness of human folly.

"One gets used to the eccentricities. One even grows rather fond of them," comments Phobos One as he lifts a forbidden cup of coffee to his lips and takes a deep and satisfying sip.

Against orders, the two Martian chroniclers go off script and start looking for ways to change the outcome of this uniquely human tragedy. They push the temporal condenser to its limits and freeze time solid. Finally Diemos flicks the bullet from its fateful path, leaving the boyfriend locked in a breathy mammalian embrace with his teary-eyed Carla. Forgiveness is all. And the thought that through this rip they have made in the fabric of the past they may have sent the universe hurtling toward an uncertain and possibly apocalyptic future bothers the newly corrupted aliens not a wit, as they walk away puffing a stash of purloined cigarettes.

For myself, I don't want to interfere with the presumed happiness of young people, but the thought suddenly grips me that I might also make some minor change in the curtain of unfolding events.

I don't recognize anyone among the crowd of bright young couples standing around the living room now, exuding copious amounts of nervous energy and intelligence; they look like publishers, ad men, or banking couples. When I asked my mother about them once, she told me, "Friends of your father. Don't worry about getting their names straight. They didn't last."

Far in the darkening background, there's Johnny Findlay's wife, in a dark blue silk dress; you can see why he wanted her, with her wide bluff stance and long, blond, under-curling hair in the style of Lana Turner. What was her name, I wonder. "Oh, that one? Don't worry about her," my mother told me. "She didn't last either."

This became a joking refrain as we paged through the slides together one evening. "Oh, she didn't last. He didn't last." "Did she last?" "Not a chance." In truth, very few of the people we saw that night have lasted. Most are in their graves now, slowly tossing and turning, or perhaps they are flitting through a dark and darkening hall, where their souls await bodies in which to return to earth. My mother and I are among the very few who attended that event that are around to talk about it now. And of course by a strict temporal observance, I wasn't there at all, as it happened a year before my birth. But a lot of us are starting to drop the old ways, and strict observance in anything is beyond us. We have lasted, that is the important thing.

As I consider how I might rearrange things, I know not to impinge too deeply. There are laws against such things, paradoxes that can't be broken. For example, if I could somehow cause myself never to have been conceived, then who would be the one causing the misconception? Still, perhaps I can send a message.

On the wall by the dining room is an ornate wrought-iron candelabrum of no doubt great antiquity, its nine candles replaced with electric wands and silken shades, which lean together crookedly like a group of chilly mourners.

I notice a woman peering at me knowingly from under a half veil; she has broken an unwritten code of decorum to make direct eye contact—a plump, doe-eyed, perky-rumped beaut in a glossy pageboy, with white blouse sleeves rolled workmanlike to her elbows. Perhaps later this grown debutante will allow one of the bachelors to transport her to a hotel room in Glen Cove. Where he will sandpaper her cheeks with his stubble, fill her mouth with his tongue, her lungs with his smoke, and her soul with his deep and earnest longing.

The procession drifts into the yellow-painted dining room, where enormous fans of narrow sandwiches rest on platters. Someone has left a pack of Chesterfields on the table where if it remains for too long a child sneaking up from under the table will steal it. There are shouts and "ahhs!" as Mom and Dad cut the cake, smiling at the absurdity of this pumped-up applause, and with hands entwined, lift a first piece from the two-tiered wedding cake. They will have to cut very fine slices to fill all of the guests' plates, I think. Dad looks happiest at this moment. He still holds a champagne glass in his left hand. My mother leans forward to see how many still remain to make small talk with, while my father, hands clasped before him, curls his lip as if to say, "I didn't know there were this many old bags in the world!"

I content myself with one small gesture. I walk out through the tall

French doors to the patio, to where moist air warms and fills my nostrils with the smell of seaweed decaying on the shore. Night has fallen while I have been within. The ground is dark and covered with flower petals. I bend down and wedge a dime as deeply as I can into a crack between two square stones on the patio steps. Then I return to the party.

Chapter Twenty-three

Even while my stepbrother was in town taking up enormous chunks of my time, I continued to work as a freelance writer. Writing didn't come easily to me, though. A tobacco-cured voice whispered in my ear that everything I wrote was no good, that I'd never be a writer, that I might as well give up. Still I fought, day by day, to push against that voice.

I'd received an assignment to write a lengthy feature about Keith Haring. I decided to approach the assignment documentary-style, stringing together interviews and keeping my own voice out of it. This turned out to be a much harder project than I'd thought. Overall I talked to over a hundred artists and musicians who'd survived the long-lost eighties. That decade had been hidden in a fold of my brain I hadn't looked at for years, but I doggedly went around like some gray investigator in a Dostoyevsky novel, buying mimosas for aging club boys, placing calls to discarded celebrities like Grace Jones and Boy George, and tracking down forgotten graffiti artists and DJs, until gradually, interview by interview, I began to rebuild my faded picture of those years.

The East Village had been anarchic, cynical, and violent. The taste of betrayal was everywhere in the air, it had the tang of a subway token in your mouth, bitter and coppery, and cheap. You could use that token to ride out to Coney Island and walk on the cold deserted beach in January, or you could stay home in your squalid digs and listen to the thump of Richard Hell and the Voidoids rising up from the apartment below . . .

I belong to the blank generation and I can take it or leave it each time . . .

I lived in a three-hundred-square-foot coffin on Tenth Street with my art school girlfriend Robin, a small-boned, dark-haired girl with pale, translucent skin and the delicate face and almond eyes of a Balinese dancer. Our life there was full of battles and tears, but somehow we'd managed to stay together. Out of baby hunger, kiddingly, she would sometimes throw her head back and howl at the night sky, and when we went down to Chinatown in search of a meal, it was all I could do to keep her from snatching one of the cute babies in their silk jackets from a stroller.

Every night we sat on the bed and listened to screams and the sound of smashing glass out of our back window, and watched flames and smoke gush from the tenements behind us, where the landlords were trying to torch Hispanic inhabitants out of their squalid apartments. During the day I saw thirteen-year-old street gang members ping at cans with air rifles in the backyard of the Fun Gallery, which specialized in graffiti artists. Every time the gallery had an opening, another spare tire would be stolen from my car. From my point of view, the city was on the edge of anarchy and collapse. On a steaming summer night Second Avenue became a Moroccan bazaar, its sidewalks three-deep in families selling trinkets on filthy blankets.

Every now and then in the midst of all of this Sturm und Drang I'd get a call from Dad summoning me to lunch. I'd given up trying to have dinner at his apartment, because Olivia treated Robin so badly; it was something in their chemistry—they were like sodium and water together; they sizzled and let off yellow shoots of flame on contact. Dad and I always ate at the old-fashioned coffee shop on the first floor of his firm's building at 345 Hudson Street. There, surrounded by chattering men in suits, I'd down an egg-salad sandwich and a cup of coffee, while my father shook hands with everyone that walked by. He leaned forward this time and spoke across the table to me in low, vibrant tones.

Things hadn't been going well for him at work, he confided. That much I knew. When my father's first cousin, Ted Stanley, the longtime president of Bowne, had announced his retirement, clearly my father, the most able and far-seeing executive in the company, was the obvious choice to be next in line. But the man whom my father considered his best friend—Vic

Simonte—had waged a ferocious campaign for the job. (Vic was the guy who'd been with my father when he'd come to see me in Chicago a bitter lifetime ago.) It turned out that Vic had been working the plant floor like a Democratic precinct captain, building up a base of people who owed him small favors, gathering a cadre of sycophants around himself, and gently, to everyone, demeaning my father as a dreamer and an intellectual, while ingratiating himself to Ted and the board of directors as a "doer."

Vic was a family man, from a working-class Italian family; he'd seen a crack in my father's aristocratic, Ivy League–bred façade and stuck a crowbar into it. My father was blindsided. The hardest thing was that he knew that if he asked Ted directly, he could have had the job. But something in his nature—pride maybe?—prevented him from asking for the position he so richly deserved. He wasn't a guy to bang his own drum. So Vic ended up taking the prize, and my father had stayed on as VP in Charge of Planning—a title drummed up just for him, and meaningless now that Vic was top dog.

Lighting a cigarette, Dad confessed to me, "Maybe I'd better face it. I'm the kind of guy who likes to work behind the scenes. I've never felt comfortable being in the limelight."

I watched the pigeons circling and confabulating in their elaborate mating rituals on the cobblestones outside the restaurant's plate-glass window and said nothing.

"If you asked Vic who's the second in command in the San Francisco branch, he wouldn't be able to tell you. I would—I hired him for Christ's sake! I like to be the boss . . . I *am* the boss, but I don't want anyone to know it's me, see? I like to pull the strings and make the phone calls. It's better that Victor is out front taking the hits, shaking hands, and having all those goddamn meetings. All that's just a distraction. I'll never know how he gets any work done."

I couldn't help but notice that Vic and a bunch of his unctuous cronies had pushed together a couple of tables by the front window of the coffee shop and were noisily playing a game of matching the numbers on dollar bills. Their loud guffaws echoed throughout the room. Clouds of cigar smoke wafted over our table.

I guess as a way of showing he didn't care, Dad took me over to say hello.

Vic favored me with a flash from his large, expensive-looking glasses and took my hand in a moist handshake. His manner immediately became familiar and proprietorial. If Franz wasn't going to act like a father toward me, then he would.

"Glad you finally saw reason and cut your hair. You look a hell of a lot better than you did in Chicago. Jeez, I thought you were a girl. Still haven't learned to wear a tie and jacket, though, have you?" Vic said, showing a cemetery of white teeth. "There are no guarantees in this world. You'll learn that eventually, just like your father did. We all swim in the same aquarium. Am I right, Franz?"

"Whatever you say, Vic," Dad growled. "And each fish has to eat the long trail of shit coming from the asshole of the fish in front."

As we hit the sidewalk, Dad looked back to the plate-glass window where Vic and his henchmen were still hunched over their crumpled dollar bills.

"Look at those crazy jerks gambling right out in the open. It might as well be Macy's window," he grumbled, and I saw that the sight was like a slow poison seeping into his veins.

"Let's go," he commanded. "Follow me!"

We took the Number 1 to Times Square and then the shuttle across town to Grand Central. From there I trailed my father, completely mystified, while he proceeded to get his shoes shined (he boasted to the shoeshine man how his handmade English shoes had lasted him twenty years to and from work), had a haircut, and took a side trip to Brooks Brothers, where he bought a dark wool overcoat. There was something strange about this concatenation of small errands; I couldn't tell what it all was going to lead to. And why did he need me to be there to see this?

Finally he came out with the truth. He'd decided to resign his position at Bowne and Company, he told me. Clear out his office and sell all of his Bowne stock, since he had no say in how the business was run. I was shocked. My father had worked at Bowne for almost thirty years—all of my life and most of his.

"What will you do now?" I asked.

My father told me he was going into consulting. This was the reason for his haircut, the new overcoat, the shoeshine. He was having his first interview today.

"How much can you make?" I asked.

"A man like me with my experience is worth five hundred dollars a day," he said, deadpan. "That's what I'm asking."

That seemed like an enormous fortune to me.

I left my father on Forty-second Street. As he headed for his first interview, I noticed for the first time his stooped shoulders, the bags under his eyes, and the white stubble on his reddened cheeks.

The consulting business didn't pan out for my father, though. Under his regime, Bowne had bought up most of the competing companies long ago while he was still vice president, and there weren't many up-and-comers willing to pay a retired executive to tell them how to bury their competitors and modernize their plants. Financial printing was a shrinking business, anyway, thanks to the onslaught of computers, which Dad had championed.

I imagine that my father had trouble articulating what he had to sell, as well. When you hired Franz, well, you got *him,* his irreverent mouth, his bug-zapper assessments, his blindsiding jokes, his incessant tinkering with new gadgetry, his far-from-impartial judgment of the size of the brain pans of every damn knucklehead on the plant floor. Dad kept it all in his head, which vice president knew his ass from a lump of pig lead, what kind of rat poison the accountant's son was on, why the client's daughter's choice of contraceptives had been a bad one, the sticker price of the expensive jewelry the head of the union's wife wore to the company picnic, and who was fucking the new waitress downstairs. Every single employee at Bowne could have told you that Franz knew how it all fit together, and why he was essential. But it wasn't something my father could put in words.

A few weeks later I went up by myself to the vast apartment on West End Avenue to visit Dad, and found him alone, sitting in a yellow overstuffed armchair with *The New York Times* in his lap, sipping one of his tall patented gin and tonics.

"I thought I was going to have my royal Bavarian rest," he said when he saw me, and shrugged. He didn't have to explain what a royal Bavarian rest was, though I'd never heard him use the term before. I knew what he'd had instead. *Tsuris.* Trouble at home. A dozen years of hard trouble. Nothing but strife and worry. And it didn't seem like any of it was going to get better anytime soon.

Good old back-slapping Vic! A few years later, we discovered that, like every toppler of statues, he was no damn good at governance. He broke up, he blathered, he took sick, and leaked internally once he took over the helm of Bowne, and in the last year or so, my father had to fly back from Rome (to which he'd "retired," to help Olivia finish her dissertation on seated muses), more than once to mop up the messes Vic made. Eventually Dad was reinstated and given the job of president that he'd deserved in the first place. But that was later.

Chapter Twenty-four

One Friday evening, during that squalid era when I lived in the East Village, my father roused me out of a subterranean torpor to suggest that I hop a jet and fly with him to Haiti. No special reason, he said, just a short vacation from everything. It seemed like a completely random idea, but I had nothing special to do that weekend. In terms of my relationship with him, I wasn't against dropping another quarter into the pinball machine to see if the targets would line up differently.

We flew to Miami and switched to a smaller jet. As we were about to land in Port-au-Prince, an embarrassed stewardess walked backward down the aisle spraying us with clouds of insecticide, apparently following some inane local law that visitors arrive in Haiti vermin-free.

As soon as the jet's door opened we were crushed by sweating baggage handlers who shouted and grabbed at our suitcases while taxi drivers argued over who had seen us first. My father's face reddened and a look of bullish anger crossed his face. I found to my surprise that I was more at home with this kind of chaos than he was. I chose a taxi driver from one of the characters who ranged around us and we jumped into his car.

Soon we were switching back up a hill surrounded by palm trees to the Hotel Oloffson, a tall Victorian wedding cake built with a white lacework of carved wooden balustrades around a columned swimming pool. In the room we shared, with its tall ceiling and slowly turning fan, darkness echoed like a dry cough, the way old-fashioned rooms in the tropics often do.

Being alone with my father at close quarters was vaguely disquieting. My father wasn't really that old, in his late fifties at most, but to me—runner, vegetarian, ascetic, boulevardier, Alphabetville savant—he'd long passed over the crepuscular precipice, and was sliding downward fast. As we dressed for dinner, I tried to avoid staring at the shapeless display of stomach fat hanging over his voluminous boxer shorts, his flat, almost nonexistent buttocks, his splayed legs and dangling testicles.

Every one of my girlfriends had been treated, at one time or another, to a display of my father's pendant globulars. For example, at his country place in Canada, he'd often without warning turn, strip off his bathing suit, and take a pee on the edge of the gravel roadway while maintaining a conversation over his shoulder. It was a rite of passage they had each had to pass through, and most of them went through it bravely, with the humor and worldliness that well-brought-up girls can usually summon.

The next day drizzled, though the pellucid Haitian morning light helped dispel the cobwebs of our hangovers. We took a car up into the mountains near the border with the Dominican Republic to a market set into a steep muddy slope. We slipped up and down between the blankets of wares but there was nothing to buy; wan, prematurely aged women sat on blankets and little boys sold tiny cubes of four Chiclets gum packets wrapped together in cellophane. The sight of "Baby Doc" Duvalier's smirking police, the Tonton Macoute, with their spotless khaki shirts and wraparound mirror sunglasses, struck no fear into me, probably because, living in the East Village, I had learned to see nastiness as a legitimate form of self-expression.

Then we took a taxi back to the center of Port-au-Prince, where another market dealt in wooden furniture and crates. We watched a man saw a board with deadly accuracy, cutting with a peculiar motion away from himself, and my father commented that his brother, Ulrich, had once worked only with hand tools and you'd be surprised how accurate he could get with them.

We bought a set of mahogany plates, as everyone does when they visit Haiti. To my surprise, as I haggled with the peddlers that besieged us, I found a workable patois emerging from my lips.

"I thought you didn't speak any French," my father growled.

I suppose I remembered something from a dim semester studying French in eighth grade and from afternoons spent in the cool shadows of my grandmother's living room at Peacock Point playing a card game called Spit! with my Normandy cousins: ". . . *un . . . deux . . . trois, crachér!*"

"I'm not so sure it *is* French," I replied, as we got into a taxi with our plates wrapped in brown paper and tied expertly with twine.

That night a pretty, middle-aged woman, Christine, with oversized sunglasses and an attractive tangle of dark shoulder-length hair, perhaps attracted by my father's gift of gab, invited us to a demonstration of *vodou*. We accepted gratefully.

The ceremony took place after dark, in a little cove surrounded by a rock jetty. A tall, dignified man in a spotless white suit, whom I had understood to be a tourist agent at our hotel, claimed our tickets. Before us a bonfire burned hotly in the sand. The sand drawings upon the ground of Voodoo Loa, or spirits, lit by flickering candles, seemed primitive and ominous.

Sweating dark men began to drum on hollowed-out logs with bent sticks. Two men and one woman who had been lackadaisically pushing branches into the fire straightened up and became immovable. Our master of ceremonies, the man in the white ice-cream suit, announced, "And now it appears that the Loa have entered the bodies of our friends."

The two men began to jerk and froth at the mouth. One waded into the bonfire in his bare feet and kicked the logs apart. Sprays of orange sparks flew up into the black sky. The other, a thin black man with a mustache, swigged from a bottle of rum, then broke the bottle on a fallen tree trunk and began to chew its neck, spraying bits of glass all around him.

"Do not be concerned for our people, for they are not susceptible to pain or burns as you or I would be," said the man in the ice-cream suit.

The woman's eyes were like black marbles. She lifted her skirt and began to wade out into the surf. Soon, she was beyond the reach of the firelight. Her high, crazy voice sang to us out of the darkness of the sea.

Things appeared to be getting out of hand. The man in the ice-cream suit stood up from his chair and walked calmly to the middle of the beach. He gave an almost imperceptible jerk with his right shoulder and lifted his hand. The first man responded as if yanked by strings; he rose up out of the flames of the fire where he'd been rolling and came to the side of the master of ceremonies. When the ice-cream suit man moved his left shoulder, the other man also staggered forward as if marched by invisible strings. He stood by him, panting and spitting small pieces of glass from his mouth.

The two drummers put down their sticks and waded out to where the woman floated up to her neck, her dress surrounding her like a white lily pad. They took her arms and led her back to the beach, where she simply lay where they left her on the sand.

Suddenly it was over. The man in the ice-cream suit thanked us all in a deep voice and we filed out from our rows of metal folding seats to our drivers and cars. When I looked back, I saw the woman who'd been possessed sweeping the sand with a twig broom.

"What did you think of that? A lot of crap if you ask me," said my father as we began to drive back to the hotel.

"You," he said suddenly. "You in the front seat."

The taxi driver turned around and peered back at us, in the Haitian back-road darkness, his yellow eyes shining like scimitar moons.

"Yes, monsieur?"

"I like your Tyrolean hat," Dad said.

"It is not a Tyrolean hat, monsieur. If it were it would be made of wool. That would be too warm in this part of the world. Mine is of straw."

"Well, I like it. I wore a Tyrolean hat once myself, but we called it a Bavarian hat. Now, tell me, kind sir, what do you do for fun at night in this country of yours?"

"What do I do?"

"Yes, what do you do?"

"I go home to my wife and children."

"Very commendable of you."

"Yes. But that is what I do. What I suggest for you is that I will drive you to a dance hall where the girls are very friendly," he said. "Frequently my customers go there and they are never disappointed."

"I'll bet the girls do more than dance."

"That, sir, depends on your negotiating skills."

"Don't worry about my negotiating skills. What'll it cost?" persisted my father.

"You will like the price. Everyone likes the price. I will wait for you in the parking lot with the other drivers and bring you back to Mr. Oloffson's later."

Dad turned to me. "What do you think?"

"I think we should go back to the hotel," I said. There were a thousand and one reasons why I didn't want to enter that cat house, not the least of which was the thought of listening to my father grunting on the other side of a plywood partition. I didn't suppose it would have done me any good to bring up that Dad was married, or that I had a girlfriend at home whom, despite the never-ending drama of our relationship, I was starting to miss in a warm way.

The driver leaned over the back of the seat.

"Perhaps he is not a fan of black girls," he said.

"Is that true?" asked my father. "I wouldn't have thought that of you, being prejudiced like that."

"Yes, that's it," I said. It wasn't true, but I was willing to say anything to get out of this situation by then.

"My son here is ashamed of me," my father said to the driver.

"That is a son's prerogative."

"A damn pansy, that's what I call him."

"He will get over it later and you will both laugh at this. Meanwhile where do I go?"

"You might as well take us back to Oloffson's," barked Dad. "This guy's no fun."

Dad remained pissy for the rest of the evening, and out of sympathy the cabdriver eventually called me the French equivalent of a *maricon*. But the worst thing, for me, was the realization that Dad hadn't cared who the hell I was—he was just damn eager to get into that bordello and have his choice of meat. I wouldn't have been surprised if he'd hatched this little idea when he'd first planned the trip. At best I'd been his excuse, an unwitting shill—a means to get away from his wife.

In the last day or so, Haiti lost half of its magic. At the beach the German homosexuals assumed we were lovers and asked us how long we'd known each other, as if we'd just met at some tiki bar. The commonplace conversations, the casual gruffness of the way my father talked to me, the dinner with my mother's cousins, who were staying at the hotel, the odd conversations with other guests, and the shared room all unnerved me. Despite the excellence of the gin and tonics we were drinking, I longed for the cramped safety of my East Village apartment.

When we got back to JFK, I was surprised to hear my father tell the pinstriped businessman, an acquaintance of his, with whom we happened to share a cab:

"Haiti? Fantastic! It did what a vacation is expected to do. I didn't think about a thing the whole time we were there."

Chapter Twenty-five

After I left the East Village, I drove back to Kansas City, where I still had a few friends from art school days. First I worked in construction, then video production, and then installing large-screen television sets in an older locust tree–lined suburb where the streets were all named for Indian tribes.

Kansas City had an ancient, pedigreed underground that stretched back to the days of Tom Pendergast. Most of the people I knew supported themselves on less than five thousand dollars a year, a sum which even in Kansas City was easy to come by, and that left plenty of time for thinking, reading, driving, painting, barbecuing, and making music. Everyone seemed to be connected to everyone else through a mass of branching, threadlike fibers that crisscrossed under the dark rich loam. You could easily find yourself sitting at a picnic table with a bank president and a man who made his living selling cocaine, and discover they had gone to school together and knew each other well.

The city was circled by suburban towns whose populations spanned the spectrum from easygoing Republican country club members to rank-and-file apocalyptic survivalists, religo-cryptic child abusers, and abortion-clinic bombers. But the bohemian enclave in which I found myself had settled into an inner ring of unwanted, though sumptuous, nineteenth- and early-twentieth-century homes that stood all around the gutted center of the city. There, artists bought and fixed up houses for very little money and supported themselves through small-time renovation, working in used record stores, and by starting Greek restaurants and world-music bands.

It was in Kansas City that I first started to write. Originally I started on a Smith Corona manual typewriter that a Chinese friend in New York had advised me to buy, "since you may have to go out to the villages where there is no electricity." That sounded like practical advice to me. One day I sent a book review to *The Kansas City Star*. The next week I looked in the Sunday arts section and saw my byline printed there.

When I called my father to tell him, he snorted and said, "Just like Jackson Payton!" Jack was a neighbor when my father was growing up back in Greenwich who'd called himself a writer, but as far as anyone could see, had never written a thing. Thereafter, whenever my father heard about me publishing another article, he'd repeat, "Just like Jackson Payton!" and snigger, as though he'd cracked a tremendously clever joke.

Every once in a while my mother would fly into Kansas City to pay me a visit. As I was driving her back to my apartment from the airport one night, over endless miles of dark highway, she opened up, as people tend to do when they are on the road at night. She began to tell me the story of the war years, how as a fourteen-year-old she'd shared an apartment alone with my grandmother, Froggie. Her sister was away at boarding school, and Big Ward was in the Pacific. It was during those years, when Ward was away, that Froggie transitioned from formidable social drinker to nearly full-time falling-down drunk. The story my mother told was of finding her mother passed out in the bathtub; how by herself she'd had to pull Froggie out, dress her, and put her to bed. What does that do to a girl, I wondered, just when she needed to rebel and pull away, to scream and call her parents names, to find her mother suddenly transformed into a helpless and insensible stranger?

I felt a chill run down the back of my neck, because I had heard this story, or variations on it, many times in the past. Sooner or later, it seemed, each of my girlfriends would get around to telling me a version of the exact same tale. How she'd found her mother, or father, unconscious, or raving, on the floor of the bathroom or the shower, or on the toilet, naked, pissed upon, incoherent, covered with vomit, and by herself would have to hose her mother down, drag her out of the bathtub, strip off her clothing, and put her to bed.

I wondered about myself. Was there a *type* of woman, discernable to my unconscious mind, that magnetically drew me to form a relationship? Was it really true that a man eventually tries to marry his own mother? By what pheromone-sniffing process, actually, had I *found* all of these girlfriends?

I couldn't answer these questions. All I knew was that the woman I was sharing a house with then in Kansas City, I loved like a sister—but nothing more. Like my girlfriend in the East Village, she wanted to have children. The physical process of becoming pregnant, however, of watching her stomach stretch and grow bulbous, and then having a team of doctors crowd around her to pull the squirming infant out from between her legs—all of that repelled and confused her. So it was her fantasy that someday we would grow a baby inside of a bubbling glass orb set up in our living room. Arm in arm, we would watch our baby bob in a warm vat of nourishing medium until it reached birthing age. Then we would gently fish it out and give it a name.

Her plan awaited technical developments. Meanwhile, I knew that if we went on as we were, we would soon be married.

I continued to write reviews and feature articles for the paper, sometimes working as a stringer for the suburban "zone" offices. The writer William S. Burroughs was living near Kansas City in those days, in the scrub suburbs of the college town of Lawrence, less than an hour's drive away. When Burroughs came out with his next book, *Queer*, my editor at *The Kansas City Star*, Steve Paul, sent me out to interview him. Burroughs had been my hero since I'd read *Naked Lunch* as a high school freshman. I knew enough about the man to fear him, to know that he did not suffer fools gladly. Walking up the steps of the small, dark bungalow into which he'd fallen back, I felt as though I were about to have a root canal without anesthesia. I'd stayed up most of the night devising questions to ask him, but my only wish now was to jump forward magically an hour into the future, when the interview would be over. The balding writer who came to the door was not the tall, wrathful specter with waxy gray skin I'd expected, though. Burroughs was bent into an "S" shape, and had sensitive, rheumy eyes; he seemed older and more delicate than either of my own grandfathers had lived to be.

"I've always been maladroit in amorous areas, oddly enough," Burroughs confided to me over a cup of tea. "Doing the wrong thing, saying the wrong thing. It is not my area of expertise."

"Have you ever thought about committing suicide?" I asked, after I'd conversed with him for a while and felt I'd gotten to know him.

"Oh, merciful God, no! No!" he replied, appearing visibly aghast at my question. "I keep a .45 caliber revolver in the next room, but the thought of turning that upon myself gives me the horrors!"

In a kindly way, Burroughs repeated to me the words of Gertrude Stein, that everyone should have a métier. For him it had been writing. Having a métier had saved thousands of people, he said, and had been his own salvation as well.

Chapter Twenty-six

My father divorced Olivia during the time I was living in Kansas City. After she moved to Idaho and bought a rafting expedition company on the Snake River, Little Peter followed her there. This opened what was to be, perhaps, a fruitful and something approaching happy chapter of my stepbrother's often frustrated and sidetracked adult career.

In Idaho my stepbrother's life turned indolent and easy. The West was full of eccentrics like him who fought hard for their right to be left alone: rattlesnake men, prospectors, truckers, ranchers, one-worlders, and world-enders. Had always been that way. Men who mumbled to themselves and slept under blankets up in the hills. Men who earned a living one way or another, or got by without one. In Idaho, the term, "rugged individualist" was practically a brand name.

If you squinted one eye and closed the other, you could have mistaken Little Peter for simply another educated young man rambling out a few feckless years before job, family, and maturity set in. In Korea they have a word for this, my mother-in-law says: *mujung yohang*, which means "traveling to nowhere," or perhaps more accurately "traveling with nothing in your pocket." No money, no expectations, just a fervent desire to drift and let the world come to you at its own pace. For Koreans it's a coveted time, a gap year, a walkabout, a break most people long for, but never get around to having. Sometimes he worked for Olivia, sometimes he just lay in his bunk and stared up at the flies on the ceiling. Like Little Grasshopper in the *Kung Fu* TV series, he wandered the parched grass of the prairie, hallucinating strange scenes from his past and impressing the locals with his mental and physical prowess. He acquired cars casually and lost them casually. He flew to Hawaii for a few months, to house-sit a shack owned by my sister Olga, until he got in trouble with some surfers and came back. During this time he reconnected with an old friend who'd been a counselor at Spring Lake Ranch on one of his stints there, Dave Arnott.

Arnott was a Montana-raised psychologist, writer, photographer, and musician who had issues of his own, and at Spring Lake Ranch he and Little Peter came to a strange understanding right away. Together they honed a lifestyle at odds with the rigid structures of the ranch, which was, after all, a psychiatric hospital. They played piano all night on an old Steinway, guzzled tall cans of beer, skied like maniacs, took girlfriends from among both patients and staff, and spent their afternoons souping up one of the ranch's trucks, which they "borrowed" for wild all-night treks into the woods and mountains. Arnott's native Montana outlook saw nothing out of the ordinary in this kind of behavior, nor did Little Peter find much to complain about.

After Arnott was fired for crash-landing the truck into the ranch's parking lot, he returned to Montana, bought an old school gymnasium in the tiny town of Moccasin, and turned it into a recording studio. One day when he was standing lookout on the roof of the gym, he spied a lone figure in the distance walking over the fields toward him. It was Little Peter, still on his *mujung yohang*, his journey to nowhere. Right away, my stepbrother found a home in Arnott's gymnasium among an ever-changing roster of musicians, poets, painters, and vagabonds who tarried there.

There was something in the particular chemical makeup of Arnott's kingdom that had allowed Little Peter's talents for once to shine over his social deficits. After hearing my stepbrother tell many stories about his Montana years, I grew curious and tried, unsuccessfully at first, to contact Arnott. Finally I managed to leave a message with a brother who owned a sound studio in Salt Lake City. Within a day I received an e-mail. Arnott was more than eager to tell me about his friendship with my stepbrother, he wrote. My inquiry seemed to open up a floodgate in a lonely and pent-up soul. He began posting me three or four long, detailed e-mails a day, most of them at early hours of the morning. In fact, as the e-mails multiplied, I began to suspect him of harboring mania. Sometimes he'd end by saying,

"Jesus did you ever get the dump!" He also sent me a PDF novel he'd written about a vengeful female ninja and a set of dramatic Technicolor cloud form photographs he'd taken while camping in the mountains. It was never entirely clear to me whether David Arnott himself had a home, because he seemed to travel incessantly.

What intrigued me was that the picture of Little Peter Arnott painted in his e-mails was so completely at odds with the person I, or my family, might have recognized. He was a much fuller, rounded individual. My father would have been flabbergasted to learn, for example, that Little Peter had sustained several long-term relationships with young women who were not only educated, good-looking, intelligent, and artistic, but seemed to have liked and accepted Little Peter as he was. Arnott himself was comfortable with a complex view of my stepbrother, whom he seemed to idolize and pity in equal amounts. Finally he simply appeared to enjoy his company as a friend, and the Little Peter I knew had few friends.

"Well, he was handsome as the devil and funny," Arnott wrote describing Little Peter as he was at Spring Lake Ranch when he first encountered him. "He was the most athletic person I ever met, the finest downhill skier, and I've seen a few. One winter night he RAN down the railroad tracks into Rutland and back for beer."

Arnott was impressed by Little Peter's uncanny ability to calculate numbers in his head. In late-night drinking sessions in the closed office, they played a game where Arnott would type two long strings of numbers into a calculator, while Little Peter carefully watched his fingers without being allowed to see the screen. Arnott would multiply the numbers and try to read off the answer before Little Peter could say it out loud, but not once did he beat him.

"I found that underneath [Little Peter's] hostile exterior lived a very bright, very funny, unusually sensitive person," he went on. "I recall Peter had a girlfriend there named Michele who was a former staff member and had attended Dartmouth.

"There was a kind of small-town hoopla about Peter and Michele," he went on. "They were smitten. They played a lot of four-handed piano during their courtship. Since he could sight read ANYTHING he always played the bottom of the keyboard. He was so patient. So understated. That was a sweet romance to see. Honestly. It was touching.

"Not just a looker, she was a fun, bright young lady. She came to visit once when Franz happened to be there. Peter and Michele were just returning from a bicycle ride when I was visiting with Franz in the parking lot. Franz only wondered what a woman of that quality saw in Peter."

As a psychologist, Arnott expended a lot of digital type trying to define for me what Little Peter's symptoms meant. Since he rejected much of his own training, and admitted to periods of near-madness himself, he seemed torn.

"Peter fits the diagnostic criteria for Asberger's much closer than schizophrenia," he asserted. "The mathematical and music skills just fit that profile so perfectly. Also the issues with social skills. Paranoia is a pretty broad topic. I'm a little paranoid myself. A lot of people have it. And as he didn't really ever have outright hallucinations I question schizophrenia. As for the 'psychotic' episodes, is flipping your lid now and then a sign of schizophrenia? Especially if [the episodes] are temporary and usually with a quick recovery?"

"I don't believe Peter ever had a 'disease,'" Arnott was to write to me later. "My opinion is that he was born a genius, a savant. Then he was shamed, neglected, ignored, and abused. Even Franz, whom Peter considered the only loving parent he ever had, could not contain himself from speaking in a condescending and dismissive manner of Peter in Peter's very presence.

"There is nothing more painful and destructive than being labeled 'bad' as a little child. There is just no way to know how he might have turned out had he been raised in a loving, attentive, and thoughtful environment."

In Moccasin, Little Peter started a second, rather wistful relationship with a young painter I'll call Kathy, who quickly moved into his small room at Arnott's gym. "Peter and Kathy were of the same cloth, at the same level, in the same league, birds of a feather, who spoke the same language," Arnott remembered. "Kathy was an all-around advanced soul."

Together, she and Little Peter founded the "Poetry Pantry" in Little Peter's room at the gym, reading and writing verse together at all hours of the night. During the afternoons they played "Shoot from the Seven," one of their incomprehensible games, where they both stood on the #7 shuffleboard square in the gym and tried to shoot baskets, a distance of thirty feet. Each basket meant you got a "Lucky Point for Life." Little Peter and Kathy shot baskets for hours a day, and days in a row, racking up innumerable "Lucky Points" . . .

In Arnott's gym, Little Peter also founded the Stars Only Repertory Theater, another wacked-out idea only he and Kathy, apparently, could truly understand. The rules were: no audience, no cameras, and no script. If Arnott happened to walk through during one of the rehearsals, the players would freeze until he'd left. Strange and exhilarating Bohemian pageants were enacted in which Little Peter and Kathy would lead a parade around the gym holding a goat's skull attached to a six-foot boiler rake, a frightening totem that everyone called "The Thing," until Arnott finally got hold of it and tossed it into Lost Lake.

Meanwhile the three improvised recordings together, singing along with Arnott's wheezy Hammond organ, compositions that were like acid trips without drugs. "Peter joined a gang of brilliant, creative, adventurous, athletic, and good-looking people because he was just like them," summarized Arnott.

Living in this offbeat mountain town surrounded by artists, musicians, and friends seemed to soften and open up my stepbrother. When the sad news reached Montana that my father's sister Olga had taken her life after being diagnosed with brain cancer, one might not have expected Little Peter to write my father a letter of condolence. His life was not composed of such polite niceties. It had been a year or so since he had spoken to Dad, and probably more years since he'd written a letter to anyone. Still, he insisted. A woman in town gave him paper and helped him draft the text, and the postmistress made sure he correctly addressed the envelope. The postmistress also lent him money for the stamp. Ultimately his letter became a community effort.

My stepbrother's Montana downfall, like that of many a hero in a cowboy flick, was money—too much of it, and too fast. This happened when Olivia cashed in a mutual fund that had been started for him as a baby, and gave him all $17,000 at once. With this windfall, my stepbrother bought an old Mustang and began five long months' worth of seriously corrosive partying. A bartender in Hobson, Montana, would report that he'd seen Little Peter feed $750 into a slot machine over a single evening. One afternoon Little Peter pulled over at the edge of a field—rye or wheat, he wasn't sure which, though it was tall and ready for harvest—and fell asleep. When he came to after the sun had risen, his Mustang was dead, so he walked out into the long grass carrying his sleeping bag with him and settled in for a nap.

The harvest combine came up with little warning. There was no transition: before the accident he was a wanderer, a "Little Grasshopper," still in his voyage to nowhere, his *mujung yohang*; afterward he was a tragic statistic, an urban variable, part of an invisible herd.

He left behind a group that had looked up to him as some kind of New York genius. Arnott provided a last impression of this prelapsarian time: "I have old recordings of Peter playing Bach on the gym organ that sound like liquid silver and shooting stars. My opinion was that he was the most talented piano and organ player I had ever met in my life. I used to joke that playing the piano was the *only* thing he could do right.

"There was, of course, the combine incident, which kind of hit people hard. When his hands got taken away. And that's just the way that it goes, isn't it?" Arnott wrote. "If you were the finest organ player in the state of Montana then your hands would get cut off . . . This for me is just one more cruel joke too many. That Peter's hands got taken away. That fucking hurt."

When Arnott's e-mails stopped abruptly, I figured he'd simply run out of things to say. It seemed in keeping with the serrated zig and zags in his character that he would bite off our correspondence as cleanly as a plug of tobacco. A few months later I learned through a search on the Internet that he was dead. Arnott had gotten out of his vehicle during a snowstormy night on the highway near his home in Montana and been hit by another truck. A friend of his I spoke to on the phone told me that in the weeks leading up to his death, Arnott had been drinking quite a bit, and his mental health had declined. But he'd also been spending a lot of time with his teenaged daughter, whom he'd come to see as an important part of his life.

"This culture has a 'disease,' and now it's dying," Arnott wrote to me in one of the last e-mails he sent. "Archeologists point out that the bones of people living a hundred thousand years ago indicate that tribesmen who had been completely disabled lived up to forty years afterward. This is because these cultures took care of their own. We don't. We let them die in culverts alone. We are resentful of brilliant people. We punish them. Shun them."

Part Seven

Space is a swarming in the eyes; and time a singing in the ears.

—Vladimir Nabokov

Chapter Twenty-seven

A bright, sunny Sunday morning in Greenwich Village. The wan March sun streamed in through the slats in our bedroom, while outside the street remained still and quiet. Hali lay asleep with a folded black T-shirt over her eyes, and Maya, curled between us, was a dark smudge of hair on the rumpled sheets. Even though it was near 10:00 A.M., I was still in bed—but Little Peter's voice was rasping in my ear.

He'd called from Miami Beach, where he'd been for about a week—at my recommendation—and at the moment, he was standing at a pay phone in a town called Bayside, a tony little shopping area in Miami Harbor. And things were spinning out of control for him; it was worse than I could have imagined. The scenery he was painting for me was apocalyptic—drugs, cops, racial violence, poisoned food, the sun on retreat from the earth, pestilence, the kind of naked fear that causes people to die mysteriously while alone in their rooms with the door locked . . .

It was pretty apparent that I was going to have to go down to Florida to perform some kind of rescue operation. Because the terrible prospect of his disability check—nearly five hundred dollars—being automatically deposited into his ATM account on the first of the month, was only days away. With five hundred dollars my stepbrother could wreak awful havoc upon himself in a place like Miami, where cocaine is almost as cheap as lemonade, and I was starting to worry about his ultimate survival.

"I told you about the scene down here," he said, breathing coarsely into my ear. "I confess that the money you sent me, I spent most of it on coke—I'm being honest with you. I wasn't going to, but I spent the day running around downtown Miami, trying to find a Western Union office. Then I ran into my friend Bobby and while he was making himself useful, he more or less helped me find creative ways to spend my money.

"Like always, the first part was good," Little Peter went on. "It was really, really good. We went up to Overtown, and got a rock and brought it back to the bridge to smoke, and it was like strips of coals glowing in the back of my head—extremely pleasurable. But then something happened. I really don't want to go into it in a whole lot of detail.

"After that, things got really, really bad, and they stayed like that for a long, long time."

Little Peter had apparently suffered an epiphany down there in Florida while pawing the sand on the soda straw–strewn high-tide mark. He'd decided to go into drug rehab. He babbled something about how "effective communication is the solution to all the world's problems," sounding like a dropout from a Dale Carnegie course, except for the fact that he was sweating and probably coming off a bad high.

Still sleepy, I drifted away. His words entered my ears, morphed into animal cookie shapes and floated like clouds before streaming off into the air. I'd gone into my stepbrother's head, or he'd entered mine, and I saw myself in the hot Florida sun with the seaweed in my shoes, working off a toxic flash. Seconds later I woke up with Little Peter's voice still in my ear:

"Here's a message to my mother: Why am I out here eating out of garbage cans if you love me so much?"

My friend Jim, who'd developed a creative yen to take more pictures of Little Peter in his "natural habitat," flew down two days before I did, and began staking out the downtown area and Miami Beach, looking for my stepbrother in all of the likely locations. He called on his cell phone, saying, "I'm in Bayside and I'm standing right next to the bridge you described that Little Peter was sleeping under."

"How is it?" I ask.

"Glorious!" Jim says. "There are palm trees and boats and beautiful women wearing bikinis. I wouldn't mind living here myself."

A few hours later he called in another report. "I'm at Second Street and Ocean Drive in the park, and there's a guy sleeping here wearing cut-off jeans, cheap high tops, and a plaid shirt. I'll just wait until he wakes up."

An hour later, he called to say he'd been talking to a news vendor who swore he knew Little Peter, but of course it turned out he didn't.

I began with the depressing certainty that I was going to spend the next three days tromping the man nests and underpasses of Miami like a blind scarecrow, until I was sick of myself and our self-appointed task.

In order to save a few dollars, I'd chosen to fly Tower Airlines, an outfit that Jim described as "a Third World airline operating in the First World." When I arrived at the Tower terminal, I found the experience on another planet altogether, though. The seats in the waiting area were orange-colored and shabby; the walls were lined with dated eighties artwork. My flight was canceled at the last minute, and I was bussed from JFK to another terminal in Newark Airport, where no one had ever heard of me—nor could they find any trace that my ticket had ever existed. Three hours later, after some audible grinding in the gears of my misfortune, I stepped off the plane in Miami.

I took a cab to the Airport Best Western; Jim stood waiting for me outside the room, holding up an ancient strobe light held together with adhesive tape. No doubt he wished to capture the look of trauma on my face. I was in for another shock: Little Peter had already arrived, and the two were sharing a Coke on the motel room's tiny dining table.

It had only been a week or two since he'd left New York, but Little Peter was hugely and boyishly glad to see me; it would not be a large exaggeration to say that he felt a miracle had taken place. He kept exclaiming that the world had a reason for everything; we were meant to find each other today.

In truth Little Peter and Jim had walked up and down the same narrow strip in Miami Beach for days, narrowly missing each other. Just today, however, Jim had driven to photograph the lunch line at a homeless facility called Camillus House and there had found Little Peter outside on the sidewalk.

When Little Peter stood to shake my hand, though, his short-sleeved T-shirt revealed the extent to which his arm had been damaged by the harvesting combine in 1992. His forearm was bloated, lacking in muscle tone, a bag of loose flesh covered with parallel striations. And his grip, as he held my hand, was the rubber grip of a glove filled with warm water.

"What do you think?" asked Jim. "Your brother cleans up pretty well, doesn't he?"

I had to admit that, even so, Little Peter looked pretty sharp now, showered and shaved, with his deep tan, wearing a pair of baggy Bermuda shorts, a T-shirt from his mother's river rafting company, hiking shoes with fresh white socks, and a Cayman Islands hat. His unbounded enthusiasm at seeing me made him look younger. He'd jettisoned his pack and lost some of his beggar's stoop. He was, in short, indistinguishable, at first glance, from any of the ten thousand debauched college men who'd descended upon this resort town for spring break.

You'd never guess he'd woken up that morning in a bed of flattened beach grass and had his first meal out of a trash receptacle. Only when I looked into his face closely could I see the gulley lines incised by the endless runoff of outdoor living, cheap drink, drugs, and Dumpster cuisine.

We stopped at the hotel desk to take a second room for Little Peter. There was the usual confusion about our sharing the same name: we decided to call ourselves Peter von Ziegesar the Elder, Peter von Ziegesar the Younger.

I slid into the backseat of Jim's orange Neon rental in order to let Little Peter enjoy the full experience of riding in the front seat of the car. Once in the backseat, as I listened passively to Jim and my stepbrother bicker over control of the radio; a curious lethargy took over my limbs. I was transported to the uncertainty, the social insecurity, the not-knowing-what-was-going-to-happen-next of my high school days. In a few moments, Jimi Hendrix's "Purple Haze" took over the heavy bass speakers, thunderous, joyful, demanding my full attention. I felt the deadening swerve of pot fill my head, though in truth I'd only had a cup of motel room coffee. Jim drove as if he were gripping the joystick of a machine in a video arcade, putting a full body English into every spontaneous lane change, speeding up to the car's maximum velocity whenever the lane ahead was clear, reacting with a jerk to car movements that were hundreds of yards ahead, but ignoring those that were dangerously immediate. All the while he cursed bitterly about the criminally deficient driving skills, dead reflexes, and subhuman intelligence of Miami drivers. He came to an abrupt halt at a highway entrance, completely bamboozled by the loops and contradictions of the Miami road system. He and Little Peter completed a weird nonconversation:

"I'm not sure where we are," Jim said.

"That's why I despise this place," Little Peter replied. "Miami is so wide and full of distances that a man feels lost."

"If I turn left and head east—"

"I'm definitely going back to New York."

"That turnoff is the right one, I think."

"But maybe I'll go to Canada first."

"This street wasn't there before . . ."

"You guys think I'll go crazy if I stay here another month?"

Jim swerved off. We made our way downtown, parked the car at a relatively swanky shopping mall, with views of the harbor from the jewelry stalls. This was Bayside, the place of Little Peter's desperate call to me. Next door, the Port Boulevard Bridge stretched away; underneath which Little Peter had slept for several nights, and where his suitcase and sleeping bag were still stashed (along with, I assume, his glass crack pipe). We trudged several times back and forth between the tinkling upscale mall and Peter's dank cryptozoic hiding place; I became aware of how much I myself needed to be recognized by the people we encountered as a middle-class American, how afraid I was to be mistaken for the Other—what my stepbrother has become. Everyone in our world believes in upward mobility, but downward mobility is a shameful thing, a taboo never spoken of.

In New York I probably wouldn't have felt this way, but here, surrounded by potted palm trees and kiosks containing sunglasses, lotions, engraved jewelry, and portable disc players, I found myself stiffening whenever we passed a cop. We were crossing and recrossing a border not normally traversed—at least not in a single day. Society demanded that Little Peter go through a rigorous program of self-denial and transformation before he was allowed to reenter. Today we'd accomplished the change by means of a few cosmetic touches. How long could we sustain this charade?

Little Peter had spent a week living on a rusty, abandoned container vessel called the *Ocean Freeze*—it was about a hundred and fifty feet long and registered in Belize City. We saw it ahead of us, floating in a narrow strip of water within sight of the Bayside shopping mall, in the center of a rutted and treeless waterfront stretch that would someday be called the "Bicentennial Park," if it was ever completed. Little Peter told us the sheriff's department had impounded the *Ocean Freeze* when they found it, a few months ago, floating in the Inland Waterway, with a cargo hold full of cocaine. They towed it into the harbor, and there some of the most impoverished and desperate of Miami's homeless had colonized it, swarming through a warren of small cabins in the bridge above decks. Each cabin had its own private head and sink. A Rastafarian named Dread had even taken over the Purser's Office; he'd put a lock on the inside that he claimed was impervious even to the weighty kicks of Miami policemen.

A few nights ago, Little Peter had ripped an enormous coil of copper wire from the engine room of the *Ocean Freeze,* burned off the insulation in a small deck fire, and walked six miles through the croaking heart of the Miami night to trade the copper to a shifty scrap metal dealer for $9.40—only enough to buy a small lump of crack. Like slumming tourists, we strolled over, so that Jim could take a few pictures of the upper decks. There was no hint of life onboard, and the gangplank had been torn off and lay broken and rusty on the dock.

Back in the car, we headed across the causeway for Miami Beach. Our course took us over endless three-dimensional loops of sandstone-colored highway, done up in self-conscious Deco style. We skirted the exclusive enclave of Fisher's Island, then navigated along Miami Beach's Ocean Drive. There we skimmed by a strip of pastel-colored hotels straight out of a gangster film of the 1930s—their bright colors were supposed to instill the idea of tropical enjoyment and loose living, but it was easy to see things through Little Peter's eyes and find only raw, basic greed and cold indifference behind the amusing façades.

A triad of young men, ostensibly on the make, we prowled through the still delicious lotion-scented air, up over a sandy path in the sea grass to a beach growing luminescent in the waning orange sun, then as we tripped and staggered down toward the enormous ocean, we marveled like urban rubes at the thong suits and bare breasts of the native girls (who were natives of New Jersey, at least) and the muscles and bikini pants of the boys.

It was fascinating to watch Little Peter revisit the habitats of just a day before, now as a fully franchised citizen with money and a couple of pals, where that very morning he'd skulked, a lost and hopeless hazard. I tried to imagine what it was like to be destitute in the midst of such surface opulence, to be ugly and deformed in such crowds of perfect, tanned young bodies, to be depressed and uncertain in a culture of perfect narcissism.

A young, tanned cop in shorts gave Little Peter a hard look. "Yeah, this is a great town if you don't fuck with the locals," Little Peter said with a harsh laugh. "They get to know you after a few days, if they see you eating out of the trash cans. That one's probably wondering what I'm doing with you guys, if I'm pulling some kind of scam."

We were taking our sweet time along a kind of sandy strip that ran just at the top of the beach. Jim hung back to take a picture of the row of decrepit apartment buildings that rose along that end—shabby but picturesque low-renters, with flaking pastel-colored paint and concrete balconies, exuding a depressing romanticism.

As we walked, maybe it was the sweet air, the scent of coconut oil coming off of the fair skin of the bikini'ed teenaged girls, but Little Peter loosened up and began to tell me of his lost college career—he'd lasted less than a semester at the University of Vermont. His classes were scheduled all in the morning, as it happened, and Little Peter, not a morning person, decided that he would sleep through them—but read the textbooks on his own, relying on his photographic memory, and come in just to take tests.

"Well, that didn't work!" Little Peter said. "After a short time, the textbooks started making no sense to me at all. I panicked and realized that I had to start attending lectures. The first one I went to was a typical freshman survey class in a huge amphitheater, filled with shouts and slamming books and loud echoing noises. All those students jammed into one place gave me the willies. The instructor's words might as well have been in Swahili for all I could make out of them. I left after a few minutes."

From then on, he told me, he stayed in his room during the day and went out only to buy beer and pizza at night. Just before Thanksgiving, Dad sent him a ticket to fly home to New York for the four-day vacation. When he got to Logan Airport, Little Peter had about three hundred dollars in his pocket. He bought something to eat, had a few beers, and missed his plane. This turned out to be a fortuitous happening, perhaps a turning point in his life. He entered a fog, spent the next four days drifting around the airport, sleeping on the waiting room seats, eating in the cafes, talking to no one, and avoiding the airport police. He remained in his own world—while the rest remained in theirs. He wasn't unhappy, in fact, just the opposite. He'd enjoyed an unusual sense of well-being.

Little Peter halted suddenly in the sand and gave me an extraordinary leprechaun smile that pulled all his immense, demented features together at the top of his face. It was a smile that I'd seen on a couple of my friends' faces before when they'd done something wrong and knew it: a smirk, an admission of a total and complete fuck-up, and yet a request for understanding and forgiveness, an inward—and perhaps inbred—grin that said, "Oh, well, it's only me and I'm a bit peculiar, you know, too!" And he asked me earnestly, with that smile yanking most of his red face all up behind his ears, "Do you think I can live in my own world for the rest of my life?" (I think he meant, ". . . and get away with it?") And my reaction was to say, "Well, Peter, ahem, yes, I believe some people *do* get to, the very lucky ones, the ones who don't compromise, and who are lucky enough not to be crushed or arrested for it." I could think of one or two then—I can't now.

We tired of the beach and walked south toward the jetty as the sun faded into warm haze. Here the city, in an effort to keep the beach clean, had lined the sandy strip with wire mesh trash baskets. Little Peter seemed to have X-ray vision. He'd say, barely glancing, "Don't bother with that one." Or he'd nod his head slyly and ask, "Did you notice the bag of chips in the can seven cans back?" I couldn't decide whether it was ESP, or some idiot savant trick like Dustin Hoffman in *Rain Man* instantly knowing how many matches there were on the floor when you spilled them out of a matchbox.

As Jim raised his camera, a fit of self-consciousness overcame my stepbrother and he refused to continue.

We came upon a young man with long hair, lying on a Mexican blanket on the sand between the garbage cans. He twirled the handle of a can opener around and around, as though it were the prayer wheel of his own personal religion. Little Peter told us the man was always here, day after day, no matter what the weather. To me he seemed like one of the old religious mendicants of India, a strange, wise Sadhu, using a can opener to open up the pathways of his consciousness.

At the channel mouth, we watched huge container vessels leave Miami Harbor, and cruise ships with names like *Ecstasy* and *Fantasy*, overloaded with dentists from Bayonne and insurance agents from Manhasset, the ships' sheer bulk making us feel small and lonely and unneeded.

Little Peter turned suddenly and asked, "Can you arrange for me to go on a cruise while you're here?"

"Peter, I don't think you'd like the company," I replied.

Here in the free-for-all, Coppertone-scented atmosphere of Miami Beach, redolent of ancient gangster history, we decided to bend the rules, what the hell. It was worth it to watch the sun break upon Little Peter's normally befuddled and worry-laden face, when I informed him that Jim and I were going to let him drink beer with us, as we sat down at a cheap tourist restaurant called Moe's Mexican Cantina—and to see him slowly nursing his Negra Modelo in the booth, as if he'd finally been asked to join the big boys' club and didn't want to be noticed lest he be kicked out. He was hugely, innocently delighted.

"Maybe it wasn't a good idea for me to stay in Miami, but then again, I didn't have a lot of choices," Little Peter told us earnestly. "When I got off the bus, I'd never seen a place as poor and desperate as this. I'd never seen it get so bad that people were fighting over garbage cans. You should see the black section; it's called Overtown; it's just a collection of shacks and dirt and broken-down cars; it's the worst and dirtiest and most run-down I've ever seen anywhere."

Miami was awash in cocaine, he informed us; the same two bills that fetched a pencil eraser–sized chunk in Harlem, here purchased a sizzling block of brain food the size of a pigeon's egg. As I contemplated this, I began to see evidence of surfeit everywhere, in the sheen on the upper lip of the waitress who tended our table, in the reddened nostrils of the middle-aged woman at the bank who'd handed me cash earlier that day, in the rank hilarity of the off-duty staff at the tiki bar within sight of our table, who were belting back shots of tequila to calm their jangled nerves and breaking into spontaneous line dances.

Money was no longer a limiting factor to Little Peter's intake. With lunar patience, he waited to cash his SSI check to fund his monthly binge, which never lasted more than two or three days. But in Miami, where Bolivian powder was cheaper than jug wine, though it was, obviously, in a whole other category in terms of potency and addiction, the party never had to stop; in seaweed rat holes under the causeway, in the rusted hulks of DEA-confiscated freight vessels, in the dirt alleys of Overtown . . .

"I can't vouch for anything that will happen if I stay here," Little Peter said. "I'll take cocaine and die. The cop dogs will rip out my throat. I'll cut my neck on a rusty pipe. That can happen. Most likely, I'll just go crazy.

"I just talked to my mother for the first time in a long time. It was pretty good. She wasn't as condemnacious as other times. There are reasons in my head why I don't get in touch more. When I finally break through the wall, though, it's a relief.

"I told my mother that this whole idea of going into a program for people who use drugs keeps coming back to me. Though it's in some ways an unappealing idea—just a nagging notion that I should do it.

"There's this wall: people are going to be on one side of it or the other. I've been on the outside of it so long that the idea of being on the inside is extremely difficult to negotiate. I'm used to freely wheeling and dealing, of going where I want, when I want . . ."

Jim and I set our faces and got serious. As we drank lime-flavored beers under waving palm trees we talked over the situation like two men in a Graham Greene novel with a mission to accomplish. Little Peter had discovered a violent current running through the streets of Bayside and Overtown that had shaken him to the core: an enticement too powerful for human resistance; a Tyrannosaurus rex thrashing through the shacks with devouring jaws. He was ready for rehab—so he claimed—but where and when and how and what?

The question of what we were actually going to do with my stepbrother weighed heavily on us. Little Peter changed his mind every minute or so—would he go to Spring Lake Ranch in Vermont, where he'd been before? A drug program in Miami for the homeless run by the Salvation Army? Perhaps he'd return to Albuquerque? All of this I'd been through endlessly with my stepbrother in New York over the past weeks. His paralysis made me wonder whether he was truly a psychotic. Shouldn't he be more apathetic? But New York's dangers had been relatively benign compared to Miami's.

Little Peter turned suddenly and looked very intently into my face, until I unwillingly met his eyes, and then said, "You just do what you do, and you don't think about what you're going to do next—that's what I've decided. You do it and you don't look back."

We returned to the motel to sleep on our options. The following day, we woke up almost immediately gripped by waves of boredom and restlessness. Even Little Peter seemed to have caught this malaise. He sighed and looked out the window of the car as we drove from the motel. A resort town has only so many fruits to bear on its limbs, and this morning, as we drove along the highway to Miami Beach, we already had the dread feeling we'd done all this before.

Jim wanted to photograph Little Peter standing in line at the Camillus House, where he usually had a free meal at this time, but my stepbrother refused. Like a schoolboy, he was afraid his street friends would see him with us. Somebody had the inspired idea to revisit a remote but pleasurable pursuit in Little Peter's past . . . we took him windsurfing.

We motored out the Rickenbacker Causeway to a little beachside rental place about halfway to Key Biscayne. There, a pleasant and jocular Cuban with long hair, who called himself Obed, threatened us with dire consequences if we didn't bring his windsurf board back in one piece. Against Obed's advice, Little Peter coupled the smallest and most difficult board to the largest and most unwieldy sail. He couldn't attach the sail using his ruined hands, however, so I waded out into the surf to help him, gripping the board between my knees.

Once he'd pushed his board out into the waves, Little Peter seemed to have lost his touch. He stood up on the board, flopped over, stood again, tugged mightily on the sail cord, twisted, and fell over. Then with a terrifying effort, he pulled the sail upright against his chest and began to fly against the brisk breeze.

Standing with Obed under the palm trees, watching Little Peter struggle to keep the board upright, I asked for his assessment of Little Peter's windsurfing skills. He replied, "Confidentially? He stinks!"—a line I recognized, with a kind of crazy delight, as coming from an old Moss Hart play, *You Can't Take It with You.* Clouds drifted in, low and puffy, their loose skirts skimming the water. Soon the breeze turned rough, and a sprinkle of rain raked the slate-green water. Long thin rollers came in, one after another, like hand-rolled Cuban cigars. Nevertheless, a few hardy windsurfers continued to skip back and forth over the sound, resembling water bugs.

Little Peter took the board out a couple of hundred yards; there he floundered and collapsed. After a long struggle, he lay on the board and paddled with his hands to keep from drifting downwind. I began to change into my bathing suit in anticipation of having to borrow one of Obed's sea kayaks to rescue him. If Little Peter floated any farther, I saw, he'd be pulled under the causeway bridge, where he'd face dangerous tidal currents.

At last, by main force, my stepbrother wrestled the soaked triangular sail upright and induced the wind to push him to shore. The physical strain of holding the curved boom to his chest showed in his face. He jumped out of the surf, and stamped around the coral beach for several minutes, talking to himself. Then he called Obed over, exchanged his board for a bigger, more stable one, and pulled on a pair of rubber nonskid boots.

This time things went better for my stepbrother; in a trice he was out half a mile; he sliced back in a fast tack to shore, and cut away again. But his hands had lost the ability to grip; I saw that he hooked his right elbow over the boom pole in order to maneuver his board.

A few minutes later, Little Peter returned. He yanked the mast from the board, pain distorting his face. "I've never been this tired," he complained. "My hands are slipping off the pole!" He stood under a tree, arms tightly crossed, for the next ten minutes.

Soon, however, I saw gears begin to turn in his head, a new resolution forming. He walked stiffly to Obed's rack of sails and turned one over in his hand. He chose a new board, lifted it up, and sighted down its length. He went to where Obed leaned by his truck and they stood together talking for a minute or two. When Little Peter placed a triangular sail in the surf, I observed that it was one of the smaller ones. He slipped the new board up to it, and called me over to help him fasten the mast.

"I've had time to think now," he said.

He pushed back into the waves. The board and the man turned together. He reached the end of his tack, lugged the sail around, and set off. It wasn't beautiful, but it sufficed. After a few cuts he returned.

"It's coming back to me, I can feel it," he said. Something in his face showed that he'd gained something.

Nevertheless, as we drove back to Miami, we were pressed down in our seats by the enormous weight of the still unmade decision regarding Little Peter's future. Jim and I had tickets to fly back to New York the next day. I saw that Jim and I might simply have to drop Little Peter off in downtown Miami and drive away in our rented Neon, leaving him to the uncertain mercy of drug addicts and cops—but that eventuality was too horrible to contemplate. The radio waves were full of Dylan; his howling, bipolar, pre-1969 intonations echoed our miserable presentiments about being left in this derelict resort town: *"Awwww, how does it feel?"* he asked, *". . . How does it FEEL? . . . to be without a home . . . like a complete unknown . . . like a rolling stone?"*

We discovered that Dylan himself was performing that night in a small theater a few miles away. Only because I needed to indulge myself, to touch base with something familiar—both Jim and Little Peter were completely indifferent—we cruised by. Despite the radio's announcements that the concert had been sold out for weeks, I pushed through the line of Dylan hoboes camped outside a dirty door and from a web-encrusted window bought the last three remaining tickets at the least expensive level.

We were ushered upstairs, for reasons I couldn't explain, to the VIP section, where we found seats behind a black-painted bar that sold rum and Coke near the stage. I kept Little Peter supplied with cocktails to assuage his anxiety, afraid that the crowds of shouting Dylan fans were likely to set off major paranoiac alarms in his head and cause unpredictable actions (so might alcohol, however . . .). Every now and then, I snuck a peek in his direction, but Little Peter remained solidly deadpan throughout the show. With his arms crossed on the bar, his deeply weathered face, and bill hat, he gave a perfect imitation of a cruise captain taking his glum, end-of-the-day sundowner. He never cracked a smile, even when Dylan sang of cocaine "running all 'round" his brain:

> You take Mary, I'll take Sue,
> Ain't no difference twixt the two.

Only in the middle of the third encore, when Dylan was beating through an inspired version of "You Go Your Way and I'll Go Mine," did Little Peter turn to me. A sad and hopeful grin split his face from ear to ear, and he asked, "Do we have time to go windsurfing again before you leave?"

That night I called Hali. Eventually it came out that, yes, we'd just been to a Bob Dylan concert.

"Well, you boys have been having a lot of fun down there in Florida, haven't you," she scolded, with a bitterness that surprised me. "Can you tell me what *else* you've been doing?" I realized I had brought myself a long way away from my wife and two babies, without a very convincing reason. If I got back on that plane tomorrow, however, leaving Little Peter in Miami, what would I have accomplished, beyond having given Jim the opportunity to take a few pictures, feeding my stepbrother a couple of nourishing meals, and getting him up on a windsurf board again? The possibility of complete ignominy swept over me like a dark weather front.

"Listen," I said, "I don't know what's going on with Little Peter. I never do. But we're going to figure something out."

"Will you try to remember to bring back something for the kids?" Hali said. "Try?"

The next morning arrived, despite a number of persuasive indications that it wouldn't. An agent from Tower Air called at eight to say they'd canceled my return flight—their only flight to New York that day. Shortly afterward Little Peter knocked on our door, to announce that the pressure of our impending departure had wrought on him, of all things, a decision. He was willing to go into rehab right away.

I reached for the telephone. My first call was to Spring Lake Ranch, where Pam Groves, the admissions director, held out the slim possibility of accepting my stepbrother back *only* after he'd completed some kind of bona fide drug rehabilitation program.

I got busy with a copy of the Yellow Pages. Before long, I'd found a hot-line and a list of names of what are called "dual diagnosis" centers—places that cater to schizophrenics with drug problems. Soon, I narrowed our choices down to a single one, a private rehab facility by the Miami River called Windmoor Healthcare. By chance, it was near the airport, so we piled into our car, conveniently forgetting Little Peter's foul-smelling back-pack and coat, and with a few twists and turns and a little more body En-glish (Jim was still driving) we rolled into the driveway.

Ahead I saw a low, boxy, decrepitating sixties-era hospital block whose walls had been painted ripe cantaloupe. Because it backed onto the river, its surroundings were incredibly lush, and somewhat romantically molder-ing. A huge banyan towered from an island in the center of the parking lot, but on closer inspection, the tree turned out to be stone-cold dead. I walked Little Peter up to the front door, lost in detective novel fantasies of icy marble corridors; an evil, bearded doctor dispensing drugs to all that desired them; strong, obedient orderlies; screams muffled by blankets; and a deep and abiding corruption lying between whitewashed walls.

But things did not turn out to be so dramatic, or interesting, as usual. We were asked to sit in a waiting room whose door was labeled ELOPEMENT PRECAUTION. When I tried the door, I found it was locked from the outside. Within moments of our entry, Little Peter went completely passive—he simply sat in his chair with his fists under his chin, and did whatever was asked of him.

A young, crew-cut Cuban-American named Manny came through the door holding a clipboard. His eyes widened. I could see wheels turning inside his head. Which one of us was the client? Jim and I had taken on much of the outward appearance of my stepbrother in the past three days. Jim's face and limbs were sunburned and peeling, his normally tall and rangy frame was stooped from carrying his heavy camera case, and he'd picked up a virus somewhere, along with chills and stomach troubles. As he stood in the middle of the room waiting for someone—anyone—to make a final decision, his eyes fluttered dangerously. As for myself, the minute-to-minute strain of catering to the moods of a thirteen-year-old trapped in the body of a thirty-year-old had rendered me unable to concentrate or speak coherently. All of three of us, to some degree, had started to ramble.

Manny quickly sorted things out, and got through the intake paperwork. Then Little Peter was led into a private office, where Caron Helfner, a competent, no-nonsense psychologist, interviewed him. After that, Manny and Caron called Jim and myself into the empty office of the director for a money conference. Little Peter was long out of insurance, so we'd have to cut a deal. Caron started with an opening bid of five hundred dollars a day for a thirty-day stay—fifteen thousand in all. She and I batted that idea around for a while until eventually we came up with what I considered to be a more reasonable plan: three hundred and fifty per day, plus fifty dollars a day for the doctor, and a ten-day sojourn—a total of four thousand dollars. Little Peter would have a chance to dry out, get back on meds, and straighten out his disability payments, and Manny and Caron dangled before us the future prospect of housing, job placement, and a raft of other post-stay benefits. I told them, "You've got a deal."

The drawback was that Windmoor wanted the whole payment in cash. When I offered two thousand now and the rest later, I got cold fish eyes. So, Jim and I headed out to the rental car, and I began to make calls. First I secured a promise from Olivia to pay me back from Little Peter's rapidly draining "education" fund. This she readily agreed to. Then I started dialing local banks. I don't want to bore the reader with the complexities of how one comes up with four thousand dollars in cash in Miami, especially when one is from out of town, knows nobody, and is wearing spotted camping shorts, dirty Teva sandals, a soiled Hawaiian shirt, a bent visor hat that reads NANTUCKET FILM FESTIVAL (an event I've never been to), and a three-day stubble. Suffice it to say that most bank employees assumed that I was rounding up cash for an unexpectedly plum drug deal, and were not unsympathetic. The money could be raised, I found out. It just took a little persistence and a cellular telephone.

We returned three hours later and found Little Peter in exactly the position we'd left him in on the sofa behind the "Elopement Precaution" door. His fists were firmly knotted up under his chin. An institutional torpor had settled over him. His eyes were glazed, I noticed—perhaps they had already started to give him medication.

"Well, Peter," I said, taking a seat. "You never know what life is going to throw at you. Last night you're at a Dylan concert; today you're in a mental ward."

He let a half minute go by before replying:

"Ironic, isn't it?"

Part Eight

There is only one question: When will I be blown up?

—William Faulkner

Chapter Twenty-eight

After Little Peter graduated from the Windmoor psychiatric facility, he flew to Spring Lake Ranch, that old, familiar work farm in Vermont he'd attended as a teenager (this was all paid for with the last dregs of money left for Little Peter in Olivia's divorce settlement with my father). But Little Peter's demons followed him wherever he went, it seemed. He chafed under the work program, hated the food, developed a serious crush on one of the secretaries, and despised the therapy. After two weeks he freaked out in a movie theater during the film *Armageddon,* and evaporated. A few days later, he called me from a pay phone outside of Albuquerque. He'd just talked to his mother and was, predictably, in despair. He brought up suicide, but at that point, I couldn't make myself care.

The one thing I'd prided myself on all along was being the person in our family who looked at my stepbrother realistically. (It helped that I was also the only one who wasn't completely burned out on him.) I wasn't looking for Little Peter to pick up his violin and head on to Oberlin College to resume his concert career one-handed. I wasn't expecting him to start picking up a phone and selling bond futures like half his old friends from Dalton and Choate probably were. But I *had* expected out of all the effort and money that had gone into Miami that *something* would have turned up. That's where my father and stepmother were way ahead of me. From then on I vowed to take Little Peter on an ad hoc basis, situation by situation. He'd done a great job, in my opinion, of adapting himself to the homeless lifestyle. As he told me once, with a kind of pride, "My life got so much better after I learned to live without money." From now on, I was going to stay out of his way and let him do what he did best.

Just to turn up the heat on that resolution, the next I heard he was in the Denver County lockup awaiting transportation to Leadville on an outstanding warrant. Typically, during the arrest he'd also lost his wallet, including his bank card and driver's license.

I wasn't actually that worried. Little Peter had ended up in the tank quite often during his travels, for reasons that were generally unfair, but not always. For example, once he was picked up in a snowbank near Ketchum, Idaho, after getting drunk and breaking into the home of the rock musician Steve Miller to steal a pair of moccasins. When the cops searched his pack, they found the picture ID of a woman believed to be a victim of a serial killer who for the past few years had been picking up prostitutes in Kansas City, cutting them up, and strewing their limbs along the banks of the Missouri River. Despite my stepbrother's protest that he'd only shared a jug with her in a parking lot and found her wallet on the ground, the prosecutor was sure she had a live one and set his bail for $500,000.

Little Peter's defense was weak, but I didn't think he had what it took to be a mass murderer. I'd known two serial killers in my life and my stepbrother wasn't much like either of them. There was John Rice, a pimply guy I'd shared a biology bench with in high school. He was a slow-simmering resentful guy. He'd woken up early one morning and snapped, killed his brother with an ax, knifed and hacked his mother, bludgeoned his grandmother with a hammer, and strangled his sister with a tie. He'd awakened somewhere in Oklahoma a few days later in his station wagon with a completely wiped memory. Then there was Bob Berdella, whom I'd gone to college with and who ran a bead and trinket store in Kansas City where my wife used to buy ankle bracelets and dangly earrings. She had befriended him and even given him a ride home now and then. Luckily Bob wasn't interested in girls. He'd formed the habit of cruising Cherry Street for male drifters, whom he'd take back to his bungalow, tie to a steel bed, drug, sodomize, and dismember, in basically that order, then put their parts out in green plastic bags for the city to pick up. Bob was more the steely methodical type. But as I said, my stepbrother didn't resemble either of these guys. The person he was most likely to kill, in my opinion, was himself, and even that seemed to be taking an awfully long time. Soon Olivia was able to pull out years of phone and bank card statements that proved he couldn't have been in Kansas City *all* of those times.

So Little Peter's bail had been lowered overnight from half a million to seventy-five hundred and eventually he was sprung. Before he left jail, I asked him one question.

"The last time you saw that woman in Kansas City?"

"What are you talking about?"

"She was alive, wasn't she?"

"Of course! What do you think?"

After Little Peter had been arrested a few times, it'd reached the level of a routine for me. I'd get on the phone, then gamely start dialing the sheriff at the jail desk, who'd be more or less accommodating; the public defender, who would be to a greater or lesser extent useless; a local bail bondsman, whose advice was usually invaluable; and the judge, who'd be sympathetic or (sometimes) not. But even though I learned I could often pry my stepbrother loose from corrective custody with time and patience, I wasn't sure this time it was the right thing to do.

In truth, I was still licking my wounds in the aftermath of Miami. I realized I had come to some conclusions fairly soon about how much anyone could really "do" for my stepbrother. The honest answer was, very possibly, nothing at all.

I'd promised to call Olivia to see about paying his fine and getting him out. But when Olivia came to the phone, she just gloated.

"I *love* it when Little Peter lands in jail!" she told me. "This is the only way he ever ends up in therapy. He gets regular meals and sleeps inside. I'm not going to pay the fine. Let him sit there until he agrees to go back to Spring Lake Ranch."

"You want me to tell him that?" I asked, unbelieving.

"No, don't tell him that. Let him figure it out for himself. He's a smart boy."

The telephone rang that night, just as Hali and I had put the kids to sleep, finished cleaning up the kitchen and washing the dishes, fallen into bed, and dropped a rented video into the VCR, hoping to watch a movie for the first time in what seemed like a century.

"Am I catching you at a bad time?" Jim asked me.

"That's okay," I told him.

It turned out that Jim was delirious from being in the darkroom all day printing up the photographs he'd taken in Florida. His talk grew so wild and garbled that eventually I rolled out of bed, grabbed a sheaf of loose paper, and started to take notes.

"Peter is the Big Enchilada!" he enthused. "It's prophetic, don't you see? In a lot of ways, Little Peter *is* the all-American boy!"

"What the hell are you talking about?" I asked.

"That photograph I took of him in the Miami Beach restaurant, hoovering up the enchilada?" Jim asked. "Behind his head is like a map of the universe. The horizon line is *right* behind his head. It's like one of those photo-realistic star maps you see in *Scientific American* of the universe. The whole thing wrapped up in a soft corn tortilla!"

"Jesus, man!"

"I don't know how you say it in New York, but this is what we say out West when we mean 'the whole damn thing.' You know. Everything! Everything there is! The Whole Enchilada!"

I called a short time-out to fill Jim in on new developments with my stepbrother.

On hearing this, Jim laughed.

"That just means we have to drive out there to catch him getting out of prison," he said. "Can you imagine it? The Rockies in the background, the county lockup, which is probably some depressing pile of concrete blocks, full of stringy deadbeat prisoners, the tourists from Iowa looking on. Can't you see? It's perfect!"

"Perfect for what?"

"Listen, Peter, I've been printing for ten hours and I feel like we're getting back to the relationship between you and your stepbrother, but getting deeper. I mean, put it this way: he's a burden to you, but there's the desire that you have to help him, so that he's going to get better. I mean, the interesting thing is that he is this person who is, without any reservations, pursuing the two basic things that everyone else in our society has given up long ago—i.e., the pleasures of getting high and the bare necessities of survival. So you as his brother experience him as a hero, a person who has no inhibitions about doing what he wants, dropping out of society, not caring a whit about social norms, and so on. Get it?"

"Huh? Maybe."

"There is definitely a two-way relationship. That's what I'm getting at. It's pretty interesting. It's pretty *damn* interesting. This enchilada thing has a lot of seriously great metaphors in it."

"Okay, Jim," I said, when he'd wound down a bit. "I'll be up for a while. Let me know if you have any more flashes of insight."

Little Peter called me the next day, incensed that his mother had refused to pay his fine. He begged me to buy his freedom myself.

"This is very little money . . . you can afford it! Oh come on, man, this is my life!" he cried. "Do you understand what it's like to be inside like this? They brought an Indian guy in my cell for public urination and he smells like he hasn't taken a bath for months. I can't think straight!"

I asked if he'd be willing to go back to Vermont, as Olivia was demanding.

"Listen," he said. "Better send the money sooner than later. It will save me a lot of pain and humiliation. It's going to get worse in here soon, and I don't want to go through it."

"How do you know it's going to get worse?" I asked.

"It always does."

I was tempted to just pay up and get this thing over with, even though I'd promised Olivia I wouldn't. For the time being, though, I wavered. Since Olivia had been paying the bills, I figured she had the right to call the shots. I decided to stall the situation and see what shook out.

I called the Denver County Jail and got a woman behind a desk to agree that she *probably* had my stepbrother in custody, but would tell me little else. Than I called the Leadville lockup, whose number I had in my notes from the year before, when Little Peter had been imprisoned for breaking down a tavern door (in truth a bunch of drunken locals had used his head as a battering ram). The woman there placed her hand over the receiver and came back to say I could wire the money via Western Union, since there was a Safeway in town. "Just send five hundred sixty-seven dollars to the 'Leadville Municipal Court,'" she told me. This seemed wildly improbable.

That night I talked the whole thing over with Hali, including the idea of my driving out to Denver with Jim to free my stepbrother. She was getting ready to travel to Albany the next day to give a speech on family violence in the Asian community and was scheduled to leave at 5:00 A.M. The kids had taken a long time to go to sleep, and so we were left, as usual, cleaning up the dinner mess at about 11:00 P.M.

Hali insisted that I absolutely should *not* pay Little Peter's fine. "It's important to make boundaries, and that this should be one of them," she said. I agreed. If anyone should bail my stepbrother out it should be Olivia, or possibly my father. But I hadn't asked my father about it. I didn't want to bring him anywhere near this harebrained and morally ambiguous situation—yet.

Little Peter called the afternoon of his court appearance.

"How'd it go?" I asked.

"The judge said he won't let me out until I pay."

"That seems a little unfair. How are you supposed to raise the money if you are in jail?"

"The judge said he hasn't seen one person yet who'd stayed there forever."

"Funny."

"Look, if you can take care of this for me, I can pay you back a little each month."

I told him I wasn't going to send him anything.

"Why not? You've got pots of money. Just send it to the county sheriff. You can use Western Union."

"Look, Peter, it's time for you to get out of jail. I *know* that," I said. "I'm working on a deal with Olivia."

"Why are you talking to *her*? She just wants me to do something I don't want to do. I don't want to go into a program. Just send me the money. *Send it!* If you tell me it's going to be another week, it might as well be forever!"

Finally I saw red. "Look, Peter, I'm trying to get you out of jail. If you don't like the way I'm doing it, you can call someone else!"

Little Peter called again on Friday, bitter and sarcastic, saying, "You know how to buy a money order, don't you? You just go to the store, give them the money, slip it in an envelope, and send it to me."

Then on Saturday the family and I drove out for a stay with my father at his condo in Sea Bright, New Jersey—an episode that wound down to a typically prickly and boozy ending.

Dad greeted us by the pool in his black bathing suit, his skin a welter of red spots and encrustations. His stomach, unbound, looked like something hanging off a prehistoric lizard. The day began with a blazing sun, a hundred-degree heat, and sopping humidity, and finally broke down into rain and electrical thunderstorms that exploded over our heads like unfriendly fire. We spent the remainder of a restless and crabby afternoon stuck inside the condo with Liz and Dad and the kids.

By 10:00 P.M. I found myself half drunk and sweating in the kitchen, having first absorbed three combat-grade gin and tonics and as many glasses of wine. Foolishly I picked that moment to present Little Peter's predicament to my scoffing and equally boozed father.

Dad was wearing his seersucker jacket and a faded madras shirt. His face sometimes took on the expressive simian characteristics of a seasoned Hollywood actor. If in my childhood I'd once seen him as a worldly and skeptical Humphrey Bogart, he'd now, I thought, successfully morphed into a boisterous, clowning Anthony Quinn—the foolish, even faintly ridiculous, aging woman killer of *Zorba the Greek* and *The Secret of Santa Vittoria*. Whenever my father drank in a restaurant these days, if a few bars of music should happen to waft in to him from somewhere, he'd pick up the nearest woman—Liz, my sister, a waitress, whomever—and whirl her around in a staggering dance. The subtext was that he might have taken on an encyclopedia of human frailties, but whatever fool he had turned into, he was still possessed of the kind of earthy wisdom that was forever unavailable in books, and an unwavering zest for life as it was truly lived.

Even as Zorba, my father had no sympathy for my stepbrother—or me for that matter—and thought jail was too good a place for him. "Little Peter's the kind of guy that when you do something for him, he kicks you in the face," Dad steamed. "Then you wonder *why* you did anything for him. He's just like my brother Ulrich, a first-class pain in the ass and a moocher."

I did my best to sit back and listen to my father's mumbled harangue. The mere mention of Ulrich's name was likely to twist my father's guts into paroxysms of frustration and rage. I had always tried to defend my

234 | Peter von Ziegesar

uncle's rakish ways against my father's disparagement, though. A tall, handsome, cadaverous man who spoke with a booming stage-worthy basso profundo, my uncle, who lived in Hollywood, a decrepit and faintly bohemian beach town north of Miami, was spending much of his time driving from place to place in his old Chevy, visiting a string of tottering "lady friends." Some people are born spendthrift grasshoppers, I argued, and others are born industrious ants. There's nothing you can do to make one into the other. But grasshoppers have a role in this world, too. Our planet would be nowhere near as interesting a place without grasshoppers.

After three hours of fending off waves of negativity, I joined my wife in bed and fell instantly into a deep and toxic coma. I woke up at about 5:00 A.M. to find that my son had somehow crawled under the futon and was whimpering to get out. I struggled up, pulled Alden out from under the bed, gave him a hug, set him down in front of the TV, and put on one of his animated dinosaur tapes (*Land Before Time*). Then I staggered to the toilet and threw up a half pint of gin-scented battery acid.

Back home there were eight messages on the machine from Little Peter. Each started out with the same robotic voice saying, "*Hello! This is a collect call from . . .* (his real voice:) "*Peter!*" . . . *To accept this call, dial one or hold on. To refuse, press zero. Thank you for using Ameritel . . .*" Then I'd hear, for a moment, his scratchy voice questioning, "Hello? Hello?"—behind which would be recorded the hollow sound of prison inmates arguing over the television in the rec room.

The telephone rang every fifteen minutes. Each time I picked it up, and the recorded voice began, "Hello! This is a collect call from . . ." I'd hang up, and a few minutes later the phone would ring again. I went out for lunch and there were ten more messages waiting for me when I got back. I was beginning to see my stepbrother as a diabolical force, the epitome of a jailbird harasser.

I let fifteen more calls go by unanswered, telling myself I was sick of trying to play God to my stepbrother, who, I was convinced now, was in reality just a hardened criminal. When Hali came home, she said I should probably talk to him, though. "He might actually have something to say."

I picked up the next call.

Little Peter said: "Good, finally you're back. I just want to apologize for sounding angry before."

"That's all right, I'm sorry that I got angry, too."

"I called up my mother and told her that I'll go to Spring Lake. She's going to call them tonight to find out if they'll take me."

"Good."

"The only thing is, I don't really want to go. I don't even see why they'd want me. I don't want to end up living in Rutland, Vermont, in some apartment with a job. That's where it's all heading toward there."

"Nobody thinks that a guy like you, with your kind of brains and the experiences you've had, is going to be happy in Rutland, Vermont."

"Well *they* do. If I can get myself out with my bank card, will you help me?"

"If I did, I'd never be able to talk to Olivia again without lying."

"She wouldn't have to know."

I changed the subject. "Jim is on his way to Colorado to see you."

"You're kidding me. Where is he now?"

"I'm not sure, but he'll call me from on the road tonight or tomorrow and I'll let you know."

"He'll have some money on him, won't he?"

"I'm sure he'll have some money."

"We're about to get cut off," Little Peter went on. "I just wanted to say that I am really sorry for making you mad before."

"I feel bad about that, too. Call me any time."

I also had a message that Olivia had called . . . I got through to her at about 10:00 P.M. "I sent Peter his bank card today so he could pay his own fine," Olivia said. "But he doesn't realize the sheriff won't let him use the card. They'll get the letter, realize there's something shiny and hard inside, and take the card away from him."

"Are you sure?"

"Of course I'm sure."

Meanwhile, Jim was driving toward Colorado at seventy miles per hour, having started Sunday night. I reached his cell phone in Youngstown, Ohio, and described my conversation with Olivia.

"Little Peter's probably going to be letting himself out," I said. "This was completely unforeseen, that Olivia would send his bank card. I can't understand why she would undercut herself like this. It makes no sense, since she wants him to go into therapy."

This new twist had left Jim in a bad position, I thought, with the likelihood that Little Peter would have vaporized by the time he got there. But Jim philosophically decided to stay on plan.

"Hey, I'm going out to the part of the country I love the best. I'm just going to keep on driving until I get to Denver."

"You're a good man, Jim."

"You're a good man, too, Peter."

"I don't feel like one. I feel like a louse."

When I next called Jim to see how he was doing, he was tootling down a little two-lane blacktop called Route 86 in the flatlands of Colorado about sixty miles outside of Denver. Life was good. The sun was peeping in and out of little puff clouds, he was doing about eighty-five miles an hour with some light jazz on the radio, and there were no cops in sight.

"I'm trying to avoid the interstate because I'm sick of it," he told me. He'd spent the night in Limon, Colorado, a mile down the road from a cattle feed lot, so he'd had to breathe the foul odors of urine and fecal matter all night. "I don't know where they get off charging me seventy-two bucks for *that*," he said.

I'd had a dreadful premonition the night before that Little Peter might try something violent with Jim . . . try to steal his money or his cameras. I hoped not. Little Peter told me he'd never stolen anything, and I believed him. Still, I remembered what happened to Olivia when she'd tussled with him over money. Little Peter had swung at her forehead with a piece of firewood.

"Little Peter isn't normally a violent guy," I warned, "but be careful. He has been pretty aggressive in the past."

"What do you think might provoke him?"

"Alcohol and money. In that order. Sometimes both at once. Look," I said. "When he pays his fine, he'll be flat broke. What he really wants is to go into Denver after his dry spell in jail and have two or three hundred dollars to spend on partying."

"I can give him a ride into Denver, but I'd really like to go up into the mountains for a day or two and enjoy nature. Maybe he'll bite for that."

"Just don't give him anything more than a small handout," I warned. "Twenty dollars, max."

That night Hali and I allowed ourselves the luxury of going to the movies. Afterward, as we strolled down Second Avenue in the East Village, everything we said to each other sounded like a line from David Mamet, and so, we were giggling . . .

I felt my cell phone buzz and it was Jim. The connection was crackly. He was in his car driving through the mountains above Leadville, taking pictures. I pictured him spinning under granite cliffs in the chilled darkness of a Colorado evening.

He said the altitude was bothering him. His head ached and his stomach was acting up. This is the way it is with Jim. Whenever he gets into a new place the first thing that goes is his stomach, then any sense of contact with reality. It all goes out the window. Somehow the work gets done, and it's always excellent.

"I dreamed about money last night, after what you said about Peter," said Jim.

"As humans we must dream," I replied.

"And when we dream, we dream of money," Hali finished—a line from *The Spanish Prisoner*. We both burst out laughing.

"What's that?" asked Jim.

"Nothing. Let me give you the number of Little Peter's jail," I said.

"Hold on," Jim said. "I don't think I have a pen with me."

I heard him swearing and tugging at his pants pockets and his shirt, then rifling through the glove box. I imagined the car drifting slowly across the shoulder of the road and then a dizzying drop.

The line was quiet for a long time. Finally I let it go.

"It's the blind leading the lame," said Hali, as we went into a restaurant.

The next morning, Jim called again, but he didn't sound at all right. "I'm in front of the courthouse now," he croaked. "I talked to Peter . . . they passed the phone in to him. He hasn't gotten his bank card yet. Hold on . . . I think this oxygen deprivation is doing something to me."

I waited a minute, listening to him gasp.

"I've been sick for the past two days," he confessed. "The food goes right through me. I have a room for tonight, but after that I don't know if I'm going to be able to stay around here."

I felt the pit of my stomach drop. "Jim, did you get your health insurance straightened out?"

"Right now I don't have health insurance," he replied calmly.

"Well, Jim, that scares me," I scolded. "Who do you think is going to have to pay for you if you get sick? Me, that's who! I couldn't just let you lie there in some welfare hospital with the rats and cockroaches crawling over you. Could I?"

But Jim had stopped listening. "Hmm, a drive with Little Peter up over the mountains and into some high country might be pretty interesting, from the photographic point of view. Pretty *damn* interesting!" he mused. "What do you think about the idea of the two of us springing him tomorrow, even if his bank card doesn't come?"

"I don't like it!"

But Jim still wasn't listening. "Hmmm," he said. "Maybe he'll say something, too. Maybe I'll write it down . . ."

Chapter Twenty-nine

The World Trade Center towers exploded into fire and dust on the first day of our son's kindergarten in the Village. I left the classroom and went outside onto Washington Street and stood with a group of Tunisian nuns to watch the black smoke billow from the North Tower. When the second jet hit, it came from the south. A brilliant burst of yellow flame billowed out, a boiler explosion, I thought, a propane tank in the building. There was a collective cry of ineffectuality and pain from the crowd around me like when a car slips its brakes and starts rolling down the hill toward a child.

We milled around in the street, not knowing what to do, so I went up to Horatio Street to check on Hali and Maya, who were helping to clean out Maya's preschool classroom.

They were fine. As I walked back to Alden's school, I became the victim of a strange optical illusion. From that angle, from that particular spot on the sidewalk, the two World Trade buildings had lined up, so that it looked as though there were only one. Black smoke still poured from the north building; the flames, instead of burning out, if anything had grown brighter and fiercer. I returned to pick up Alden in his classroom. Without being told, all of the other parents had returned as well.

For weeks the children drew pictures of the towers, somehow getting them exactly right in details they could not have noticed, though there were no models to copy from anymore. The image of catastrophe must have flown from kid to kid in their elementary school with the swiftness of thought: the antenna spike on the North Tower, the striations of the windows. *No Jumping*, Alden scribbled below these pictures, penciling his first written words: *N-Jmpg fr wInDws*.

The day after 9/11 the sun burned incredibly bright. As we walked down the river, flowing with the crowd, Alden regaled me with theories about the men on the planes. It was the cops in the second jet. They were chasing the bad guys. The bad guys took a wrong turn and crashed. The bad guys were not bad guys. There was only one bad guy. He made the others go bad. And so on, he went.

There was a notorious tavern in the neighborhood of the school, called One Potato, a two-story building housing a cabaret that featured the most base of entertainments, lip synchers, cross-dressers, and pole-dancers. The roughest and oddest sort of men in wigs and gowns were pictured on the billboard out front. We had to pass this place every day in order to go to the church in which his school had us dropping off and picking up. One morning Alden stooped down to pick up a flyer from the ground. It was a flyer from One Potato.

"That's them!" Alden told me fiercely.

"Who?"

"The bad guys. The World Trade bombers! I know where they are now!"

He dragged me over to the squat brick building on the corner. Yes, it was true. The men on the flyer were the same ones depicted on the decrepit marquee out front.

"See! That's him! That's him!"

I looked. The guy on the top, the frowsy wig, the sharply cut cheekbones from too many poppers and too much ex, the stubble, the faraway Riker's Island stare. Yes, I could see the resemblance . . .

"Bin Laden!"

Yes, bin Laden and all his gang, right there on the billboard. I don't know how we'd overlooked it for so long. And it was all I could do to drag my son away, so great was his conviction. Alden wanted to storm the citadel forthwith, find the bad guys, and lock them up. Singlehandedly, my son, taking on a cadre of seasoned al-Qaeda operatives and meth-sniffing transsexuals. Saving the country and setting things right. So of course what I did was try to head him off in some way, easily.

"Yes, of course, we'll get them, but first, don't you remember, we have to check you in with your teacher? She doesn't like it when we are late. We'll get the bad guys later. I've got the flyer right here; look, I'll fold it up and keep it in my pocket. Plenty of time to save the world after school." Thus we subvert our children, day by day, and lead them from their natural path of war and bravery.

Every night just before Alden went to sleep, I would hear him mumble, "I don't want to have any dreams. I don't want to have any dreams. And I don't want to *think* about it." This last came from the year before when he had also been afraid of having dreams and Hali had hit on the idea of telling him, "If you *think* about it, you can tell yourself not to dream."

I never found out what happened in those dreams. They weren't things that could translate themselves easily into words, apparently. In them, did bodies drop from the windows of tall steely towers? No, I don't think so. What I think he confronted endlessly were the brick walls of the maze we were busily constructing around him. As contradictions and ironies of his life gradually closed in on my son, his dreams may have turned to raw fear: of becoming civilized, of the monsters of rationality and polite behavior lurking nearby, the claustrophobia of obeying rules. As I say, I never found out.

Alden was a kid, I found, who hated contradiction of any kind. In this he took after me, I have to confess. It both pained and humored me to see the thoughts flicker so nakedly across his face. Like when he learned at school that Martin Luther King had resisted the police and been put in jail for it. The paradox that police were virtuous and principled sometimes (as we'd taught him) and unscrupulous and sinful other times was impossible to solve. "The police are good," he said, carefully choosing his words, "but sometimes they're bad. But the police have guns, and I like guns. But the bad guys have guns, too. And I like bad guys."

Watching him work his way through this moral issue made my heart alternately spring up to my throat and drop down to my feet, which pretty much describes my everyday relationship with him. But the next day Alden was cheerfully singing a new song as we walked hand-in-hand to school.

> Bad is good, good is bad!
> Bad is good, good is bad!

Of course I was helpless in terms of discipline and rules; there was no point in even discussing it. It didn't help that my son and I were joined at the kidneys by a pair of barbed fishhooks and an invisible length of line, so that anything that hurt him hurt me twice as badly. I understood that children shouldn't run out into the street, or eat small metal objects found on the ground, otherwise I was completely lost. Fortunately, to Hali the instruction manual, though written on air, was a complete and detailed document, full of precedents, interpretations, and exceptions, all as fixed and permanent as the orbits of the planets.

As I watched my son's uncompromising mind develop, I lived in constant awe. He was always finding new uses for words, stretching them, making them fit. For example, his word for "a lot" was "never-run-out-of," as in, "For my Christmas list, I want never-run-out-of tinfoil." Tinfoil being a substance that he had landed on for I'm not sure what reasons as a being of immense value. Alden's guns always contained never-run-out-of bullets, and his Batman's wallet always contained never-run-out-of money. Just how much money *was* never-run-out-of money was a question I put to him one day. His answer was he didn't know, since it would take never-run-out-of days to count it.

At times he scared the shit out of me, though. "Dad, sometimes when I'm crossing the street, I see myself walking like another person."

"Where are you, are you floating up above?"

"I see myself, Dad. I see myself down there. And at night, I don't sleep at all. I'm never asleep. I'm awake all night."

"But when I get you in the morning, you are asleep, aren't you? You look asleep."

"No, Dad, I'm awake. I'm always awake."

Hali of course twigged right away that the person I was fretting so much about was not really my son, but myself. Alden was an entirely separate entity composed of our two gene sets put in the blender and switched on *frappé*. He was growing up sturdy and strong like a bright green pepper plant in a pot. No, it wasn't Alden I really worried about, but cold, lonely me, ignored, left in the car in the parking lot, hungry, starving, uncared for, uncared *about*, sent away to a clammy New Hampshire boarding school when I was too young to fend for myself, staggering along stony pathways of some remote mountain.

"You've got to separate yourself from him," she urged. "First of all he's not you. And second of all, he's *all right!* And third of all, this is not about you! Do you understand? He's fine! We are *good* parents!"

But I could barely hear her, I was too busy grinding up the food from our meal in the baby grinder so I could feed it to him mouthful by mouthful, like a tiny fledgling bird. *Grind, grind! Grind, grind!* If that were true, why was I having so much trouble getting a breath in? *Grind, grind! Grind, grind!*

Part Nine

Visions! omens! hallucinations! miracles! ecstasies!
gone down the American river!
Dreams! adorations! illuminations! religions! the whole
boatload of sensitive bullshit!

—Allen Ginsberg

Chapter Thirty

For my mother, Peacock Point held a particular brightness and excitement in the years before the war that it never regained later. The best thing then was the game of Hare and Hounds. The game was hard and wild and ranged over the whole estate, and even into the surrounding estates, and probably only could have happened during the time it did, in those few years. The war itself pried apart the boards of whatever remained of the old esprit at Peacock Point and was a demarcation point for what came afterward, the particular dreamlike sense of being frozen in place, of being unable to move one's feet or arms or move away.

Hare and Hounds was the great blending of everyone, my mother recalled, the only time when the generations collaborated except, perhaps, when young and old stood in the drive in front of the Big House at Christmastime waiting for Santa Claus to pop his head out of the false chimney. The game had been extremely popular in Victorian England, so it was easy to imagine that it satisfied something in Peacock Point's deeply Anglophile nature to re-create that pastime.

At the time, she and her sister Allie led an unruly and almost completely autonomous gang of tomboys who roved the grounds in jeans, zippered leather jackets, and shoes with red rubber soles. The look was relaxed and depression-chic and very Amelia Earhart, whose flight across the Atlantic had thrilled them. For kicks, they shimmied out on branches and chinned themselves far off the ground, their legs swinging. Their ferocious games of Kick the Can lasted for hours on the hot pavement, along the many bays of the garage.

Allie was the oldest and adored by everyone and was therefore their uncontested leader. Both she and my mother were tall, leggy, athletic girls, who grew taller and leggier with every passing year.

The other two main gang members were their first cousins, Diane and Cynthia, who were the adopted daughters of Alice and Di Gates. Diane was a match for my mother and her sister in looks and spunk; she was sporty and lean and if anything blonder than they were. She was an intelligent girl, but a pace or two removed from reality. She could talk for hours about events that had never happened and on subjects with which she had little familiarity.

A story is told about Diane, that, for a year or two, after her parents had moved to Washington so that Di could become Assistant Secretary of the Navy for Air, she went to live in the Big House with my great-grandmother Goggie. It so happened that a distant cousin named Nito moved into the Big House from France at the same time, so that he could continue his studies at Columbia. Diane soon developed a fixed idea that her French cousin should notice her. To this end she began to feign sleepwalking through the hallways in the early morning hours, babbling in a loud, hollow voice. She would drift into Nito's bedroom, strike a pose with one hand on her forehead, then after delivering a soliloquy worthy of Lady Macbeth, fall into the astonished Nito's arms. (This bizarre tactic actually worked: the two later married and produced seven children.)

Wandering thus in the halls one night, Diane happened to run into Grace Mann, my great-grandmother's secretary, a confirmed insomniac. Being English, Miss Mann was fascinated with the Other World, a place that she would shortly explore in person. Sure that Diane was receiving messages from the Great Beyond, Miss Mann pulled out her notebook and began taking down the girl's wild speech in shorthand. This only caused Diane to redouble and then triple her verbiage. As the nights wore on, Miss Mann filled notebook after notebook, until the stack took on the heft of one of Mark Twain's posthumous novels. But it was all a fraud, a spinning out of a loosely-tethered adolescent mind, and Miss Mann eventually spun betrayed and weeping to her room.

Cynthia, Diane's sister, was delicate as a wood nymph, with pale skin and dark, coiled hair, a sweet girl whose conversation unfortunately tended to run in circles. When I was young, I thought her the smartest of my mother's cousins, because she didn't bray on about silly things as most of the others did, but stayed put and made short pithy observations in a breathless voice. It had been easy then to mistake simplicity for common sense.

My mother's girl gang only grew fiercer and more independent after the two oldest cousins, Danny and Cottie, who were large, sporty, and *very* serious, went off to Groton, imitating the English manner of starting boarding school at the age of eleven or twelve. At Groton they would hang their clothes on wooden pegs, sleep in open stalls, and imbibe great gulps of "Muscular Christianity" along with their cold-water showers. These were the traditions passed on by the famed rector of Groton, Endicott Peabody— who also lent his genetic material to the boys, being their maternal grandfather. My mother's cousin Danny especially resembled the fierce old master, with his smallish head, flat forehead, narrow sad-dog eyes, and the apologetic set of his lips.

They were quickly replaced in her rowdy tomboy pack by a pair of younger cousins, Jimmy and Gates, who were much more fun and daring. Gates was the youngest of Uncle Trubee's boys, chubby and humorous, always saying outrageous things and getting the giggles, with a large head, wide frank forehead, and thick pendulant earlobes inherited from his grandfather, Harry Dear. Jimmy, the youngest overall of the cousins, was tall, lean and good-looking, and in possession of a wicked sense of humor. The most useful way to put it, considering the era, would be to say that they were boys who liked to play with girls.

Homosexuality was one of three subjects that could never be brought up at Peacock Point—the others were alcoholism and cancer, which would figure more after the war—and so, of course, the estate was rife with queasily closeted men. The English butler for decades, Bedford, was gay, and I personally remember, as a young child, attending the magnificent wedding in a large Catholic church of a handsome chauffeur with an equally comely serving girl, although it was common knowledge that the driver had just completed a steamy affair with one of my mother's male cousins.

Nevertheless, to my grandmother Froggie's great relief, the stodgy dinner hour had taken on color, laughter, and artistry in recent years, thanks to the introduction of two fairly flamboyant young men whom she had championed. They were bald as eggs, though as different from each other as a quail and a peacock, and not close friends. The first was Luco, a distant cousin, the grandson of the Breton writer Anatole le Braz, who'd married a bohemian sister of Harry Dear in Paris. Luco had a huge, booming, happy laugh, and lived part-time on an island in the Caribbean with the famous jeweler Jean Schlumberger.

The other was Froggie's close friend and confidant, the young and talented decorator George Stacey. Tall, pallid, scathingly funny, and always dressed in black, George could usually be found wandering the paths alone in the Sunken Garden like a disdainful and reclusive monk. He attributed his success as an interior decorator to convincing his female clients he never lunched, since he would have been required to pick up the tab. Froggie had impulsively rescued George from another decorator's dismal employment by giving him the task of filling out her outsize octagonal living room with Louis Quinze and Chinese lacquer. Meanwhile, George somehow contrived to hole himself up in the estate's squash court. From this bohemian outpost, he steadily built his client list, which was to include the cream of the social world: Babe Paley, Grace Kelly, John Hay Whitney, Vincent Astor, Viking Press publisher Harold K. Guinzburg, W. Averell Harriman, Ava Gardner, and so on, mostly friends of my grandmother or her sister Alice.

My great-grandmother Goggie held a surprisingly tolerant view of these men, though they obviously didn't fit into the manly Groton mold. Perhaps her marriage to Harry Dear had given her time to ponder what it was like for a woman to be solely at the mercy of a man's man. After George joined the war effort, as every man at Peacock Point did, and was thrown out of the army for behavior unbecoming a soldier (one can only speculate what that was!), Goggie surprised everyone by writing him a calm, affectionate letter, insisting that he was a brave man for trying, and assuring him that he would always be a welcome guest in her home. And later when my great-grandmother's sons tried to reclaim the squash court for themselves, Goggie defended George's squatting rights on such strong terms that he was able to remain the sole inhabitant there for three full decades after her death, sleeping in the loft and filling the court to the skylights with dusty pagodas, carved mirrors, and gilt armoires.

The game of Hare and Hounds was played on one or two Sundays in autumn, after the formal luncheon at the Big House had finished, after the roast beef had been taken out and finger bowls lifted away, after the portraits of god knows which relatives on the bright yellow walls in the vast dining room had nodded and fallen asleep. No program or schedule would have been made. The idea would spring spontaneously like a sinkhole on Fifth Avenue, or one of those irresistible happenings in a Jazz Age novel: a kiss, a drinking match, a duel, a fistfight, a stampede of Spanish bulls.

Impatient, the girls would begin to toss their shoulder-length hair from side to side, and I suppose the boys would toss their bangs. Amid great hilarity the chattering posse would tumble from the dining room and begin to divide up into teams as someone recited:

> *Eeny, meeny, miny, moe,*
> *Catch a nigger by the toe.*
> *If he hollers let him go,*
> *Eeny, meeny, miny, moe.*

This useful counting ditty was considered to have no special negative cultural resonance and therefore safe for children to use. Then, repairing to the flagstone terrace that overlooked the blue Sound, the teens began frenziedly ripping up newspapers and magazines into one-inch squares. Armloads of homemade confetti were stuffed into leather shoulder bags that resembled newsboys' pouches.

My great-grandmother Goggie would not have participated in the game of Hare and Hounds, as it was rare for a woman of her age to walk beyond the precincts of her garden. But many of the adults jumped up with enthusiasm: Froggie, Ward, Alice and Di, Uncle Harry and his wife Anne, Luco, and perhaps a few of the lunch guests, such as the displaced Russian countess Ishka, who was not yet confined to her wheelchair by multiple sclerosis.

Ward and Froggie were still in their thirties then, and thus quite childlike and spirited themselves. My grandmother was at the height of her powers. No one dressed with her imagination, or talked with her hilarity, or drank and smoked with her daring, and thus, you could say, she stood all alone and untouchable in her set.

My grandfather Ward would have hesitated visibly before he decided to join, however. Ward wasn't yet transformed into the relatively unbuttoned grandfather we knew as kids, who'd show up to dinner on the patio in his bare feet and chase my cousin Sondra across the lawn in shorts. He was a sober businessman, charged with keeping the family silk mill afloat just when artificial fabrics such as rayon were appearing on the technological horizon. People of his generation spoke of Ward's warmth and generosity, but at home to his daughters he was remote and chilly. Perhaps he joined the Hare and Hounds only once or twice in all those years, but the memory of each of those brief engagements would loom large for my mother.

After five or so Hares had been chosen, the remainder Hounds numbered perhaps a dozen. Depending on their ages, the Hounds would begin to laugh and cheer, and to take on corny English accents and say things like "Cheerio!" and "To the Hounds!" and "Pip, pip!" According to the rules they were to remain in place for fifteen minutes after the Hares took off.

Choosing her moment for maximum effect, my great-aunt Alice reached up and brought her arm down to start the game. To everyone's cheers of "Tally-ho!" the Hares scampered down the short slope toward the water, silhouetted themselves for an instant against the sparkling Sound, then veering off the way birds do, all together as if with one mind. As they ran, the Hares reached into their bags and tossed handfuls of white confetti behind them to create a trail.

Di, the former Yale football star, would have liked nothing better than to run with the Hares, but a sense of gravity held him back. He stayed at a table on the terrace, his long legs out, and dropped two cubes of sugar into his iced tea with a pair of silver tongs. Across from him, his brother-in-law Trubee also sipped iced tea, his cane leaning against a chair within reach. They were old college buddies. They'd been in Skull and Bones together, and helped start the famous "Millionaires' Unit," of Yale flyboys, who'd careened planes over the cove in hopes of joining World War I as pilots. Di went on to become a war hero, an ace, but Trubee broke his back in a watery crash during training and remained home.

"Filling out nicely, aren't they?" Trubee commented across the table.

"Who's that?" asked Di.

"Frankie's girls. And your set, of course."

"Can't see it," Di replied, pouring cream into the tall glass and watching the thick liquid fall through the tea in Florentine swoops and curls. "Don't understand the pants. I like my women in dresses, the way God intended. Shows their rumps better."

"My God, you're an old-fashioned lout," grumbled Trubee. "You'd better have your glasses checked real soon."

"Call it what you like. I'd like to see mine married off someday. No real man looks at a girl in trousers."

The Hares ran until their hearts pounded in their chests, until they had to pant their hardest to fill their lungs with air, until transparent motes swarmed in the blue sky above them and until the green leaves of the trees overhead glowed like spearheads. The pack scurried almost to the white Casino, hesitated, then dropped down to the beach, and galloped along the sandy crescent below the grass tennis courts. Then they zoomed up through the curiously parched and prickly patch of grass behind the Tea House. Reaching the tall iron maypole, they each took a handle and spun a half twirl, their feet leaving the ground.

As she galloped, dutifully tossing a fistful of confetti up into the air now and then, my mother kept thinking, picking up possibilities, discarding them. Not the monastery that hemmed in the estate on one side. Not the swamp. There was a small bunkhouse by the clay courts built as a sleeping hut for the older Davison boys. Out of the girls' territory. Avoid *that*.

Her thoughts turned to the British thriller *Rogue Male*, by Geoffrey Household, which she'd just finished. In the book, a British sportsman on vacation in Germany decides to stalk Hitler just for the sheer pleasure of placing the mad dictator in his sights—although he never plans to pull the trigger. He is captured and nearly tortured to death by Nazi agents, but escapes somehow. Broken and bleeding he is pursued like a wounded rabbit over the heaths. As he races, his mind keeps working. Clearly only by using his wits can he hope to escape his ruthless tormentors. He just needs to find the right place to hide. Where? Where?

The Pump House—a phalanx of pipes set into the ivy-covered slope on the way to the Casino? Hidden but not enough room. The dank and nearly abandoned changing rooms under the Casino? Creepy and hopefully avoidable. The crawl space under the Tea House? Too obvious and hard to get into . . .

At twelve or thirteen a girl's hips start to fill out. Centrifugal forces come into play. Suddenly her knees don't push back and forth smooth and straight like the pistons of a machine, as they have all her life, but swing pendulously from side to side. How did all of this, well, *bottom* get in the way of things? she wondered. When did this startling change take place? Who knows? Was it relevant? Never mind. *Run! Run!*

Back at the terrace the Hounds were getting restive, accompanied by the gentle tinkle as servants cleared the last cups and saucers and dessert plates that had followed them out onto the terrace. Luncheon over, the servants ate their fill and began to scrape the remainder into the trash bin: great bushels of rolls, parsleyed potatos, green beans, and thinly sliced slabs of pink roast beef. The Great Depression had not reached Peacock Point, of course. Not even a crumble or a flake of consciousness had flown in through the front gates. My mother's uncles were great believers in letting Nature take its course. Everyone knew that drought followed plenty, and that plenty would eventually follow drought. The Bible had put man over the birds of the air, and things that crawled on the ground, and it was natural for a few men to rise to the top and for other men to work for them. The poor would always be with us. In the White House, Franklin Delano Roosevelt, a traitor to his classmates at Groton, was hard at work doing everything that was *wrong* for the country: coddling misfits and stifling banks with unnecessary rules.

Finding solutions to massive unemployment or hunger wasn't something the sons of Henry Davison spent a lot of brainpower on. My mother had a wealthy friend whose chauffeur drove her family out to the center of the vast homeless encampment in Central Park every day or so and stopped. There she and her siblings got out of the limousine and stood in the open, handing out warm, cooked potatoes to the shabby men, who, anticipating their arrival, had already formed a polite line. That wasn't much of a solution, though it was amazing to see how much of a positive difference a warm potato in the stomach could make on the outlook of a man who was starving. But at Peacock Point the Davisons kept their baked potatoes to themselves. They had to keep their strength up to assume the mantle of leadership when the country came out of this slump, which it most positively would, as long as FDR and his make-work programs didn't inflict too much damage on the economy.

"Two minutes!" Alice called in a loud voice. Froggie disappeared into the Big House and returned wearing her mother's old-fashioned long blue overcoat and one of her indescribable hats.

The Hounds quivered with anticipation. There was a fair breeze blowing in from the water and below them, a few flakes of paper turned and spun on the lawn.

Looking at her watch, Alice raised her hand high for the second time and let it drop. "Go, Hounds!" she shouted.

Giving tongue to *"Hallo!"* and *"Let's make tracks!"* the Hounds burst from the flagstone terrace.

Froggie struggled to keep up, weighted down by her mother's heavy blue coat and her own hilarity. She and Alice already had the giggles. Froggie tripped, bringing down Alice with her, and Alice, reaching out, brought down Luco. Then Allie and Diane jumped back up to have a go themselves, and soon everyone was tumbling head over heels down the grassy slope to the lawn, clawing at one another.

When all of that got sorted out, the Hounds, baying and halooing, spun off toward the sparkling breakwater.

Doubling back to round the maypole, the Hares crossed the gray drive near the croquet court, ran past the white string hammock, giving it a spin while passing, and shot suddenly straight under the protective skirts of the House Tree, the enormous weeping locust whose misshapen shoulders loomed over the Big House. When they left the House Tree, they separated into three droves, each laying a different paper trail. Which trail was the real one, none of them knew.

Overexcited, taking up the rear, Jimmy shook out the whole bag of clippings behind him and the little squares of paper floated this way and that over the lawn.

My mother threw her arm around her father's shoulder and whispered for a moment. He tore away from her down the side of the pond, around the squat dark Supervisor's House and out of sight. He tossed out handfuls of paper squares as he ran. Ward always could run. At Yale, he'd rowed crew, and he still had the long, lanky, crewman's body. Once out of sight he ran with the energy of a released rabbit, with long stretched legs and long stretched arms. Friends remarked about how Ward could dump all dignity by the wayside now and then and just let loose. Of course, no one married to Froggie could be a complete stranger to frivolity.

As my mother, separated from the pack, scampered through the Sunken Garden, she paused to genuflect to each of the mottled, gray stone statues there, a longstanding habit. *Run! Run!*

The Hounds, arriving by roundabout route to the House Tree, came upon the three paper trails splitting like the sparks of an errant firework.

"Oh, my gosh. So clever. Which way should we go?" asked Alice.

Diane put her nose down. "This way!" she urged, pointing to the track that curved back toward the beach and then up into a sparse orchard. "This way!"

A few minutes later, all of the Hares met up at the fishpond's willow tree. They climbed a split-rail fence, then another, and reached the black-tar service road. Another road belonging to the neighbors, the Guthreys, snaked just beyond.

In *Rogue Male*, the wounded British sportsman finally comes up with a desperate plan to dig a dark burrow deep into the ground, big enough to plunge himself in and hide until his Nazi pursuers gave up. My mother was looking for just such a hiding place around this time.

There it was! A small shed surrounded by wild honeysuckle, leaning to one side, its sloped shingled roof with a hole where a stovepipe had once been stuck. The shack was almost hidden by old orchard trees that had grown up wild around it. Windows were boarded up on the inside, their glass panes cracked.

She wrenched open the door. They had, of course, been in this shed before. It was an old shed of the Guthreys'. Or had they?

"It looks like a crapper," someone said, peering in. They ducked inside and crouched in a row in the dark. There were a few boxes and something like a bench. The only light crept through long thin cracks between the boards. Ten long minutes went by.

"How long will we wait?" my grandfather asked calmly, sitting in the dark.

"As long as it takes!" my mother would have replied happily.

The door swung open suddenly with a shriek and the silhouette of a large head with particular thick-lobed ears appeared.

"*Gates!*" my mother called out in a whisper. "I thought you were a Hound!"

"I just thought it would be more fun to be a Hare!" Gates said, as he snuggled in next to her. And my mother would have given him a delighted hug.

Although they were close then, in later life, my mother and Gates were to drift apart. She went off to a progressive, even vaguely socialist, boarding school in Vermont, where students dug manure with pitchforks and built their own dormitories, while Gates followed his brothers to Groton, where he must have quivered with fear of exposure. Later he would run with a rather wealthy and flamboyant social pack, whose leader was Sharman Douglas, the socialite known for her ties to the British royal family and for a two-year affair she was said to have had with Princess Margaret. Alcohol was a big part of Gates's life then, as well as a certain kind of fast, frivolous talking that made my mother nervous.

After his father, Trubee, died, Gates gave up drinking. He wasn't able to avoid the illness that had killed so many of his friends in New York, though. At his funeral, in 1990, when a niece walked up to one of his sisters-in-law to ask if it'd be appropriate to donate to an AIDS cause in Gates's name, the grand dame drew herself up and replied, "Hush, we don't speak of such things here!"

The Hounds, racing along the lawn toward the back of the estate, encountered a small cloud of scattered white scraps, blown hither and thither by the breeze. There was absolutely no way to tell where they had come from or which way they led.

Diane stopped so suddenly her heels skidded on the grass. She peered ahead. No one knew the grounds of the estate like she did. Sheer energy had spread her marauding band across every square foot of the grounds. She thought of the shack in an instant, saw it all perfectly, the old shingles, the trees, the honeysuckle, had it all visualized in her mind, and knew.

"Hey! Hey everyone!" Diane called. "Follow me! Now I know *exactly* where they are!"

Inside of the shack, Gates began singing the work song from *Snow White and the Seven Dwarfs*. "How long do *you* think it'll take to find us?" murmured one of the six now squatting in the shed. Through the board cracks, the autumn light had begun to dim and grow blue. "Not long," said another.

Hunkered down in darkness, my mother heard pounding footsteps, panting, and a thud. The door was thrown open for the second time. A bright mass of hair appeared and shouldered its way in.

"Allie!" sounded my mother with joy.

"I couldn't leave you guys here all alone!" she cried, catching her breath, before she squeezed in next to my mother.

In later times, my mother and her sister would diverge sharply according to their temperaments. Allie would enjoy shopping in fancy boutiques and department stores, while my mother would browse carefully in thrift shops. Allie would marry a finance man and stay at Peacock Point, while my mother would marry a Hun and move to the suburbs. But at this point you could hardly tell them apart.

Two smiling portraits of my mother and her sister that had been painted when they were girls hung side by side in my grandmother's living room for many years. With their shoulder-length blond hair and bright expressions, the pair were almost identical. Inexplicably, on the day Allie died, the surface of her oil portrait broke up into deep crackles. My mother's portrait, hanging right by its side, remained as it was.

"I found the trail! I found the trail!" someone far away seemed to be calling.

"Who was that?" asked someone in the dark shelter.

"Diane, I think."

"She's the best tracker."

The inhabitants of the little shed traded glances. You *wanted* to get caught, of course. You *wanted* to give the Hounds a problem they could solve. You didn't want to be so clever with your false trails as to create a maze that the others couldn't follow.

Diane yanked the door open and threw it back. The inside was a black rectangle too dark to see inside of.

"Come on! Come on!" she called, waving her hands wildly.

One by one, the Hounds gathered behind her, breathless. They all peered in at once. "Holy mackerel!" breathed aunt Alice. The shack was empty and dank, full of cobwebs and spiders. Diane's clairvoyant vision had brought them to a shack, but it was apparently the *wrong* shack.

Overhead sun was just peeking over the red-limned trees. A chill was beginning to spring up from the grass.

"Oh, screw it!" said my grandmother vamping in her mother's long blue coat. "Let's go back and have a drink, shall we?"

"Sure, they'll come out when they are good and ready!"

"Ow-WHOOO!"

"Whoop!"

The Hares listened as the baying of the Hounds slowly faded away.

"Strange, I thought they were *so* close."

Huddled together in the dark shack, the Hares looked at one another. Should they go, or should they stay? Perhaps the maid was even now rolling the cocktail cart out and preparing a flight of ginger ales in tall glasses with long green perfect sprigs of mint. But it would be ignominious as hell to be caught trudging across the grass of the Polo Field in a discouraged pack.

"How long do we wait?" asked my grandfather Ward, pushing his shoulders up against the scratchy boards. He was enjoying the dark, actually. It rested his eyes.

"As long as it takes!" my mother replied again. Almost everyone she cared about most in the world was crammed into the close air of the shack now with her.

And so the Hares waited, and the minutes ticked by. The last rays of autumn light, filtering through the cracks between the boards, made dim curling patterns on their faces. Floating motes of dust made their noses twitch.

Had they really been abandoned? How sad. Perhaps someone would remember the shack and send an emissary to free them from their exile. Everything was in the future, really. It was hard to tell how things would unfold.

Part Ten

A story should have a beginning, a middle, and an end . . . but not necessarily in that order.

—Jean-Luc Godard

Chapter Thirty-one

When Hali started shaking in the cab, I knew she was going into shock from loss of blood.

"I'm afraid the baby's heart has stopped beating," she said.

"The baby's okay," I said.

"Is she bleeding all over my seat?" asked the cab driver.

"No," I lied to him. "She's fine."

"Are you sure about the baby?" Hali asked.

"Yeah."

"I'm cold," Hali said, pulling her coat around her. "I'm cold."

Hali had gone through a partial abruption, which meant that the umbilical cord had separated from the placental wall, causing a hemorrhagic flow. It was a condition that usually only occurs to women with extremely high blood pressure, or crack addicts, neither of which accurately described my wife. After the emergency C-section, the nurses called our child the "miracle baby." In any other era, baby and mother would have died in childbirth.

I got back to the apartment at dawn, having left Hali in the hospital drifting in a cloud of morphine. I expected our bedroom to look as though Charlie Manson had staged a party there, but found the walls clean and the sheets fresh. Hali's mother and father had spent most of the night scrubbing the bedroom down and washing the sheets. When you have kids, you might as well reconcile yourself to being knee-deep in body fluids for the rest of your life.

As with each of our previous children, we flew the baby to Colorado, to present to Hali's grandmother. She took him into her lap, turned him over, carefully studied the whorl on the back of his head, and pronounced him unusually fortunate. He would be rich, famous, musically talented, not only that, a great athlete and a scholar. True, she'd discovered auspicious whorls on the scalps all of our children, but none so providential as this. She pried open his tiny fist and pointed to the lines in his palm. They only confirmed that he was a remarkable child.

Chapter Thirty-two

Through all of this I continued to sneak down and see my friend Lester Bergamot in his sordid apartment. Sometimes I'd go for a month or two without visiting him, but sooner or later my shoes would find themselves steering down toward his seamy pad, as if working on their own. As often as not, if it'd been more than a few weeks, I'd end up on my knees in his filthy bathroom cubicle worshiping the porcelain goddess. In fact, vomiting was a fairly common event for me to experience in those days, since street dosages were so variable and my tolerance remained—on the scale of things—fairly low. At a predictable rate I ran with sweat pouring down my face from movie seats, Broadway plays, restaurants, and the dinner tables of friends. Other side effects of powder were a dry smacking of the mouth, a gray bloodless face, a hoarse croaking in the throat, itching at the beltline, sleeplessness accompanied by a thousand cartoonlike half-dreams, an uncontrollable urge to defecate, and an inability to reach orgasm (this Lester actually considered a positive effect). Probably applying only to myself were two more curious symptoms: an irrepressible urge to tidy up our apartment—and strangely, to buy my wife flowers. My wife, a doctor's daughter, who can discern seventeen shades of color in a man's face, and take the temperature of one of our children by merely brushing her lips across her forehead, would look at me and demand to know, "Are you using?" I'd deny it up and down, claiming a headache, stomach cramps, or viral flu, but she'd know, and a certain amount of distrust quite naturally built up between us over time.

I would take powder and go for a run so as to lose my pallor, an exercise probably not recommended in the jogging books. You'd be surprised how well you can run on junk. In a very real sense you're floating on air, and when you take a shower afterward, it feels as though your skin is being massaged by the hands of a thousand tiny kohl-eyed houris.

Sometimes I'd sit in a chair and dream until dawn like Sherlock Holmes in *The Hound of the Baskervilles*. Out of those lost hours, a single idea might emerge, a thought, a string of words, an unnamed species of cabbage moth fluttering among my ruined garden of exotic plants. I'd wake up knowing I'd squandered another of my last few nights on earth.

"Listen, you don't like to get sucker punched, do you?" Lester would ask as the TV set burbled behind us.

"What?" I said. When the powder finally came down, it was like a hot lion's tongue licking the back of my neck. I stared into the tabletop, stunned at the absolute rightness of what I was feeling. This was exactly where we had been trying to get all of our lives. I was sure of it.

"No one wants to get blindsided, right?" Lester repeated. His patrician upbringing made him stubborn. "You're on the floor, your head is spinning, and you don't even know where it came from. You're out before the fight's even started. It's an overwhelming feeling. And you don't want it to happen again, not after that first time. So what you do is, you start getting ready. Your muscles tighten up. Your heart is working. You're always staring blindly ahead into the dark. That's why you feel tense all of the time. It's a natural reaction. Internally you're always preparing for the worst."

"What's the worst?" I asked.

"You know what the worst is."

"Oh, listen to this wise old asshole," said Arnie. "He has no idea what he's talking about, does he? Stoned out of his gourd."

"The next punch. That's gonna be the worst," said Lester, his eyes half shut. "That's why you can never let your guard down."

It's true that heroin helped me to relax from a state of constant vigilance. Lester had it right. The asteroid was always about to collide with the

Earth, the sun abandon her children to the void of space. The lava was beginning to well up from the sewer grates in the sidewalk. In other words, small setbacks often incurred in me a feeling of calamity and global change. This was, if I were to be honest, a mechanism I shared with my stepbrother. He sought street drugs to put the planet back in its course. As for myself, in my more cautious way, I now and then took a pinch of snuff.

Naturally, at some point, powder had begun to compete with my work schedule. Oh, I still ran around my usual dizzy circle of phone calls, deadlines, interviews, and rush jobs, but it was hard to compete with the pure stillness of perfection brought on by the distillates of the opium poppy. When I was sitting at my computer, I'd feel the need of it waft across my face like a draft of warm, flower-scented air. I never wrote when I was high, but the urge to feel that burn in my nostrils grew sharper with each passing hour. Many times I forced myself to stand up, go to the shelf where my stash was kept, and cut up each of the little rectangles methodically with scissors, flushing the whole bundle down the toilet—knowing if I didn't my entire week would be ruined. Lester would have been horrified at the waste of precious powder, but there was always a next time.

There comes the moment in every user's life when the effects are no longer what they used to be. Junk molecules tend to gum up the pleasure receptors in your brain cells, and eventually the sun doesn't shine as warmly as it used to and a meal no longer summons up the same reflexive pangs in your saliva glands. Still, there were times when I'd be running out the door on my way to an opening, having just taken a line or two of powder, and remind myself, as Lester had before me, "It's the best feeling ever!"

When I started hiding my sheaf of tiny green plastic envelopes at the very top shelf of my closet to make it more difficult for me to reach, that was the first circle drawn in the game of Hangman I was playing—the head. When I joked about how well I handled heroin to a relationship therapist Hali and I had gone to see at the beginning of our marriage, that was a thin pencil line drawn for the neck. When I stopped telling Hali what I was up to, that was the oval that made the body. And when I started going to the East Village and finding my own connection, without even telling Lester, that was the last of the stick arms.

Out in the kid park, I nodded to a mom I recognized from another lifetime, a Brillo-topped blonde whose pair of coffee-featured daughters I'd assumed were adopted. I'd learned though, never to make any assumptions about consanguinity in a New York City children's park.

Long ago, back when she'd lived in the East Village, she'd introduced a friend of mine to powder. It had all seemed like so much fun at first, but it had turned out badly in the end, of course. She flagged me over.

"Have you seen Lester lately?" she asked.

"Not in a while."

"I'm worried," she said.

"What do you mean?" I asked.

"If there was one guy I thought was in control, it was Lester. He used to be able to make a gram of cocaine last a month. He could take a puff of a joint and put it out and save it for the next day. He thinks he can handle heroin, too. But it's not the same as other drugs. You can play that you know it. You can string it along for a long, long time, but fundamentally it's different. The way it works. The way it goes through your head and gets inside your body. How it takes you away from everyone else."

"I'll check up on him," I said, as much to end the conversation as anything else.

"It won't do any good," she said.

What happened in the end was, I got a call from another old prep school friend who told me Lester had gone into rehab and was trying to fix up his life and get back with his ex-wife and kids. These things get around somehow. I knew that the story was eventually going to reach Hali, including my part in it, and that didn't bode well. I decided to go to her first, hoping that an apt and properly worded confession would head off the worst.

I arrived in the bedroom full of mirth and self-mockery, thinking that I was going to tell her a funny story about the misadventures of a couple of old friends, a humorous updating of the Peter Pan myth ("I'll never grow up, never grow up, never grow up! Not me!"). But Hali saw immediately to the heart of the tale. I had lied to her and deceived her, kept dangerous drugs around the house. Been under the influence. Pretty soon I knew how a rabbit feels after it has been gutted, skinned, spitted, and slowly turned on a stick over the licking flames of a campfire. I'd seen this delicacy prepared a couple of times on hiking trips. When properly roasted, the rabbit turns a particularly unpleasant red color. Its flesh is charred in parts, and it begins to seep precious bodily liquids that should safer be left inside. There are few things on earth that look more pathetic or naked.

I saw the bitterness and revulsion on Hali's face, and my own bravado gave way to a growing intuition that my married life was on the balance. The apocalypse was here, at our home, the fiery rain falling around our doorstep. Like my father, I had been keeping a double life for years. I had only one argument I could make against the face of Hali's rage. It wasn't a very good one, but it was the best I could summon up, and it had the flavor of truth. "I know the difference between fantasy and reality," I told her late that night after hours had passed and everything else had failed. "Doing drugs and hanging around with Lester is a fantasy. My real life is here with you and the kids."

"Okay," she said at last, the weariness showing on her face. "Okay."

Somehow it worked, to buy me some time anyway, until I could gain her trust back. I knew I'd just barely squeaked by, though. And the margin for error in the future would be very slim.

Chapter Thirty-three

Meanwhile, Olivia seemed at the end of her rope. In Colorado, Jim had sprung Little Peter loose from his jailers, then had spun off on a road trip through the mountains that had alternately turned revelatory and disturbing, filled with lunar landscapes and odd misplaced government towns that didn't seem to have any people in them. The photographs Jim had sent me had been ecstatic and jaw-achingly beautiful. After a long, gritty, picture-taking trek, he'd dropped Little Peter off with his mother in Idaho, who, strangely, hadn't seemed that pleased to see them. Had she asked us to drop her son off with her like an errant puppy? Not really. She'd wanted him persuaded back to Spring Lake Ranch where he could be watched over, or taken back with us to New York where he could at least find decent homeless services. Now she was delivering him over to me permanently, she wrote in an e-mail—washing her hands of him forever:

> I am totally tired of Peter's flushing money down the toilet as if there was no tomorrow. I'm tired of his taking up my time and energy with his interminable phone calls, always in need of more dollars and for some asinine reason.
>
> If you want to deal with him you have my blessing, but I am finished. At this point I'm not even convinced he has schizophrenia. I think he's just an alcoholic, probably a drug addict, and a moocher and sucker.

Little Peter's life was a Chinese puzzle, I thought. From the outside it was a smooth and polished piece of wood, with no lines or cracks visible anywhere. If I kept twisting and turning, though, pushing on this depression, pulling out that knob, eventually I thought, eventually a hidden drawer would slide open, and soon I'd have the secret solution to his existence revealed. Or so I told myself. At any rate, I was ready to try a whole new tactic.

At the end of 2001, Jim and I bought a small three-chip Sony "prosumer" DV camera. The idea was to record our encounters with Little Peter, guerrilla-documentary style, and let the scenes spin out wherever they needed to go, into fiction, surreality, quasifiction, or abject confession. The camera was small enough to pass in the street as a tourist camera, or slip invisibly into a homeless shelter, but sharp enough to take broadcast-quality footage. Making a film with Little Peter would allow us to shape our time with him, I thought, without feeling we were merely wasting it, as I usually did. His stint in Arnott's gym in Moccasin, Montana, had shown that he could be a creative artist in the old underground mode: with this film I would try to engage him on that level. I also secretly hoped that my stepbrother would benefit from his exposure to a pair of working artists—even such a questionable pair as Jim and myself.

In the seventies the French anthropologist and pioneer filmmaker Jean Rouch had made a famous improvised movie with a trio of Nigerian chicken vendors, one of whom, since Rouch had saved his life as a boy, felt that Rouch was responsible for his upkeep. *Cocorico! Monsieur Poulet* took the form of an African fable; the three men have to cross the Niger River in a tiny two-horsepower van three times in order to take their chickens to market. For some dreamlike reason they forsake the bridge. Once they simply push the car across the river, blowing water out of the pistons on the other side and driving away, the second time they wrap the tiny truck up in a tarp and float it across like a raft, and the third time they inflate the tires like balloons. Rouch gave the illiterate Nigerians absolute creative control and the results were an almost perfect blend of outer and inner truth. I wanted to see if between us Jim, Little Peter, and I could make a modern fairy tale as powerful and innocent and sweet and random as what Rouch had done.

The project sounded a little naïve, but naïveté could legitimately be said to be part of our aesthetic. At HBO, cinema verité maven Sheila Nevins had been buying up films made by amateurs using any kind of camera, super-eight, DV, BetaCam: the old rules of professionalism didn't matter, what was important was that the film had heart. Hali and I had made some contacts in the documentary world, including HBO, so I thought there was a fair chance that the film would get seen.

When Little Peter arrived into town in the dead of winter—his usual modus operandi—I explained my idea. In my mind, the film would be a collaborative effort, where Little Peter would be as much a participant as a subject, where we handed the camera back and forth to each other improvising scenes. It would be part ethnography, part confession, and part political statement in the manner of Jean-Luc Godard.

My stepbrother thought about it. He put his fist to his chin and screwed up his face. He tried the other fist.

"Will we be able to videotape the police?" he asked tentatively.

"Of course."

"Hah! I'm in," he said.

As it happened, our film idea dovetailed neatly with his new ambition to gain "financial stability," he told me. That spring he'd spent weeks at a Rainbow Gathering in the Okala State Forest in Florida. Under a cathedral of Spanish moss, while topless, mud-smeared women danced around a roaring bonfire, Little Peter became a festival hit singing improvised songs like "Old Number Seven Jack Daniel's Mississippi Blues" on a borrowed guitar. Now that he was back in grimy, cold New York, he wanted to try his luck as a street musician. He was even thinking about calling his mother and asking her to send his old violin.

"This is just a first step in a much larger idea," he told me enthusiastically. He would get a passport and play at Rainbow Gatherings around the world: Europe, Australia, Asia. "I've got a realistic plan," he said earnestly. "I just need you to help me formulate it."

There was a nugget of possibility to Little Peter's idea that I liked. He claimed he'd start paying for his room at the Jane West Hotel—which I also liked. I was amazed at how well things were falling into place, for once. Exulting, I took the train uptown to buy a Harmony guitar in a Times Square pawn shop. It wasn't the best guitar I'd ever seen, but Harmony had an old-fashioned reputation as a street musician's instrument, and I felt it was perfect for the occasion. My stepbrother's attempts to break into the subterranean music scene in New York could be the glue that held our film together.

Jim and I arranged to meet my stepbrother at a rehearsal space on Thirtieth Street. Stepping around the pierced and tattooed members of a Jersey heavy metal band we entered the sound studio we'd rented. Once inside, Little Peter began to pace the chamber's perimeter watchfully as a cat that's just come into a strange house. He tapped each of the cymbals and the drums, took the guitar out of its case and put it back, and finally crossed to a dusty window to stare down at the street with a troubled expression.

At last he turned from the windowpane, crossed the room, and sat down at the electronic keyboard. Despite some awkwardness with his frozen right hand, he moved the dials to a setting called "Hearts of Space." Soon the chamber filled with otherworldly twitters and howls, like a shortwave radio tuning in stations from the Siberian archipelago. His face grew serious and focused, as if he were drawing together everything he'd ever seen, felt, or learned from books for one monumental effort. He began to run his left-hand fingers rapidly over the keys, cupping his right hand as a crude flipper to depress improvised chords. With his disheveled hair, his intent eyes, and his ripped jeans, he looked like an avant-garde composer preparing for an important solo recital.

The music he played for the next forty-five minutes was half Bach and half soundtrack for an as-yet-unwritten science fiction film. I thought I could see the plot unfolding in Little Peter's gnarled grimace, his brilliant farseeing eyes: scruffy warriors racing in rusted vans across yellow desert wastelands to confront electronically sophisticated nomadic tribesmen, homemade bombs igniting, shrieks of torn metal, dull percussions of red fire and smoke, and feral children howling and gnashing their sharpened teeth, as they tore flesh from animal bones. The piece ended with an aural explosion of feathers and sparks. When the last flutter died, Jim and I both applauded.

"I should do this more often," Little Peter said, a shy smile pulling his lips. I was overjoyed. This seemed like a promising start to our movie.

The afterglow of my stepbrother's extraordinary performance was only slightly dimmed as we left the building, when Little Peter noticed a paper plate of macaroni and cheese resting on a street barrier. He picked up the white plastic fork on the plate and was just about to shovel a mouthful of brilliant orange goo into his mouth when a chorus of howls from Jim and me arrested him.

He looked at us curiously.

"Want some?" he asked.

———

Over the next few days, Jim and I roamed the city videotaping musicians in the subway and the streets to use as background for the film. Meanwhile Little Peter was showing increasing proficiency on his cheap Harmony guitar, his maimed right hand gripping the pick loosely, his left hand crawling up and down the frets like a nimble spider, the music an easy, streaming mixture of classical and jazz chords.

Jim was spending nights at our apartment, which was sometimes an iffy thing. Despite my wife's acceptance of him as a family member, I never knew when he was going to drive her to the kindle point. Jim had a habit of standing up whenever Hali stood and sitting down when she sat—an auto-response, resulting from his grim military-Catholic up-bringing, I suspected. Sometimes when he called and Hali picked up the phone, he got so nervous he acted as though he didn't know who she was.

"Your friend is retarded," she said.

Yet I knew Jim to be honest, sensitive, and intelligent—as if such things mattered anymore in the world we live in. That spring he'd taken a beautiful set of photos of the kids during cherry blossom season at the Brooklyn Botanical Gardens, which had softened Hali's response a bit. But that only went so far.

From the start Hali had looked at our film with deep suspicion. She suspected that I mistakenly romanticized my stepbrother as a Kerouac-style hero. There was the not inconsiderable fact that every time I went out with Jim and Little Peter to shoot our real-life video, I left her alone in the apartment with three screaming children. And ever since the Dylan concert in Miami Beach, she'd begun to look upon any artistic endeavor I engaged in with my stepbrother and Jim as an excuse for three full-grown teenagers to get together and have a party.

Of my children, it was Alden, the oldest, whom I usually took along to connect with Little Peter when he was in town. Often I'd walk with my son to the old Chinese restaurant on the corner of Perry and Hudson, now of course long gone, to meet his step uncle. This time, by prearrangement, Jim was there with our DV camera, when Little Peter, red-faced from drinking sake, suddenly loomed up, huge and lumbering, from his chair to shake the hand of my small and agile son.

Alden, with a smiling oval face, sleepy eyes, and long brown hair, had quickly learned to call my stepbrother "Uncle Peter." The growth of their relationship was hampered, though, by reason of their vastly divergent political opinions.

"Where are the weapons of mass destruction?" Alden taunted, crawling up behind Little Peter's seat. "Well, where are they?"

"I wish you wouldn't keep asking that," my stepbrother grumbled. "And what do you know anyway? You're just a kid."

My stepbrother was a Bush Republican ever since he'd watched the whole of the Republican Convention on TV whilst flat on his back recovering from his combine accident. Onscreen, speechmakers had reviled Bill Clinton and the Democratic Party. Coming one after the other, these vitriolic harangues had wormed their way into Little Peter's cerebral cortex and found secure root there.

Alden, on the other hand, had been exposed to his parents' oft-repeated utterances of dismay at the actions of George W. Bush: his senseless war in Iraq, his dismantling of social programs, his phony Texas drawl, his kowtowing to the religious right, his sanctimoniousness, his allowing torture of detainees, his underhanded way of entering the White House through the back door of the Supreme Court.

"Why is there a war, anyway," Alden persisted, shoveling a dumpling into his mouth, while Jim filmed. "Why is there a war?"

"Quit playing with your food," Little Peter said. "Anyway, how do you know there is a war? And if there is a war, I'm sure there is a good reason for it."

"I know why," my son piped.

"Okay, why?" Little Peter growled, cradling his sake bottle in both hands uncomfortably.

"Because George Bush is a liar!"

"You shouldn't say things like that about your president."

But this time Alden crawled down under the table.

"Why not, it's true!" he called from below.

"You, what do you know about it?"

"George Bush said that there were weapons of mass destruction. But there weren't! He lied!"

Little Peter looked at me embarrassedly.

"Probably right," he said. His eyes shifted around the room and his face became a mask of fear and watchfulness. "I have the feeling we are being watched."

"No one in this restaurant cares about us," I said.

"It's not them. It's the guys who work for the last president, Clinton." He ducked to look under the table, where Alden was tying his shoelaces together. "Hey, you get up from there!"

To me he said, "I remember when I was his age, I liked to stay under the table too. Once during a dinner party of Franz and Olivia I crawled under the dining room table and spent the whole night there while everyone ate. I don't know why."

"Maybe because you wanted to escape somewhere where you couldn't be found," I said.

"It's true," he said. "I wanted to be an animal living in a hole. And now I've gotten my wish."

Alden stuck his head up over the top of his dish of pork dumplings and shouted, "George Bush is a liar!"

"I really wish you'd stop saying that." Little Peter sighed. "And whatever happened to manners?"

Alden crawled up on his chair: a big naughty-happy smile on his face, reminding me suddenly of how Little Peter and his brother Erik had looked when they were his age.

"Hey there, you little kid. Where'd you get all this information from anyway? Do you read the newspapers?"

"No-o-o! My mom told me."

"Figures. Well, you tell your mom that she shouldn't be saying that kind of stuff about your president in front of you."

"Even if it's true?"

"Well, *especially* if it's true."

The next scene on our list was to document Little Peter's demimonde existence in the Jane West Hotel. It was from here that he set off each day on the tiny and mysterious errands of his life.

It was twenty degrees above zero when we checked in around 10:00 P.M. The wind was howling in the street. Since Little Peter's room was too small to film in, Jim and I had taken a double on the same floor. Our accommodation came with a pair of slit windows that overlooked the ice-laced Hudson River and a television set that—like my friend Lester's in the East Village—only seemed to play ancient episodes of *Star Trek.*

Jim, who had begun to develop the flulike symptoms that for him always accompanied a busy production schedule, lay down and immediately went to sleep. I puttered around with our equipment, attaching microphones to cables. Even though our camera was small enough to fit in my hand, when fully rigged with a shotgun microphone, it looked like the ray gun used to contain errant poltergeists in *Ghostbusters.*

Little Peter soon knocked and with great enthusiasm threw himself into the task of adjusting the television aerial to get better reception, only managing to make the blue and red bands that crisscrossed the screen snap and twist like the electrical arcs in a Frankenstein movie. He began to ignite sticks of incense. Tendrils of musky-smelling smoke curled through the room. I lit a dozen candles and stuck them to the surface of the small table.

Jim came awake and joined us; we handed around a pint of Seagram's vodka. I fiddled with the camera until it seemed to be adjusted properly and then without telling anyone I switched it on. For a minute or two all went on as before: three tired men sitting around a table in a sordid hotel room, drinking and joking, and then with the power of a silent thunderclap we passed through an invisible curtain and entered our movie.

Surrounded by burning candles and tall sticks of smoking incense, my stepbrother looked like a mad Russian monk, a Greenwich Village Rasputin.

"What are we doing here?" I asked.

"That's easy," my stepbrother said. "You are an artist. I am an artist. I am helping you make art."

"That may be the most patronizing thing you've ever said to me," I said.

"I guess I don't understand the film," he admitted.

"Well, it's about you, I guess."

"*No!*"

"It's about me, then," I said.

"No, it has to be about the universe!"

He took a candle and held it to his cheek—so closely that the hair of his greasy bangs sizzled.

"Look!" he ordered. "Go ahead, look!"

The candle flame flickered millimeters from his bloodshot eyes. I realized that he meant, quite literally, for me to slide the camera into the expanded black lens of his pupil to record the clockwork gears in his brain. I pushed the camera to within an inch of his eyeball.

"I can't see anything in there," I complained.

"Bring it closer!" Little Peter insisted. He held the flame perilously near to his glistening iris. "Okay, then. Look deep within the retina of the left eyeball and you will see the damage that's been done," he said, "to the natural memory of the human organism. See? Want to see more?"

"Stop!" I begged. "You're going to damage your eye!"

"No, it's not going to damage my eye. Look, I've had the laser beam cameras in the deepest part of my soul."

"Enough," I said. "Stop!"

The room flipped dizzily and when it settled, Little Peter was sprawled on the bed and Jim was holding the camera. My stepbrother seemed electrified. The ends of his eyebrows corkscrewed up to the corner of the ceiling.

He began to make his pitch. What he was asking for was forty dollars to make a run up to Harlem. The idea was that he'd return to the hotel and *we would continue to film while he smoked* . . . we would share the sacrament. It would be a crack film, in other words, the first of its kind, a *landmark!*

But he didn't say that, not in so many words.

What he said was that he was about to perform a feat of *unparalleled daring*. The journey up to Harlem—in twenty-degree cold—to streets unknown at three in the morning would be an adventure with the outcome uncertain, but he felt up to it. He'd been drinking vodka since nine o'clock and he was *energized*. His eyes crackled with the powers of Mothra and Gigantor combined!

Jim and I gave each other appraising glances over the camera. This was what we'd set out to get. We'd already received lectures from a photo editor friend of mine about *getting the shot*. The temptation to set him loose was overwhelming. As a father, though, I just couldn't make myself do it. My reflexes were honed from years of gouging razor blades and small marbles out of the mouths of small children, and explaining why it probably wasn't a good idea to hang from your knees and drop headfirst into the sand from the top of the jungle gym. I could picture my stepbrother in handcuffs being pushed head down into a squad car. Even more clearly, I could see him bludgeoned and bleeding on the frozen pavement of some uptown alley.

"Peter, you know I don't care what you do," I began. "If I could snap my fingers and repeal all the drug laws in this country, I would. But I can't let you go out at night when it's twenty below zero to meet up with criminals you don't even know."

"What are you saying?"

"It's obvious. You're going to get killed. You're going to get arrested. You're going to get stabbed. You're certainly going to get ripped off. It's just a question of how much violence they'll use when they do it."

Little Peter made a sound like the warning jangle in *Jeopardy*.

"*Wrong!*" he shouted, springing off the bed, Jim just barely rescuing the camera from destruction. My stepbrother quivered with compressed energy. He looked like he'd drunk a bucket of rocket fuel. "I'm going to DO this thing. Because I've got the *power* and I've got the *desire*! And nobody can stop the power of desire once it's been turned on. No one and nobody!"

I could see where things were going from here—out of control. I remembered with helpless distance that each of my stepbrother's assaults had followed some bleary combination of alcohol and money like this. He began to nudge my shoulder. Insistent. Hard.

"I'm sorry, Peter. I'd like to . . ." I began.

Each nudge with the thumb of his clenched fist pushed me a few inches forward on my chair. Little Peter wanted his drugs. *Thud!* We wanted our video. *Thud!* I wanted my crack! *Thud!* He wanted his money! *Thud!*

"I want to, but I just can't . . ."

And then suddenly the moment broke . . . A wide, shamed grin opened up on Little Peter's face.

"All right, I'm embarrassed," he said. "I'm embarrassed to say what it is I want. So I guess I'm not going to get it." The curtain slid down on our movie and its magic was replaced by the bleary reality of three tired men drinking late in a sleazy hotel room.

Later I showed an edited version of our confrontation with Little Peter to Maryse Alberti, a tall, blond French cinematographer who'd shot *Crumb* and *Joe Gould's Secret*. Maryse had shot videos of homeless culture in the tunnels of New York, and wasn't the slightest bit squeamish about getting close to the dirty and naked. I'd been trying to interest her in shooting some of our footage, though I knew we couldn't afford her. When I told

Maryse that we were getting ready to show HBO a short edited from our documentary, she straightened up in her chair, thought for a moment, and said, "Well, you've got the right kind of sleaze right there."

The next scene was with Cecily, Little Peter's half sister, who was also my half sister. (She and I shared a father, while she and my stepbrother shared Olivia.) Cecily had grown up to look like her mother, with blue eyes, ice-blond hair, and a square jaw.

Amazingly she agreed to make the shoot with Little Peter as long as her husband Richard could be there to prevent violence upon her person. She was being an awfully good sport about it, I thought. As far as I knew she and my stepbrother hadn't seen each other since 1994, when he'd hit Olivia with a log of firewood at her house in Stanley, Idaho, and had spent the summer in the "Hailey Hilton" for it.

Cecily and I hadn't been close growing up, but she'd come to my wedding. After college she'd worked as a book editor in London, married, and returned to New York City. Her young adult novel, *Gossip Girl*, based on her experiences attending private school in Manhattan, had just come out, and was starting to gain wild popularity.

For the purpose of the shoot, I borrowed a loft from a friend in Chelsea. I moved a large round oak table in the center of the loft, hoping for a civilized Charlie Rose feel. While Jim busied himself unpacking the video equipment and switching on lights, Little Peter began to mumble darkly to himself, glowering across the table.

"Who's this? What's *he* doing here?" he snarled at Cecily.

"This is my husband, Richard," Cecily said carefully, picking each of her words as if they were pennies out of a bowl. "I don't think you've met before."

"Whether I've met him or not makes no difference. What's he *doing* here?"

"Richard is with me," Cecily said. She laughed lightly. "He's my bodyguard."

"Oh, you need a bodyguard when you are with me, do you? What are you afraid of?"

"Hey, guys!" I said quickly, sensing disaster. "Come on, Peter! This is your sister, remember? You haven't seen her in eight years. You can do better than this, I hope."

"Sure I can. I know how to be polite," he said. "But there's one thing we have to clear up before we go any further. I want *her*, over there, to apologize right now *to me* for what she and Olivia did in Idaho when the cops came and dragged me off like a dog. A dog that has to be put out of its misery."

He turned to Cecily. "You ever been to prison?"

"No-o-o," said Cecily.

"Well, you wouldn't like it. But you don't have to worry about it because they don't put people like you into prison."

He struck out wildly in the direction of the camera that Jim was by now aiming at him. "Get that thing out of my face!" Jim dove behind a column, but emerged on the other side still shooting.

"Do you know what Olivia's last words to the cops were as they led me away in handcuffs? 'Take him away and shoot him!' That was my first incarceration and I blame you for it," he said.

Cecily spoke up bravely. "Peter, I don't see why I have to say I'm sorry for something that was clearly not my fault. I didn't hit Mom, *you* did. I just happened to be in the house when it happened."

"You're the one that called the police."

"I'm not sure if it was me or Erasmo, but what were we supposed to do? You had just hit Mom with a log and knocked her to the floor. Were we supposed to stand around and wait until you did it again?"

"All of that is irrelevant. Bullshit, bullshit, bullshit." He glared at Jim. "I thought I told you not to shoot anymore," he snarled.

Jim ducked back behind the column.

"But Peter," Cecily said reasonably, "that's what we came for. We came here to make a film."

Little Peter stood. "If we all don't stop talking, if we all don't stop what we are doing right now, something is going to happen, I swear. And *none* of it is going to be my fault."

"So, what, are you going to hit *me* now?" Cecily asked calmly. "What did I do?"

"That's just it. You know exactly what you did. And the reason I know that is you are doing it again!"

"Peter, I'd like you to sit down," I said.

"I'm *not* sitting down." He made another wild swatting gesture at the camera. Once again Jim, who was just barely peeking the lens around the edge of the column, pulled out of sight quickly.

"Okay," I agreed. "You're not going to sit down. It's over then. We're stopping the shoot."

"Fine," he said.

"Just wait here," I said. "I'll be back in a minute. Don't move. Talk to Jim."

"That got a bit heavy," Richard said mildly, as he and Cecily put on their coats in the elevator lobby. "I thought I was going to have to resort to fisticuffs."

"Richard, I don't think I've ever seen you hit anyone," said Cecily.

"I mean it's not really my thing, but if I had to, I would," he said, smiling. "For *you*, dear."

"Thanks, Richard, I knew I could depend on you," Cecily said. Despite her kidding tone she was trembling and dead pale.

To Cecily I said, "Sorry about this."

"That's okay. I actually thought it was going to be good. You know, talking to Peter about things in our past."

"So did I," I said. "Too much water under the bridge, maybe?"

"I guess."

Much later, Cecily and I met at a vegetarian restaurant in the Village. I apologized again for how the taping had gone, and she said it was all right. Then Cecily told me much that surprised—and some that shocked—about her life growing up with my father and Olivia, of shouting and chasing, fists raised to hit, of waking up in the morning to birdcalls and finding herself alone with her mother in the back of the Volvo in the woods near Washademoak Lake in Canada after her mother had fled my father's violence of an evening—and of then reluctantly having to drive back home to the summer place, because there was no place else to go.

She remembered a family vacation (just days after he was kicked out of Choate), when Little Peter strode the beaches of the island of Rhodes, a muscular blond kouros, oblivious to the brown eyes and enticing bare breasts of the French girls surrounding him. Already a crack skier, Little Peter became an expert windsurfer in a matter of days. And every night, he sat down at the piano to improvise effortlessly with a European jazz combo, without written music or preparation, in a *taverna* open to the starry Aegean sky.

She also recalled, on their return, a tortured, closed-in soul, with few friends, who tapped away his afternoons at home alone on his electric piano with headphones on, filling the shadows of the empty apartment with the dry clicks of his electronic keyboard.

There had been more violence and violation. Peter throwing her up against the wall and holding her by the neck with one hand to watch as her face turned purple. Her having to watch while he laughed and masturbated into a plastic bag, and one particular incident when she was very young, when he placed her on his lap and paddled off into the reeds in a tin dinghy and she'd felt him rubbing beneath her buttocks.

It was clear that some things in our family couldn't be fixed. Little Peter would always be the slavering bugbear of her dreams. Now, like me, she was aspiring to shake the disaster of her early years to create a life for herself.

"I wished I had a normal upbringing," she said. "I wished I had normal brothers. But I didn't. As a teenager I was intent on being normal. Now that I've grown up, I am *conscientious* about it.

"I think about Peter now whenever I see someone homeless, or when I do something aggressive, or start losing my shit toward my children. He haunts me.

"I don't actually think about Peter on a daily basis, but when I do, I wish he would die. Oh, I know everybody has a right to exist, theoretically," she said. "But he causes so much pain to those I love and care about. He's this lurking threat that's always out there, and I still believe he's going to kill my mother someday—he has so much anger toward her. I keep expecting that one of these days, the way he lives, the way he drinks and rides on trains and gets himself arrested, that he'll get into a situation that kills him. That would be the best solution, really."

She stood up and began to wrap a scarf around her neck. We'd finished our meal. The restaurant that had started out full and noisy was now empty and still. The waiters were standing in the shadows waiting for us to go.

"I don't feel good about saying that about anyone, especially my brother, but that's the way I feel," she said. "I just wish he would die."

Atlantic City had been the scene of much of my stepbrother's recent intemperance, and where he went to play the slots. Our plan was to smuggle the camera into one of the casinos and see what happened.

On the drive down I lay in the backseat, listening to Jim and Little Peter arguing about which song to play on the radio. I began to feel the spirit of the film invade me. We had just crossed a bridge, for one thing, and had entered a new state. That was liberating. Turning on the video camera, I began to record spontaneous light poems, catching Little Peter's suspicious eyes in the rearview mirror and Jim's gesturing hands on the steering wheel. Why couldn't our film all be like this? I wondered. Why did we have to try hard to make sense, or any sense at all? Why didn't we simply record what happened, like Basho and his frog going plop in the pond in the famous haiku?

Suddenly Dylan's "Fourth Time Around" came on the radio, an unusual choice. It was one of the singer's most mysterious and fragmented songs, a fable in waltz time of desire and failed love:

When she said,
"Don't waste
Your words, they're just lies,"
I cried she was deaf.

Sure, words are just lies. And stories, like words, are just ways of getting around the truth. Why tell stories at all?

Halfway down to Atlantic City we stopped at a cold and desolate beach along the Jersey Shore. As soon as we halted, Little Peter jumped out of the car without a word and took off walking by himself, soon disappearing from sight. I grabbed the video camera and immediately found myself alone, lost on the white sand paths that wound through the high green dunes.

Then Jim came running up out of nowhere, panting. "Are you all right?" he asked.

"Yes," I said. "Where is Little Peter?"

"Oh, he's up . . ." Jim waved vaguely, and galloped off again.

Coming up to the top of a sandy hill, I spied Little Peter marching away across the rippled beach, a tall, sad, clownish figure with the ocean behind him. My stepbrother crossed and crossed again. Where had he come from? Where was he going to?

He soon turned and disappeared over a hill and I followed. By the time I caught up with him, he'd found a hollow in the sea grass, and had began to draw weird spirals and hex signs with a stick in the white sand, imitating, I thought, the perfect circles that tufts of tall, windblown sea grass had engraved around their roots nearby.

In his rags and with his tragic demeanor, Little Peter looked like a Pierrot character in a French drama, buffoonish and naïve. Yet his dumb play seemed to express more than he'd ever tried to say in words. The unconscious swirls and zigzags he was solemnly etching in the sand reminded me of the tiny backward twists in proteins that can cause cows to go mad, and of the similar twists in DNA that encode our consciousness and perhaps our past history. Finally they reminded me of the accidental mix of chemicals in Little Peter's brain that forever divided our two lives.

After a while, Little Peter put down his stick. With his deadpan face intact, he stiff-walked up to the camera, pushed his face into my lens— huge and leering in the viewfinder—and announced in a stagey singsong:

"It is *TIME* to go to Atlantic CITY!"

Thirty minutes later we were jogging down the lighted cattle ramp that led into the crass Christmas-lighted beehive of one of the large casinos, jostling with dentists, lawyers, long-legged cosmetologists. The mad *chigga chigga* of a thousand slot machines filled our heads. We took our free drinks in red plastic cups from a waitress in a bathing suit and dummied up to the maw of the machine.

I hit the jackpot with my second quarter. For a full five minutes, the air hummed and chattered with the musical notes of falling coins, as raw metal poured out of the gullet of the squat gaming machine into our hats, drinking cups, and the outstretched laps of our T-shirts. I've never been so surprised in my life.

Then my stepbrother said, with a seasoned gambler's mote of wisdom, "We might as well quit now. We're not going to win another dime in this place."

So we passed out of the brightly lit casino into the helter-skelter of Atlantic City at night, where Little Peter soon lost us, shouting behind him, in the dark maze of cocaine streets.

We were filming on the Hudson River, near my father's old apartment on West End Avenue.

It was one of those odd winter days that seem like the middle of summer, just because you're not used to the sun hitting so warm on your back. In reality a step into the shadows would have brought back the chill.

"So, do you think you could put me up for the night?" he asked.

"To be frank, Peter, I just can't," I said.

Little Peter leaned on the rail in a stocking cap and dark glasses (mine), trying to get a shot with the video camera of the helicopter that was hovering over the river about a half mile from us.

"How about putting me up in a hotel?"

"Maybe a night or two."

"You could ask Franz."

"I can do it—ask him. But I probably took the wrong tactic before. I implied that something was going to happen."

"What kind of thing?"

"Some kind of change."

On the Jersey side the trees were a mixture of brown and red, but mostly brown. The cliffs above had peculiar striations like the fingers of a very old person. The red sun shining on the cliffs had made me think of a painting, one of the brooding expressionists, like Rothko. Not everything is art, I had to remind myself. Some things were just things.

Little Peter looked at me a moment.

"How about a handout?" he asked.

"Sure, Peter, you can always have a handout."

A day or two later, Little Peter called from the Port Authority Bus Terminal. He sounded drunk. He said he'd had enough of New York and had a bus ticket for Albuquerque in his pocket.

I found him standing halfway up the stairs of a subway station across Eighth Avenue. I immediately stuck the video camera up to his lips. Every jagged bit of stubble on his red jaw stood out.

I realized at that moment how angry I was. The movie had really gotten under my skin. But it had never been very high on my stepbrother's agenda, I could see that.

Little Peter tried to hand me a fresh can of Hurricane Malt Liquor, the same brew he'd gotten drunk on, but I brushed it aside. He tried to hand me the can of beer again, praising it extravagantly for its taste, strength, and reviving qualities, and I refused it once more.

Luckily my stepbrother was too drunk to notice. He recited a few lines from the New Testament, just to warm up. I kept the front lens glued to his lips, so that the camera-mounted microphone could pick up the sound of his words, so that his face wobbled huge and cratered in my view-finder like a dying red planet. Finally he began to thank my father for paying for his hotel room, and for everything else—stuttering and bashful at first, but picking up speed. When I transcribed the tape later his words seemed to form the lines of an ironic prose poem, a Beat rant in blank verse. If I'd truly been paying attention, I'd have seen this was the one time in all of our hours of magnetically jiggered videotape that my stepbrother actually handed his heart to us, uncooked and beating on a plate:

Franz (he said),
If I am really talking to you,
Thank you, Franz, from the bottom of my heart.
From my heart, Franz,
Thank you very much.
And I appreciate it more than you can possibly understand.
And God bless you and
Thank you very much,
For all of the years of my life
That I've spent in uncertainty,
And wondering who the hell I am,
And wondering does my family love me,
And of course they probably do,
But like all family members
I think maybe they don't sometimes.
If I'm giving this message to Franz,
Thank you very much from the bottom of my heart.

I didn't know when I said good-bye to my stepbrother on the subway steps that afternoon, it would be the last I'd see of him for five years. Or that when I did see him again, it would be under catastrophic circumstances, although for my stepbrother catastrophe forms the tender of his daily life and therefore falls into a different category than for the rest of us.

"What about your plan for financial stability?" I asked, as he passed the Harmony guitar back to me.

"That might look pretty good on paper," he said, "but I have to travel light."

Part Eleven

And always, after the first thrills of getting under way, the
adventure develops into a journey of darkness, horror,
disgust, and phantasmagoric fears.

—Joseph Campbell

Chapter Thirty-four

At some point, while this was all going on, I started taping my mother whenever I had the chance, asking her questions concerning Peacock Point, and her remote and lost childhood on Long Island. My father didn't want to be asked about *his* life, but one afternoon he agreed to be taped too, as long as I understood that the subject was my mother and Peacock Point, not himself.

He waited calmly as I set up the camera. As soon as the tape started rolling, though, he stuck his hand toward me and waggled it, as if he had just been burned. His face grew distorted and red. Then he began to cry with deep, jagged, tearing sobs. What I think happened is that all of the cruelty, sadness, injustice, and loneliness of his early life broke open and filled his throat like warm blood from a burst vein.

"Turn it off! Turn it off!" he bawled, and I did.

My father had already started to die then, although he didn't know it. He thought he'd caught his case of prostate cancer early, and had blasted it into submission so that he could go on as before.

After his first course of radiation treatments, I called to ask him how things were going. In his typical way, he gave me an answer with far more details than I wanted to hear.

"Shitting, okay," he replied. "Fucking . . . same as always. Pissing, not so good."

That summer a badly timed bout of sciatica refused to go away. He'd suffered from sciatica all of his life, and so pretended at first not to worry. You know how it is, though, when you get sick in August. Your doctor is nowhere to be found. Others are unavailable, or vague. No one seems to be in charge. To that exact proportion that you urgently need information and someone to care for you, your professional grows lackadaisical and distant.

At some point in July, while we were staying in Canada, my father called to tell me that his brother Ulrich had paddled out into the middle of the Intracoastal Waterway behind his apartment in South Florida, put the barrel of a newly purchased rifle into his mouth, and pulled the trigger.

To me, on the phone, my father said, "Ulrich always was a misfit. Imagine killing yourself like that. I can't. It makes me shudder to think of it."

It was one of those days that only a death in the family can bring, icy cold, with rain lashing the windows. I stayed in my room all day, reading, writing, and thinking about Ulrich, while Hali and the kids made Korean dumplings, filling up the rooms with the smells of cooking pork and garlic and kimchee.

I don't want to overstay my welcome, Ulrich had written in the note he left behind. *I began life in an institution with callous warders and choose not to end up thataway. Besides, I'm down to my last pair of white socks, because the ladies at the lavenderia keep losing them.*

At two o'clock the phone rang again to disturb my reveries. This time it was my mother.

"Whatever happened to Ulrich started at age two," she said. "They were the most unpleasant people," she added, meaning my grandparents, Hatti-Hatti and Mimia. "They were impossible."

On Sunday, I called my father at his home, waking him from a nap. Still groggy, he let his guard down and admitted to me for the first time that his prostate cancer had revived and spread. The "sciatica" that had been making walking and driving so painful for him since the spring was actually a series of tumors growing in his hip bones and spine. His doctors were giving him five years to live, he said, actually more than he expected. The tough thing was that he'd already received as much radiation as they were willing to allow him, so they were prescribing testosterone inhibitors and might even have him take estrogen. He prepared to mourn the end of his sex life, but he said there was a chance the cancer would even go into remission.

Oddly, being given five years to live lifted my father's spirits. The diagnosis hadn't done much for his pain, but it had ended the uncertainty and worry that had plagued him for months. Five years at his age seemed an awfully long time—he'd already outlived his father, Hattie-Hattie, who had died at the age of eighty-one while taking a nap in a hotel room. Five years would take my father almost up to the age of ninety. Five years wasn't a sentence, it was a reprieve.

From his study my father started a new pursuit, one that interested him greatly. He began to track down and contact his former lovers, one by one. He found that one had become a judge who had inspired a television series. He made a special trip across the country to visit another, an eighty-year-old widow.

Calling my father once a week was a duty I assigned myself that fall. Liz later said that my dad enjoyed talking to me more than any of his male friends, that I should have seen his eyes light up every time I phoned. But all I remember is feeling wary. I steeled myself for each conversation, and waited for the verbal cut, the offhand remark that would start the black waters rising. In truth I had never learned to feel at ease with my father, and his present condition didn't change that.

Now that my father was officially on the list of the dying, all of our interactions with him took on a sense of urgency and importance they hadn't had before. The present was still a bit vague, but you could at least look the future square in the face. Hali urged me to drive out to spend time with Dad, to help out around the house and to take some of the load off Liz. My two sisters made plans to fly in from Alaska. Alerted by Olivia to the seriousness of my father's illness, Little Peter called me from Ketchum, Idaho, where he was attending AA meetings while sleeping under a bridge. He begged me to intervene with Franz for one last visit. It'd been twenty years since he'd last seen my father. Since then he'd undergone a conversion, he said. He wanted a chance to prove to my father that he wasn't the old Little Peter, that he'd changed.

"What are you going to tell him?" I asked.

"I don't know yet," he admitted. "But God will tell me exactly the right thing to say when I get there."

With this less-than-reassuring prediction in mind, I called Dad. The best I could do was to promise that I could ensure Little Peter's sobriety and good behavior. I was bluffing perhaps, but only a little. I shouldn't have expected any reply but the one my father gave.

"I'm a sick man and the doctor says I have to keep up my spirits," Dad said. "What happened to your stepbrother just makes me feel bad."

Hali reminded me again to start driving out to New Jersey on a regular basis to visit my father and help out around the house. "Liz needs a break," she said. To my wife this seemed the only natural way to behave, not only based on the way her family would have acted, but the way people generally behaved in Kansas City, where she grew up. However, I was a little skeptical of the plan.

"You don't know them," I said. "They don't like trespassers on their alien planet." But I knew I should at least make the offer. It *was* the neighborly thing to do, and in any other family it could actually have been the right thing. As it happened, even in my most pessimistic moment, I couldn't have foreseen what an uproar my day of duty in Sea Bright would cause.

Dad was lukewarm on the idea, but I pressed my case, and early in the morning a few days after Thanksgiving, I drove out to Sea Bright in my dark blue Volvo station wagon. Meanwhile, Liz had made plans to spend the day in Manhattan.

I found my father sitting on the couch watching MSNBC. As the stock market symbols raced along at the bottom of the screen, faster than my mind could have ever grasped them, his eyes flicked back and forth automatically taking in the numbers. Before him on the coffee table were the remnants of his and Liz's previous evening, an empty bottle of Frangelico, a box of Wheat Thins, and a large half-eaten bag of Hershey's chocolates. They'd watched the latest edition of the reality show *Survivor*, he explained, as soon as he noticed me.

"Why do you want to do this?" my father asked. He seemed lonely, but that only made him gruffer.

I told him I just wanted to see if I could make things easier for him.

"You're not making things easier—you're making things harder!" he grumbled. "Making me damn nervous is what you're doing."

It was Dad's idea that we go upstairs to his office. The condo was de-

signed as a three-story town house. I bounded up the stairs unthinkingly.
Then I stood at the landing and watched helplessly as my father hauled
himself up by the rail. He took over ten minutes to come up to where I
was. He was sweating and grimacing painfully by the end, but refused my
help.

In his crowded office he slid open a file drawer and began pulling out
papers. Everything was completely organized. "I'm a bookkeeper at heart,"
he said cheerily, and it really did seem that leafing through the IRS reports, statements, and folders brought up his spirits a great deal, as if for
the first time that morning he was back on his own turf.

Finally he pulled out his will. I suppose it was his way of acting respon-
sibly. I had little desire to see the document, although I was one of its
executors. But he insisted on going through it in wearying detail, page by
page.

In the end, he turned and gave me a self-conscious grin; it was exactly
the look a boy gives his mom when he's been caught with his thumb in the
cake icing. He hopes his mother will think it's cute, but he's half expecting
a whack.

We went back downstairs at the same slow and painful pace. And thus,
to my dismay, began what was billed to be a typical day in the life of my
father. The ensuing production reminded me of the kind of show of busy,
happy normalcy that is put on by the owners of a summer camp on visitors'
day. First there is the inspection, then the laundry, the lunch, the swim
meet, the archery contest, summer musical, and the campfire sing. "This is
great!" Mom and Pop think to themselves. "What are all those damn letters from Junior about hating it here and wanting to go home?"

Our first stop was the town library. I was shocked at the physical strata-
gems that my father was resorting to in order to get on with his day. At the
library Dad directed me to drive the car as close as I could to the edge of
the curb. When I went around to open the door, Dad growled, "You just
get out of my way!" and he hauled himself up out of his seat using the car
door. But he clung to my arm as he stepped gingerly onto the sidewalk.
The few steps leading up to the library door almost defeated him.

"My doctor told me not to shuffle," Dad confided as he leaned heavily
on my arm. Well, he was flagrantly disobeying doctor's orders that day. To
me he seemed very close to not being able to get around at all.

It was nearly worth the previous minutes' ordeal to see the way the women at the library's front desk hailed my father as a returning hero. Apparently my father had been taking a library class on the how-to of sending e-mails, and he'd used the opportunity to send suggestive messages to all of the blue-haired ladies in his group, to their absolute and unmitigated delight.

Wherever we went, Dad knew everyone. He seemed to be the most popular guy in Sea Bright. After the library we drove to the bank, the post office, and on to a small seaside restaurant for sandwiches, and then to Red Bank for a trim at his favorite Italian barber. When the barber held up the mirror to show him the back of his neck, Dad once again turned to look at me and put on his mischievous little boy grin, as if he'd just been caught with his thumb in the frosting.

Once we'd left the barbershop, though, Dad strode stone-faced ahead of me, swinging his arms with his legs apart. I ran to catch up, and said, "Dad, you promised me you were getting better!"

"Well, I've gotten stronger," he said, keeping up his dreadful pace. "I've been walking every day. You wouldn't believe the courage it takes to get up in the morning and face the exercises I'm supposed to do, when I'm in this kind of pain."

By the end of the day, I was shocked by his frailty. *Surely he's a lot worse than the doctors are telling us*, I thought to myself. Something was terribly wrong.

Chapter Thirty-five

With nothing new to report about Dad's condition, we left once more with the kids to go to the summer place in Canada. Then as if the summer had never happened, we were back. Things were happening at a faster pace now. My father had suddenly lost the use of his legs. In the space of a few weeks, the doctors reduced their first overly generous estimate of his life span from five years to one. Then it was three months. His pain increased until it crazed him. His brittle hip bones developed hairline cracks.

When Hali asked him what we could do to help, he answered sardonically, "Give me my legs back."

He talked of following in Olga and Ulrich's footsteps, but Liz simpered, "Franz, you promised me you would see this thing through."

My sisters flew in from Alaska. In the odd, unprecedented arrangements of hours that opened up for us now, no one really knew what to do. Timing seemed important, but like the market, one never could tell whether one was getting in too early, or was getting out too late. Nevertheless, suddenly there they were, my two sisters, great cheerful Alaskan presences. They appeared larger and more practical than Hali and I, and seemed to be breathing a thinner, cooler kind of air.

On the Sunday before Labor Day came the news that my father had suffered a massive sepsis from the catheter he'd been wearing. He was taken to the hospital, struggling, hallucinating.

Yet when we arrived the next morning, Dad had already been moved out of intensive care to a regular hospital room, and was sitting up in his bed calmly chatting with Liz and her mother while watching a tennis match on his room TV. Out of the window of the hospital I could see the wide blue Navesink River as it ran its slow course to the sea.

"We don't need you here," Liz said. "Tell them to go home, Franz."

"Yes, for God's sake, children, go home," my father said.

Even though we were getting thrown out, it encouraged me to see him so cheerful, and after all, in his regular grouchy mood. Mentally he seemed quite acute, another reason to celebrate. Unfortunately, just then the attending neurologist came in to explode that illusion.

"Franz, you look great," the doctor said in a booming voice, after glancing through the chart. "Your color is good, your temperature is down and so is your white blood cell count. All of that is excellent, I must say, though it's rather unusual for a man of your age with massive sepsis to be doing this well."

"Yes, yes," said my father, never taking his eyes from the screen.

"I just want to ask you one question, if that's okay."

"Sure," said my father.

"What city are we in right now?"

"*San FRAN-cisco!*" my father replied with great satisfaction.

Another day went by, in which my father seemed to get better under the treatment of antibiotics, then worse, almost to the point of another collapse, and then to rise to a kind of middle ground, a plateau, from which he seemed aware of us, though barely conscious.

My sister Olga had spent the night with us, and when we arrived at the hospital Liz had not been happy to see us all together. "What are you doing here?" she asked grumpily. She wasn't used to having so many family members around, nor sharing my father with anyone.

On the day before my father died, he began to rave in many languages—German, Latin, Portuguese, English. Often he called for his mother, Mimia, but she wasn't there, as always.

Liz took his hand. "Franz, Mimia wasn't that nice to you."

For some reason, he automatically pushed his lips out to kiss whoever put a face close to his. He kissed my sisters, Olga and Lisa. He kissed my half sister, Cecily. He kissed my wife, over and over.

He was also ravenous. Perhaps he was preparing for his long journey to the other side. As I fed him a plate of hospital mash with a plastic spoon, I remembered what he had said to me a dozen years before, when he watched me feed my firstborn son: "I was never that kind of father to you." I was confident in my own skills, though, for I knew well how to feed my father, bringing spoonful after spoonful of hospital food—pizza ground into mush, mashed potato, and then applesauce—up to his mouth. Thus I'd fed each of our kids: spooning just enough, bringing the handle up at just the right angle, scraping the sides of his mouth and his chin with the spoon, watching him thrust his lips forward eagerly after each swallow for more.

When I left, at 2:00 P.M., I leaned close over the bed and said into his ear, "I have to pick up the kids at school now, Dad. Take care of yourself!"

"Okay," he said, the response so quick and natural that I thought at first he'd actually understood me.

The following day, while my father lay in bed and snored spectacularly, the hospice nurse called the family members into a meeting in a large windowed room in the hospital. Obediently we sat around her in a circle. She was a tall woman of about thirty, with long, blond, carefully tended hair. As she spoke to us of our current position and options, she seemed to represent a novel corporate version of religious faith, one not based on belief, or received through ancient texts, but learned from years of hands-on experience with those who were dying, perhaps even by the use of unpublicized instruments that could reach into the minds of unresponsive patients to detect their actual thoughts and needs. While her discourse was somewhat New Age in tone, it appeared to me that she was a conscientious practitioner who had taken carefully into account the spiritual and practical needs of our family and my father, while also keeping a close eye on the balance sheet of the hospital and its underlying insurer. Hers was a wider truth, in other words, a truth not influenced by vague speculation or wish.

She began by telling us that our father was reliving his entire life now. That was the meaning of his grimaces, his ejaculations in many languages, his nonstop squirming in his bed. He was having to come to terms with everyone he'd come into contact with over a lifetime, the specters, apparently, arriving in fast motion. At the same time, the hospice nurse told us calmly, our father was hyperaware of everything going on around him. If we told him we loved him, he would hear it. If we said good-bye, he would understand. If we spoke disparagingly, or acted out of self-interest, he could be hurt.

To Liz, the blond nurse said, "Your husband is a man who wishes to die, but he has been waiting for you to let go of him. His body has been telling him that it is time to leave, but because of his love for you he is holding on until you tell him you are ready."

The hospice nurse went on to explain that when you signed the papers that placed your relative, or loved one, into hospice care, you agreed to remove him from all of the things that sustain human life, namely water, food, and oxygen. That which a patient can ingest for himself, he may have, though. Since my father had shown such an amazing appetite the day before, we mentally prepared ourselves for a long siege.

"When we came into the hospital I wasn't ready to let go of Franz," said Liz. "After listening to you, I am now."

Confident of her powers of persuasion, and perhaps of the rightness of her belief, the hospice nurse had brought the necessary paperwork into the room with her.

While Liz signed the papers, Hali and I brought the kids into the sick room to say good-bye to Opa Franz. His breathing was firm and his face held a strong blush, so that from a distance of a few feet he seemed like a healthy man sleeping. When I kissed my father good-bye though, I saw that the stretched skin under his stubble was sallow, and his cheek felt wooden under my lips.

At the moment Dad passed on, a blue light arose from his chest and flew out of the window. This is according to Liz, who was there with her mother, and is a practicing Catholic.

In the obituary notice I wrote that day for *The New York Times*, I listed my stepbrother, Peter Raymond Sluis von Ziegesar, among the survivors, even though Dad had cut him out of his will and had, to the end, steadfastly refused to see him. I wrote in my journal:

September 9, 2007
     my father died last night. he was a fossilized old grouch who
made sure that when I went out into the world i had both legs

cut off at the knees, but he was my father. when i used to spoon feed alden he would stare at us and say, "i was never that kind of father to you." and it was particularly strange and satisfying to be spoon feeding him, when he was in his own infant stage, just the day before yesterday, and have for a few minutes the role reversed. But i would never do to my kids what he did to us. Of course, what his parents did to him and his siblings can't even be categorized, it was beyond neglect—sent away to lonely foreign boarding schools when they could barely walk—and he is the only one in the end not to have committed suicide (perhaps because his wife is catholic). anyway, he died peacefully in his sleep, we were all there almost to the time when it happened, all of his biological kids (the ones we know about :-) . . .) and it was rather beautiful, actually. i took pictures. well, it was satisfying as a group effort. no one walked away feeling short-changed. i am supposed to write the eulogy for him. you can see that i have made a start . . .

Chapter Thirty-six

My father's death had been relatively swift and merciful, to my mind, but Liz told me he would have been disappointed. "He always told me he wanted to die in the saddle on the other side of the tracks," she said. In translation: of a heart attack and in the arms of a floozy, the way Nelson Rockefeller found his destiny back in 1979, in the embrace of Megan Marshack—a moment in history that had engraved itself upon my father's memory. It's said that when a Viking warrior found himself weak and old, and shamefully hadn't died in battle, he'd draw his sword and with a shouted challenge fling himself off the nearest cliff, or else risk losing his seat in Valhalla. I wondered whether Dad's best friend Findlay had been looking for that kind of heroic death in the way he chose to go. When he was found floating in the Gowanus Canal on the Brooklyn waterfront decades ago, no one had ever discovered what he'd been up to in that questionable part of town. Perhaps all old preppy warriors seek a similar kind of glory in death: "In the saddle on the other side of the tracks." Perhaps if my father's death hadn't caught him unawares, he would have found a way to fulfill his own destiny as well.

At the dinner after the memorial service for my father, which took place in a Sea Bright church a month after his death, I sat next to a pleasant-faced, youngish-looking man in a leather motorcycle jacket, who introduced himself to me as a former president of Bowne's New York branch. He related a story about my father that for him summed up Dad's later presence in the company. For a year or two before he retired, my father had been bumped upstairs to the newly created position of CEO, a sort of ceremonial posting. Around that time, this former executive told me, Bowne had taken on a huge Wall Street client. He wouldn't tell me what the name of this client was, but said I could compare it to Pfizer—*that* size. One day this former Bowne president received a call from his counterpart at the client's company.

"We love Franz," the president of not-Pfizer had said to him. "He makes us all laugh. We'd like him to come visit us anytime he wants. But please, he has to promise to stop goosing the receptionist."

Chapter Thirty-seven

In June the air around Peacock Point is richest. It glows with a clear trans-lucent light and is not yet weighed down with the potent sadness of mois-ture and heat that summer brings later on. Ancient rhododendrons as tall as houses guarded the gates of the cemetery when we arrived, their gar-ish purple blooms exploding like skyrockets from the gloom of their dark leaves, which descended like the ears of goats.

Although it was noon, the tree-thronged cemetery was full of shadows. A man lurked just behind a row of laurels with a wheelbarrow and shovel, waiting for us to be through, so he could push dirt into the grave.

We had gathered to bury my father's ashes next to his mother, father, sister, and brother in a small grove in the Locust Valley Cemetery, in Long Island, just a mile or two from Peacock Point. Dad's mother, Mimia, who styled herself the Baroness, even though she was born on 144th Street and St. Nicholas Avenue in Harlem, had wanted to be buried near her daughter-in-law's rich relations.

It had been a distressing month. A few weeks earlier my stepfather, Johnny, had fallen to the floor of his bedroom and died of a heart attack. We were all reeling in the shade of his absence. Each time I called my mother on the telephone to ask how she was doing, she'd answer, "Well, I'm all right." She meant that she was satisfactory, but not especially good, that Johnny hadn't been at his usual place at the dinner table that night; nor had he driven off with bags to the town dump, though it was trash day;

nor sought his reading glasses throughout the house, as was his daily habit; nor had he walked into the bedroom with a copy of the paper to expound upon the latest outrage committed by our president, George W. Bush. A day like this had occurred yesterday and another day was in store for my mother tomorrow.

Even though we were there to remember my father, the afternoon didn't seem to be about him, somehow. It was about the smiles and small embarrassments of seeing each other, the slightly cold tinge of the air, the strangeness of talking in the open, where the sound of our voices was pulled up to the sky. The men were in shirtsleeves, the women in black dresses, the children in sunglasses and T-shirts. At least I'd been able to talk Alden out of wearing his yellow basketball shorts. We stood in a half circle inside the small grove that contained my father's family plot. I filmed with my pocket camera as my niece Christina led everyone in singing "Amazing Grace." Then Liz placed the bronze urn into the small, dug hole. Hali pointed out to me how odd it was that Dad, Olga, Ulrich, Mimia, and Hattie-Hattie were reunited again, the original nuclear family—five stones in a row. No kids, and no spouses were buried there. There probably weren't going to be any in the future, either. After all of these decades, none of them had been able to take their lives beyond the family unit, or find warm soil for their prodigious talents to bloom in.

The size of a funeral has shrunken over the years from the time my grandmother Froggie was buried in the same cemetery, I observed. That was the kind of internment you saw in the movies, with lines of black limousines baking in the sun and mourners standing in formal wear around a hoisted casket. Nowadays it's simpler, you lift the urn yourself one-handed and drop it into a hole not much bigger than a dog might dig going after a rabbit. You wouldn't trust a priest or a minister to stand up and say few words of insincerity over the grave, because we've long since willed such people from our lives. A minister wouldn't have known my father in any case and would've taken the job merely to pick up a few dollars—God knows, with flocks shrunken the way they are nowadays, he'd need to supplement.

The first time I noticed this formal nonchalance take place was when we buried my stepsister Nina in the early eighties, after she died in a car accident while still at Bennington, and since then we have all gone into the ground in exactly this sort of do-it-yourself fashion. That is not to say that we are not mourned, for the sadness of those who stay on for those who leave is almost unbearable. There is a pattern to it, and the pattern seems to be that the ones who deserve to die the least, and who will cause us the most pain to be without, will go first. Has the ceremony grown simpler because, as my father might have said, we are tougher? I don't think so. It's just that none of us can bear anymore to place the task of burying our dead into the hands of strangers.

It is a saving grace that when you have children that you are always trying to educate them. After we put Dad's urn into the earth we went to look for the plot in which my grandmother Froggie's family is buried, asking directions from the man in the grove of trees, who had already placed his shovel in the wheelbarrow full of dirt, and was visibly impatient for us to leave.

We found the name DAVISON carved into a step in the stone path. There in a clearing within oaks and rhododendrons, we gamboled and ran in moist shadows and began to scrape up clumps of moss that we would later press into the cracks between the flagstones in our garden.

As I wandered off a few yards in search of the graves of my great-grandparents, Kate and Henry P. Davison, I was stunned to come face-to-face with a large predatory bird, its eyes alert and merciless, that appeared to hover, talons bared, just over their graves. When I investigated I found an immense bronze bald eagle, looming from the foliage, held up by a pole that was designed to fade into the leaves and disappear. The eagle was so lifelike that no birds or small animals could be seen in the silent grove. I wasn't surprised that my great-grandfather had chosen this fierce raptor to guard his final sojourn. He had made it a policy to show little mercy to those weaker than he. As a general and right-hand man to the banker J. P. Morgan, he'd grasped bankers and industrialists by the necks, held their writhing bodies over the sulpherous abyss, and decided whether to let them drop or not. At my feet, the words ONWARD CHRISTIAN SOL-DIERS were carved into each of my grandparents' gray slabs in ornate lettering. I knew no irony was intended. This wasn't like having a favorite line from a pop song engraved as your epitaph: "All You Need Is Love," or "What a Long Strange Trip It's Been!" My great-grandparents had seen themselves as literal soldiers in an all-or-nothing battle against softness, social deviation, and sloth. As a reward for their faithful service, and a token of their righteousness, God had given them ample riches, children, and servants.

Compared to these somber Episcopalian slabs, whose brown slate seemed to suck in all surrounding light and energy, my aunt Alessandra's stone, carved of pink granite in the shape of a swooping sea bird, was as bright and pagan as a tube of lipstick when I came upon it a few yards farther down. My cousin Little Ward was buried next to his mother. The dates on his stone showed he was only eighteen when he took his life in 1973. While I was standing over his grave, I recalled with a sudden shiver that Little Ward had visited me in my sleep the night before. He'd smiled shyly and brushed his sandy bangs aside to point to his forehead. There, instead of the bullet wound that should have been, was a small, pale scar, like an acne crater.

I'd been wrong about Little Ward, I realized. When I was young I'd thought his death had had a special meaning, that he'd died, somehow, so that the rest of us could live. I'd come to realize what vain, romantic thinking that was. Ward had negotiated his own bargain with Death, and my turn at the table would come soon enough.

Toward the back I pointed out to my kids the small row of stones where the Davisons had buried the servants who had died in harness. Here also I found the graves of the Russians. The extra slashes on the Orthodox crosses carved into their markers added a rakish air to my grandparents' own tree-enclosed clearing. Here by Ward and Froggie was the stone of my grandmother's lifelong friend, George Stacey—the tall, distant, wry interior decorator, always dressed in black, whose head had been as bald as an egg. Finally I read out loud the quote on my grandfather Big Ward's stone: it was Faulkner, who in 1950 had seemingly stood alone against the notion that the world was about to be burned to a glowing cinder in a nearing and unavoidable atomic war:

> I believe that man will not merely endure: he will prevail. He is immortal, not because he alone among creatures has an inexhaustible voice, but because he has a soul, a spirit capable of compassion and sacrifice and endurance.

I thought as we walked back to the car, if we do have an immortal soul, it must be transmitted the way children's chants and games are passed down from one generation to the next, by word of mouth. A child's humanity, his ethics, almost everything he is, he absorbs during his short time on the swings and jungle gym. In the end it builds and fills him. But whatever the soul is, it exists only for today, I thought. If I wanted to pass anything on, I'd better do it now. There weren't going to be any afterwards or second chances.

Ceremony done, we drove to a banquet scheduled in an old-fashioned suburban dinner restaurant where the walls were brick and the tables covered with white tablecloths. And then we took leave of our cousins and sisters, pulling one of those disappearing acts for which we are well known.

Part Twelve

After great pain, a formal feeling comes.

—Emily Dickinson

Chapter Thirty-eight

In a minute we were on the road, unheralded and unexpected, not knowing what we'd see when we got there. The gate was no longer marked with peacocks; it all seemed different, and the sizes and proportions were wrong, and even when I set our car along the long curved drive to the beach, the road did not seem as long, or the locust trees as tall or as shady, as in my memory of them.

A shimmering, robin's egg blue McMansion encroached the Polo Field, and there were more in view as we drove down farther. The old, giant weeping House Tree had grown worn and transparent—we could see inside its shaggy branches. We drove on. One of Danny's sons had taken over the groundskeeper's cottage and placed a sign out front that read, SHAQUE SUMMER. We saw a sign at another outbuilding that read SHAQUE L'AMOR.

We eventually found the two blue peacocks that had once graced the pillars at the estate entrance—now they watched my grandmother's octagonal house through a furze of bramble. The Cheney House now belonged to my mother's cousin Danny; his front door was open, but though we knocked and called through the screen doors, no one came to let us in. The house did not seem as big as I remembered—it was built in the 1920s, and what was grand then did not seem as grand now. The extravagances of my grandmother's class and time were modest compared to the extravagances we are capable of now.

We left the car in front of the white mansion and went around the fence to the beach, and walked the concrete walk on the Sound side all the way to the breakwater. The walk had lifted and broken up into slabs, after some huge storm. In the place where the Big House had been, there was only a sunken lawn with marks of an old foundation, whose footprint seemed tiny, no bigger than that of a largish suburban ranch house. The steps leading to the Sound as well as a pair of laughing lion sculptures on pedestals showed us the shape the building must have had. Uncle Trubee's house, which had been physically moved there in the sixties, had in the meantime also been torn down.

Someone had left a small wooden rowboat on the crescent beach. Its presence made the view picturesque from where we stopped at the foot of the breakwater. A fisherman was doing some kind of peculiar dance out on the water—wrestling with a long pole, almost as if he were a tightrope walker. Though I watched for several minutes, I couldn't figure it out.

The breakwater stretched before me, a hook of granite chunks reaching into the dark, ruffled water. I stepped out onto the boulders. I'd learned to leap along these rocks when I was a kid and I could still judge their shapes by feel under my feet, still jump, catch my balance, shift, jump to the next rock, without thinking. I ran a hundred feet out, then turned and ran back. Suddenly I wanted to explain everything about Peacock Point to my kids.

"Guys," I called, "look at the Casino. It's kind of falling down, I know. That's the place where your Opa Franz and Akka were married." (i.e., my mother and father: these kinds of supernumerary nicknames are traditional for grandparents in my family). "And did you know that these rocks were taken here by a barge when they dug the subway in New York City?"

"Dad?"

"Yes."

"You know the baby in *Family Guy*? Why does he speak with an English accent?"

"I didn't know it was supposed to be an English accent."

"You know the episode where Stewie tries to kill Brian by making him eat garbage?" said Alden. "It was SO funny. SO funny!"

"I like the *Futurama* where it's four thousand years in the future and the Beastie Boys' heads are frozen in nitrogen," said Maya.

"That was SO funny!"

"I used to play on the beach there," I said. "We used to have this game, it was kind of silly, where we would fill an empty milk bottle with sand and then spin it so the sand came flying out in a spiral. It's too bad you never knew your uncle, Little Ward.

"He was a good kid," I said. "His sisters used to say he was a little whiney, but I don't remember him that way. He used to be an incredible fisherman . . . used to pull in bass from the last rock of this breakwater."

"Dad?"

"Yes?"

"Did you see the episode of *South Park* where Al Gore gets dressed up in a bear suit and tries to kill them in an old cave?"

"*ManBearPig! ManBearPig!*" the kids chanted.

"Kids, I'm trying to tell you something," I said. "Will you listen for a moment?"

"Tag!"

"Got you first!"

"No you didn't!"

I gave up. They were already running down the beach away from me. Trying to catch their attention was like hooking an elusive bass from the end of a rocky pier. My children's lives revolved around patterns and plays outlined in television shows about cynical suburban families with dogs that talked. My life was turned inward, to plays and patterns lived decades ago in a place that no longer existed.

I'd thought the buildings and mansions of Peacock Point would last longer than my memories of them. Houses are made from bricks and mortar, wood timbers and window glass, brass balustrades and carved stone, but memories are just a kind of primal spit flowing between the neurons in our brains. I was wrong, though. It was the memories that endured while the buildings had all but washed away. All that remained of the familiar was the cobalt blue sky dotted with white mare's tails and the slate water gently lapping the shore.

It's said that ghosts come back to the places they haunt because they have unfinished business there; perhaps that is why I still wander the long carpeted hallways and dark locust-trilling roads of Peacock Point in my dreams.

Little Peter never set a foot in Peacock Point himself, and if I happened to mention it to him now I doubt if he'd know what I was talking about. But I think he'd understand. Inside Peacock Point I learned a kind of loyalty to my generation that has never broken. There's a kind of honor among the young that is similar to that among thieves. When we were at our most vulnerable, we learned to watch out for ourselves and watch out for the others, and when a real adult came along, with his glad-handing ways and his false, resounding laughter, we learned to dummy up fast and slip away.

I strolled back toward the place where the Big House had stood. As I stepped over the old foundation I saw a glint of metal between two worn stones. I reached down and found an old dime, tarnished apparently by many years' exposure to the weather. I looked at it closely. Oddly, the date embossed on the coin was a year from now. It must be some kind of mis-strike, I considered—it would probably be quite valuable if I knew where to take it. I carefully slipped the thin disc of metal into the watch pocket of my pants. Something tugged at my memory, but I couldn't quite pull it out.

A year from now, I said to myself, I'll be doing something different. I shaded my eyes and looked toward the water, to where my three kids were running along the shore, hand in hand in a rare show of unity. All relatively healthy and strong. Hadn't James Joyce written somewhere that no man is a failure who has raised a family?

A couple of years back, responding to the kind of unfocused real estate aspirations that are typical to New Yorkers, we'd sold our apartment. Frankly I didn't realize how devastated I'd be, and the next few months were extinguished in a damp fog of helper pills. By the end of August, however, we'd found a house on the far side of the East River on a street of tall, mottled plane trees. The neighborhood was dotted with sidewalk cafes and small storefronts, each its own crazy idea of what a store should be; one sold only church hats and another just red velvet cake. The corner restaurant ran on solar power and vended Brazilian sandwiches out of a van. I was reminded of the old, brave artist neighborhoods of Kansas City and Greenwich Village. So far I'd seen no tourists or chain stores.

As dusk fell on our first night, the warm summer air turned porous and magical. Neighbors sat on stoops, or wandered up and down the block carrying glasses of wine. Hali and I were invited to a party in someone's backyard, where we ate at a long table set in the grass, while the trees spilled their cool, dark foliage over us. A door had been cut into the fence so that children could chase from yard to yard, and the air resounded with happy laughter. So this was Brooklyn! It was like nothing we'd ever experienced before in New York! We walked up to our stoop half tipsy, taking our time. As we sauntered, our children scootered by us fast, pursuing other kids up into their houses here and there. "I'm in Number 24!" they shouted back to us, or "I'll be in 36!" And we called after them, "Wait a minute, what number did you say? What's the name of the mom, do we know her?" But it was too late, they'd already disappeared, flit-wing, into the trees and shadows. "Just look for the light in the window!" we heard them call. "Look for the light in the window!"

My half sister Cecily and her husband had moved nearby and our children visited back and forth regularly. My relationship with Olivia had repaired over the years, thanks to our common interest in my stepbrother's life. In truth, Olivia has, upon one or two occasions, been called upon to babysit our kids.

I'd heard from my old friend Jim Syme recently. He'd been diagnosed with a kind of heart murmur that causes unexplained collapses and flulike symptoms, especially under stress. I was convinced that this was the reason for the many times that he was stricken when we were filming. A few years ago he'd sold his town house in Philadelphia and taken his nest egg to Tucson, Arizona, where he'd lost everything in the first hiccup of the housing bubble. He was now driving a van at the Tucson airport, and working twelve hours a day just to get by. But he'd found a girlfriend, moved out of town, and was taking superb photographs of the southwestern desert, which had always been for him a location of dreams and visions. In truth on the telephone he'd sounded as happy as I'd ever heard him.

After Hali's grandmother died in Colorado, Hali's father and mother, Dr. T. H. and Priscilla Lee, had briefly passed through town on a nationwide tour of the coastline to find a shore condo to retire into. They briefly considered Far Rockaway and Sea Bright, but ended up settling in Jacksonville, Florida. In their absence we were trying to inculcate our kids with some small portion of Korea's vast history and culture—the invention of the Mona Lisa smile some six hundred years before Leonardo, for example; the creation of moveable type some seventy-seven years before Gutenberg's Bible; and the building of armored war vessels four hundred years before the *Monitor* and the *Merrimac*. Then there was the unassailable evidence that when the first Korean settlers landed on Japanese shores, they found only hairy monkeys living in trees. There was so much to learn and so little time. We were barely keeping up.

A few weeks after my father died, I saw Little Peter for the first time in half a decade, when I flew down to Miami to rescue him from jail. He'd gotten drunk on the beach and passed out, then thrown a punch at the ambulance driver who'd tried to shake him awake. Due to a mistake in his "Priors," his electronically kept criminal record, the judge was preparing to sentence him to thirteen months in the state penitentiary, a place in which he certainly would have gotten himself seriously hurt.

Your arrest record resembles in a lot of ways your credit score: it's kept on an immense national database by ill-paid data-entry clerks who have little at stake in making sure it's accurate or up to date. Little errors tend to creep in, and once they become part of your file, they are very difficult to expunge. Little Peter's contained a ghost felony from the time he'd broken into the rock musician Steve Miller's house in Ketchum, Idaho. The crime had been reduced to a misdemeanor, and Little Peter had been set free, but whoever was in charge of entering that information hadn't bothered to make the change. Little Peter's public defender in Miami, who handled five hundred felony cases a year, hadn't had the time or inclination to check out the accuracy of my stepbrother's record. For a flat fee, though, the private lawyer I found through a friendly bail bondsman was able to straighten things out almost overnight.

The judge appeared to be a nice lady of the country club variety, with a deep tan, strong arms, and a short helmet of silver hair, something on the model of Sandra Day O'Connor. She resembled my mother a little, to tell the truth. Before she released Little Peter into my custody, she smiled down from the bench, and asked me how she was supposed to tell *two* Peter von Ziegesars apart. I suppressed an impulse to reply that I wasn't the one in an orange jumpsuit and black rubber sandals, or sporting a gap in the middle of my front teeth, or with the four-month-old jail stubble. I was asked to stand before the court and swear that I would fly with Little Peter to Denver, Colorado, where a treatment program I'd set up was waiting for him.

That promise I found difficult to keep. My stepbrother stepped out of prison in a new charcoal gray polyester smock and the same pair of rubber sandals, clutching a yellow receipt in his left hand. Otherwise he'd been stripped as clean of possessions as a newborn baby. Passing through the prison system is like going through the birth canal.

I'd had an idea that something like that was going to happen. You don't assault an officer in Dade County (as the ambulance driver had been upgraded to) and walk away dusting your hands. The police had probably chucked my stepbrother's clothes and wallet into the nearest Dumpster right after the arrest. Luckily I'd packed a duffel bag with old T-shirts, jeans, and underwear for him to wear, along with a pair of running shoes.

When we went around back of the courthouse, we saw twenty or thirty other men in a similar plight flitting over the sun-blanched sidewalk in their gray prison smocks and flip-flops. Some clustered around a hot-dog stand chatting with court personnel, others pushed toward a tiny window where prison belongings were being distributed, until the woman inside shut the window firmly, saying it was time for her lunch. When Little Peter's turn came up an hour later the woman behind the plate glass told him she had no record of his having had any possessions at all.

At any rate, now there was no chance we were going to make that flight to Denver. Post 9/11, the airlines don't let scruffy men in beards to fly without proper ID. After my stepbrother changed his clothes in the parking lot, I drove my rental car as fast as I dared up I-95 to make the only Greyhound bus scheduled to leave for Twin Falls, Idaho, that day. The need to get Little Peter out of Dade County before something else happened felt as urgent as a full bladder. What an idiot he'd been to return to Florida in the first place—the scene of his cocaine freakout ten years ago and his subsequent lockdown in rehab!

Meanwhile, nothing had changed. While I drove too fast, Little Peter dithered and dathered, searched through the glove compartment, read out loud from the car rental agreement, then turned Rush Limbaugh up loud on the car radio and exclaimed, "My man!" We almost missed the bus while he spent half an hour shoveling sugar and other extras into his quart-sized takeout cup at a coffee shop, coffee being another one of life's guaranteed rights that had been denied to him in the lockup. He became ferociously attached to the free table where they had put out cream and other various types of condiments. I was a nervous wreck when I finally got him to the Greyhound station.

"Do you ever think about Dad?" I asked while we were still driving in the car. The serrated tops of palm trees were passing over our heads even though we were thirty feet above the ground on a highway overpass. Beyond the palm trees was a luscious blue sky dotted with bright, puffy white clouds. I could see why people moved to Florida and then hired guards to keep everyone else out.

"I pray for him," Little Peter told me. "I pray for Franz every day."

"Where do you think he is now?" I asked.

"He's in heaven," he replied. "For sure he's in heaven."

My information differed from my stepbrother's, however. A telephone psychic in Virginia named Sharon Flynn had recently told my wife that my father was working diligently in a kind of "library" in the Other World. This news freaked me out a little, because before he died my father had spent a lot of time in the local Sea Bright Library and had even raised money for a new wing. There was no way the psychic could have known that. Anyway, he was working in something like a trustee position, she said, while waiting for a body in which to return to earth. He hadn't been able to reincarnate, though, because of negative energy he'd built up in his past life. Summing up my father's current karmic position, Sharon confided to my wife, "It's not a pretty picture."

Once, a few years ago, my father called me quite late. He cleared his throat, an enormous gargle, and said, "There is a book I'd really like you to find. I read it in my youth, but I was never able to remember the title or the author."

He said, "It was about a man who'd once been quite rich and successful, but had lost everything he had in the Great Depression: job, money, house, wife, family. He drifted from town to town doing odd jobs, mostly hard labor like digging ditches or working on farms. Finally he was staying in a cheap hotel room somewhere in upstate New York. It was nighttime and he couldn't sleep, remembering what his life had been and how terrible it had become.

"The man looked out the window of the two-bit hotel," my father went on. "There overhead was a beautiful full moon, hanging like a bright, polished silver dollar. He looked at this giant moon and then suddenly without any effort whatsoever, and without even thinking about it, this guy began to rise up in the air.

"He floated out the window and pretty soon he was flying out among the trees right up there with the moon. He didn't have the foggiest idea how he did it. He just had the ability to fly. He zoomed around for a while, brushing the tops of the trees with his fingers and feeling the cool night air push against his face. Then after about half an hour he floated back into his hotel window and went to bed. He thought, 'This is fantastic. I'm really flying! What a dream!' When he got back to bed he felt great and went to sleep right away."

My father asked, "Is this story too long for you?"

"No," I said. "Go on. It's interesting."

"Anyway, the poor bugger's life turned really tough. He got a girl and lost her. He began to take the worst jobs like breaking rocks in a quarry, or working as a roustabout for a circus, or carrying bricks in a construction site. He was always getting beaten up and chased by railroad cops and company goons.

"None of it bothered him," my father said, "because every night he'd go back to his room and fly up out of the window and into the trees. It wasn't a dream. This was real. Eventually he rode a freight train out to the West Coast, I forget where, Oregon or Washington, where he found work as a lumberjack. From his hotel room on the pier he could hear the water of the Pacific Ocean lapping the pilings. When he looked out the window, everything seemed different than anything he'd ever known. The trees were as thick around as houses and they stretched up to the sky. A blanket of cold fog drifted in and covered everything.

"That night the guy began to fly higher than he ever had before. He drifted up into the branches and hung over the harbor, where he heard bells ringing and foghorns blaring. He looked down on the twinkling lights of the bars and heard the men below shouting and drinking. Then he glided up higher into the mists among the highest branches of the trees. This time he didn't go back to his bed in the hotel room. He just kept on rising into the mist, going higher and higher."

"That's the end of the book?"

"Yes, that's it. The poor son of a bitch just disappeared into the fog."

"That's a pretty great story."

"Now that you're a writer, you do a lot of research, right? You know your way around a library. Do you think you could hunt it down for me? I want to read that book again."

I said, "I don't know. I could try."

"Yeah, try hard," my father said. "And get back to me."

Acknowledgments

There are many without whom this book, and in some cases its author, would not be here. I would like to start by mentioning my wife, Hali, in whose absence, I firmly believe, the universe would not manifest itself in the morning, nor the stars run on their appointed tracks at night. My children, Alden, Maya, and Magnus, form the bright constellation by which I steer. To my mother, a modern-day Cassandra, who not only gave birth to me at an early age, but also introduced me to my first Dylan album, I promise, "Next time I'll listen!" I'm grateful to my very tolerant in-laws, Dr. T. H. and Priscilla Lee, for their wisdom and example over the years. Thanks also to Hali's grandmother, who taught us never to cut off the tails of the string beans, because that's where their life is.

I owe an obvious debt to my stepbrother, Peter Raymond Sluis von Ziegesar, who, despite all the things I said about him in these pages, is exactly himself and no one else. James Syme—gentle poet, brilliant photographer, and true friend, who lived this story with me for years and willingly became a character in my book—deserves both my permanent thanks and a medal. I might not have started this undertaking at all if not for David Schwab, friend and fellow traveler—a man who prides himself on knowing a good story when he hears one—whom one day I found staring at me through the steam of a bowl of udon soup, shouting, "That's it, you dismal fuck!" or words to that effect.

Michael Flamini at St. Martin's Press has been simply a great editor as well as a patient friend through three full drafts. I earnestly hope 2013 is a *much* better year for you. Vicki Lame has been of epic assistance in ushering the book through its last stages. My incomparable agent David Kuhn heard me out over coffee, spent weeks helping me grow this project from a tiny seed, and with tender mercy hunted down and exterminated every extraneous comma. Nicole Tourtelot in his office has been an enormous source of help and advice.

I'd also like to thank Jeanne McCulloch, graceful editor, smart parent, who read each chapter, gave freely of her insight, and threatened to savage me if I didn't produce the next. Susan Bell read early chapters and gave advice that later proved essential. Jill Schoolman did the same, and basically just *is* essential. Eli Gottlieb got hold of my manuscript in his teeth at one point, shook it, and wouldn't let go until it made narrative and human sense. In Bill Jones's enviable library I rehearsed almost every line. Don Zavelo kept (and keeps) me honest. My sister Cecily sat me down one afternoon and told me a lot of stuff that raised the hair on the back of my head, and I thank her for that and for many other things. Rick Ball and Liney Li always seem to be standing out on the sidewalk under my window with one of those outlandish firemen's trampolines beckoning when I think I'm going to fall. Olivia James and Elizabeth von Ziegesar each married my father and therefore knew many things I couldn't. Dandapani opened up new worlds for me just exactly when I needed a few. And finally, to Lord Ganesh, Master of Beginnings, Remover of Obstacles, Prince of Literature, and Ruler of Time, Memory, and Space, who generously allowed me to wander through his dark realms for, lo, these many months during the preparation of this book I offer heartfelt thanks.

The last note of gratitude goes to my generation: In the words of Leonard Cohen, "If I have been untrue, I hope you know it was never to you."